LEARN **C** NOW

LEARN C NOW

Augie Hansen

Microsoft PRESS

PUBLISHED BY
Microsoft Press
A Division of Microsoft Corporation
16011 NE 36th Way, Box 97017, Redmond, Washington 98073-9717

Library of Congress Cataloging in Publication Data
Hansen, Augie.
Learn C now.
Includes index.
1. C (Computer program language)   2. QuickC (Computer program)
I. Title.
QA76.73.C15H365   1988   005.26   88-8987
ISBN 1-55615-130-6

Printed and bound in the United States of America.

    4 5 6 7 8 9   MLML   3 2 1 0 9

Distributed to the book trade in the United States
by Harper & Row.

Distributed to the book trade in Canada by General
Publishing Company, Ltd.

Distributed to the book trade outside the United States
and Canada by Penguin Books Ltd.

Penguin Books Ltd., Harmondsworth, Middlesex, England
Penguin Books Australia Ltd., Ringwood, Victoria, Australia
Penguin Books N.Z. Ltd., 182–190 Wairau Road, Auckland 10, New Zealand

British Cataloging in Publication Data available

Acquisitions Editor: Claudette Moore   **Editor:** Eric Stroo

This is dedicated to the ones I love.
Family and friends become more important to me
with each passing year. May that trend continue unabated.

Contents

Foreword

Like most people, I consider typing a necessary evil, a subject to be taught by knuckle-banging ogres who drill their students endlessly.

Programming, however, is fun—as you already know or will soon discover. But it does require some typing. The more the typing, the more the tedium, and the more the errors. Learn C doesn't eliminate typing, but its drop-down menus and its range of useful editing commands make the typing far less burdensome. (But then what would you expect from C, a language whose name you can summon with a single character?)

When you write and edit programs in the Learn C environment, you have a host of editing commands and shortcut keys to speed the process along. Then you can compile and debug your programs without complex command lines—simply choose commands from menus and respond to dialog boxes. With a mouse, you can reduce typing to a bare minimum: Move through a program, choose commands and options, and run your program—all without touching the keyboard.

Of course, *Learn C Now* has some advantages that don't involve typing. For one thing, it recognizes how big the subject is. And although it doesn't skirt the essentials of learning to program in C, it doesn't try to be exhaustive. That would merely exhaust your patience. For another thing, it's a tremendous bargain. Where else can you get a C compiler that offers the convenience of the QuickC environment plus a multitude of learning aids for anything close to the price of *Learn C Now*?

To spare you hours of typing, all the sample programs are included on disk. You don't have to interrupt your progress through the book to type programs. Simply open them in the Learn C environment and run them.

You do have to type to enter your own programs or to experiment with the sample programs—I encourage doing both from the very beginning of your exploration of C. But I want the choice to be yours.

I want you to have many choices, in fact. That's why you're getting not only a book and sample programs and a compiler with loads of on-line help, but an on-line tutorial as well. The tutorial treats the same topics that the book covers, but it introduces the information in ways that take advantage of the on-screen presentation. You choose and combine resources to learn in your own way and at your own pace. The only thing I haven't done is devise a few drills....

Acknowledgments

The list of individuals who contribute to a project of this magnitude would fill many pages. Thanks to all who have been generous with their time and effort to make C accessible to those who are willing to expend some of their own time and effort on the learning process.

I am indebted once again to Claudette Moore for getting me involved in the project and for making the arrangements that brought the primary pieces of the project together. The management and staff of Microsoft Press have, as usual, worked above and beyond the call to produce a quality product. Thanks to Dave Rygmyr, Eric Stroo, and several anonymous reviewers who worked diligently to refine the manuscript and on-line training materials. They were working on your behalf. I would also like to thank Alison Conn and the developers of QuickC and the Learn C compiler for their help. Thanks as well to Ruth Moretz for answering my questions about the computer-based training tools and for helping me use them effectively.

This product would not exist if Dennis Ritchie had not created C. We who make a living writing about and programming in C owe him and his associates at Bell Laboratories a great deal for giving us such a compliant and capable medium of expression. And we also benefit greatly from the continuing work at Microsoft to produce excellent C compilers for PC-class systems.

Augie Hansen
July 1988

1: The Learn C Integrated Environment

Introduction to Learn C

Installation and Setup

Starting Learn C

The Learn C Screen

Using Learn C Menus and Commands

Using Dialog Boxes

Running a Program

Getting Help and Information

The Learn C Editor

Editing a Sample Program

The Learn C Compiler

Microsoft Learn C is an integrated C programming environment—all the tools you need to create and execute C programs are built into a single software package. It's your key to learning to program in C in the quickest way possible. This chapter introduces the Learn C integrated programming environment, explains its purpose and operation, and tells you how to use Learn C and its accompanying on-line tutorial.

As you read the remainder of this book and work through the on-line tutorial, you will be exposed to the essential aspects of C programming. The coverage is selective rather than exhaustive, but it is detailed enough to give you a good hands-on understanding of C language fundamentals and, I hope, to entice you to learn more.

Introduction to Learn C

Learn C is based on the popular *Microsoft QuickC Compiler*. Programs written in the Learn C environment are completely compatible with QuickC and with the full-blown implementation of the C language, the *Microsoft C 5.0 Optimizing Compiler*.

Learn C provides a comprehensive set of 191 built-in routines. Appendix D offers a summary of the entire set, which comprises the most often used routines in the standard C run-time library. Learn C conforms closely to the evolving ANSI C standard and incorporates extensive graphics support.

The Learn C package provides the following components:

- **Editor**—the Learn C editor is compatible with the widely used word processor program MicroPro WordStar. You can either type the editing commands in the WordStar form or use the equivalent Learn C command keys, which depend heavily upon the arrow keys and other special keys found on IBM PC or compatible keyboards.

- **Compiler**—the Learn C compiler transforms a program you create with the editor so that you can run the program. The compiler operates entirely in memory, eliminating the time-consuming disk access required with traditional compilers. Learn C does not produce separate executable program files that you can execute directly from MS-DOS. With Learn C, programs run only within the integrated environment.

- **Debugger**—an integrated debugger, based on Microsoft's lauded CodeView technology, provides you with instant feedback on program errors. The debugger can identify up to 26 errors during one compilation and takes you directly to the offending source code lines.

- **Help system**—at any time, you can obtain help with any command, error message, function description, or a variety of other topics related to C programming. Help is available both at a general level and in an indexed, task-specific form.

By combining a capable full-screen editor, an extremely fast in-memory compiler, a professional-quality symbolic debugger, and on-line help into a single coordinated package, Learn C gives you everything you need to learn C without having to learn extraneous detail about the operating system and about separate editor, compiler, linker, and debugger programs.

Installation and Setup

The Learn C compiler consists of several executable program files, a number of "header" files, and some sample programs. To run Learn C, you need version 2.0 or later of MS-DOS or PC-DOS. (MS-DOS and PC-DOS are, for the purposes of this book, fully equivalent. The term MS-DOS is used throughout.)

The details of the installation and setup procedure depend on your particular computer equipment. To preclude the need to swap disks when you compile your C programs, your computer should have one of the following disk configurations:

- Two standard (360 KB) floppy-disk drives
- A single high-capacity (1.2 MB) disk drive
- A hard disk and at least one floppy-disk drive

The following two procedures, one for floppy-disk users and the other for hard-disk users, describe the steps for installing the Learn C compiler and setting up your computer to run the compiler. If your computer setup has a high-capacity floppy-disk drive (1.2 MB), you can install the operating system and all the Learn C files on a single disk, with room left over for your programs. Simply format the disk as a bootable system disk and then skip ahead to the hard-disk procedure. If you do not have a high-capacity floppy-disk drive or a hard disk, use the first procedure to prepare your work disks.

❏ WARNING: *Regardless of the type of system you will be installing Learn C on, do not use your original Learn C disks to run the program because you could accidentally damage them.*

Floppy-Disk Procedure

The first task is to create a set of work disks. If you are using standard double-sided, double-density (360 KB) disk drives, you need to create three disks: a compiler disk, a compiler overlay and include file disk, and a working program disk. To create your disks, follow these steps:

1. Start your system as you normally do.

2. Format four new disks.

3. Use the DISKCOPY command to copy the files from the distribution disks to your formatted disks.

4. Label the disks according to the following lists:

    Work Disk #1: Learn C Compiler Startup

    LC.EXE   (Hercules support)

    Work Disk #2: Learn C Compiler Overlay

    LC.OVL   INCLUDE*.H
    LC.HLP   INCLUDE\SYS*.H
    EXAMPLES*.C   (Other sample files)

    Work Disk #3: Learn C On-line Tutorial

    LEARNC.COM (and additional support files)

    To avoid disk-full errors, use the fourth disk in drive B (assuming that you have a second drive) for storing programs that you modify or create.

5. Next, you need to create an AUTOEXEC.BAT file on your system boot disk or edit your existing AUTOEXEC.BAT file. It must contain at least the two following entries to tell the compiler where critical files are located:

```
PATH A:\
SET INCLUDE=A:\INCLUDE
```

Either entry can contain other directory pathnames in addition to those shown. Consult your MS-DOS documentation for further information on your AUTOEXEC.BAT file or the PATH and SET commands.

❑ NOTE: *Floppy-disk drives such as those installed in IBM PS/2 machines and in many laptop computers employ micro-floppy disks that can hold at least 720 KB. You can get the operating system files and the Learn C compiler file onto a single micro-floppy disk, which you use to boot and start Learn C; then you can use a second disk for the compiler overlay and library files, header files, sample programs, and your own programs. Alter the following procedure to suit your system's disk storage capacity.*

Hard-Disk Procedure

If you have a hard-disk storage system, you can install all program and data files at once and avoid the potential disk-swapping problems of a floppy-only system. As noted earlier, you can apply the hard-disk installation and setup procedure to high-capacity floppy disks, although you must format the high-capacity floppy before you can begin installation.

Use this procedure to install the Learn C files on a hard disk. The procedure assumes that the hard disk is drive C and suggests subdirectory locations and names. If your hard disk has a different drive identification than the one shown or you want to use different subdirectory locations or names, alter this procedure and the related information that follows accordingly.

1. Create a directory structure—the indention below mirrors the hierarchy of the directories:

    ```
    C:\LEARN_C
         C:\LEARN_C\INCLUDE
              C:\LEARN_C\INCLUDE\SYS
         C:\LEARN_C\EXAMPLES
    ```

    ❑ NOTE: *If you are using MS-DOS version 3.2 or later, you can simply create LEARN_C on your hard disk and then use XCOPY to copy the contents of each disk to that directory.*

5

You can, of course, create another directory to store programs that you write.

2. Copy Learn C files onto the hard disk in the LEARN_C directory. Place files in subdirectories of LEARN_C exactly as you find them on the distribution disks.

3. Next, you need to create an AUTOEXEC.BAT file on your system boot disk or edit your existing AUTOEXEC.BAT file. It must contain at least the two following entries to tell the compiler where critical files are located:

```
PATH C:\LEARN_C
SET INCLUDE=C:\LEARN_C\INCLUDE
```

Either entry can contain other directory pathnames in addition to those shown. If you're installing Learn C on a high-capacity floppy disk, substitute *A:* for *C:* in the entries above.

You can also set the PATH and INCLUDE variables by typing them at the MS-DOS command-line prompt or by executing a custom batch file that contains lines to set the variables before you start the compiler.

Starting Learn C

After you set the PATH and INCLUDE variables, starting the Learn C compiler is easy. Change to the directory containing your program source files. Your C program source files can be placed anywhere they will fit on disk.

If you are using a standard floppy-disk system, put Work Disk #1 in drive A and type *lc* to get started. After the compiler is loaded and running, remove Work Disk #1 and insert Work Disk #2, which contains the overlay and include files, in drive A.

On a hard-disk system or one that uses a high-capacity floppy disk, start Learn C by typing *lc* at the MS-DOS command-line prompt.

❑ NOTE: *If you get the message* Bad command or filename, *your PATH and INCLUDE environment variables have not been properly set.*

Starter Switches

You can also start Learn C with one or more optional parameters to control certain aspects of the compiler's operation. The following table summarizes the valid *option(s)* parameters. These parameters, also called switches, must be preceded in the command line by either a forward slash (/) or a minus sign (−).

Command syntax: lc [*option(s)*] [*filename.ext*]

Option	Description
/b	Displays black and white on a color graphics display adapter with a monochrome monitor or a composite monitor.
/g	Speeds up display updates on systems with a color graphics adapter (CGA) or a CGA-compatible adapter that permits fast, direct access; has no effect on hardware configured with an enhanced graphics adapter (EGA) or a monochrome display adapter (MDA).
/h	Starts Learn C in Hercules mode, which uses the greatest number of screen lines possible for the installed hardware (for example, 43 lines on an EGA display system).

If your setup has a monochrome monitor attached to a color graphics adapter, use the /b option when you start Learn C. If you have a Hercules display adapter, read the contents of the file MSHERC.DOC (located on distribution disk #1). Enter *readhere* to read the file, or use the MS-DOS PRINT command to send a copy to your printer.

In addition to these switches, you can include the filename of one of your program source files. Doing this causes the specified file to be loaded into the Learn C editor—it saves you the step of opening the program source file once the Learn C program is loaded.

If, for example, you have a monochrome monitor and a CGA card, you can load Learn C and open a source file called mycode.c by entering the following command:

```
lc /b mycode.c
```

The Learn C Screen

Now let's explore the Learn C screen. If you haven't done so already, start the program. The initial Learn C screen, shown in Figure 1-1, has three primary screen areas that are devoted to specific tasks:

- **Menu bar**—the line at the top of the screen is the menu bar, which contains the access points for all Learn C command menus.

- **Edit window**—the middle area of the screen is the edit window. It is here that you display and edit the text of a program source file.

- **Status line**—the Learn C compiler displays status information about the program source file with which you are working. The status line occupies the bottom line of the screen.

Learn C Configuration: Local Control

When you start Learn C for the first time, it uses its default screen and compiler settings. If you make changes to the default values (such as a change in the screen color), Learn C creates a file called LC.INI in the current directory and saves the settings for future use. If you want to use these new values whenever you start Learn C, copy LC.INI into the same directory in which you have placed the Learn C compiler file (LC.EXE).

The next time you start Learn C, it looks in the current directory for the initialization file. If none is found, Learn C looks in all the directories specified by the PATH variable. Thus, an initialization file in the current directory overrides any found in the directory search path. This feature gives you a measure of local control over the compiler so that you can customize it for different users or different purposes based on the startup directory.

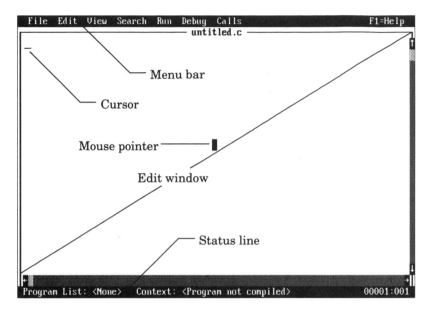

FIGURE 1-1. *Initial Learn C screen.*

The blinking underline is the cursor. It points to your current location in the file that is displayed in the edit window. If no text appears in the edit window, the cursor is located at the upper left corner.

The rectangular block shown in the middle of the screen is the mouse pointer. It appears only if you have a mouse installed.

Using Learn C Menus and Commands

You can type all Learn C commands on the keyboard, or you can choose them with a mouse. You would be wise to begin by learning the keyboard commands: You may someday find yourself working on a machine that has no mouse and need to have something to fall back on.

Exploring the Learn C Menus

Learn C commands are organized into eight menus, which you access from the menu bar. Each name in the menu bar (except Calls) identifies a set of commands.

- **File**—the File menu contains commands to create, load, merge, print, or save program source files. This menu also contains commands to run a separate MS-DOS session or terminate the Learn C session.

- **Edit**—the Edit menu contains commands for deleting, copying, and inserting text.

- **View**—the View menu has commands for customizing the Learn C environment.

- **Search**—the Search menu contains commands to find and, optionally, to replace text, to locate functions during debugging operations, and to control the display of error information.

- **Run**—the Run menu contains commands for compiling and running program source files.

- **Debug**—the Debug menu contains commands for helping you debug (correct errors in) your program source file.

- **Calls**—the Calls command is the eighth choice on the menu bar. It displays a hierarchical list of functions for the current program. When you select a function name from the list, the cursor moves to a point in the file where that function is defined or called.

- **Help**—the Help menu contains commands that lead you to information about Learn C commands and the C language.

Executing Commands

To execute any Learn C command, use the keyboard or your mouse to choose one of the menus from the menu bar at the top of the screen; then select the command you want from the menu. Function keys and other special key combinations serve as shortcuts for the most frequently used commands, allowing you to bypass the menu structure. We'll look at each method individually.

Keyboard. To activate the menu bar when you're working in the edit window, press the Alt key. The Alt key is "sticky" in Learn C, meaning that you can simply press and release the Alt key to activate the menu bar—you don't have to hold the Alt key down while you choose a menu.

If you decide not to execute a command, simply press the Alt key a second time to deactivate the menu bar and return to the edit window. You can also press the Esc key to cancel a partially completed selection.

When you activate the menu bar by pressing the Alt key, Learn C highlights the menu name farthest to the left, which identifies the File menu. You can then use the Right and Left Arrow keys to choose a different menu. After you highlight a menu, press the Enter key to pull down the menu. Alternatively, you can pull down a menu by pressing the Alt key and then pressing the first letter of the menu name.

The File entry, the one farthest to the left, is the default menu selection. If you choose this entry, Learn C displays the File menu, shown in Figure 1-2. Use the Up and Down Arrow keys to choose the required command and press Enter to execute it. Alternatively, you can press the highlighted letter of the command you want to execute. Once a menu has dropped down, you can still use the Right and Left Arrow keys to move from one menu to the next. This technique lets you see all available commands as you move from menu to menu.

FIGURE 1-2. *The File menu contains commands to create, load, merge, print, or save program source files.*

Shortcut Keys. You can execute the most often used commands by using keyboard shortcuts. The shortcut for a command appears beside the command entry in the menu. For example, the command to start execution of your program is Shift+F5, which means you press and hold down either Shift key, press F5, and then release both keys.

Here is a summary of the keyboard shortcut commands that Learn C accepts:

Menu	Keyboard Shortcut	Command
File	F2	Open Last File
Edit	Alt+Backspace	Undo
	Shift+Del	Cut
	Ctrl+Ins	Copy
	Shift+Ins	Paste
	Del	Clear
View	F4	Output Screen
Search	Ctrl+\	Selected Text
	F3	Repeat Last Find
	Shift+F3	Next Error
	Shift+F4	Previous Error
Run	Shift+F5	Start
	F5	Continue
Debug	Shift+F2	Delete Last Watch
	F9	Toggle Breakpoint
Help	F1	General
	Shift+F1	Topic
	Esc	Close Help

Mouse. If you have a mouse, you can use it to select and execute commands. Simply point to a menu name (anywhere in the name) and press the left mouse button to pull down the associated menu. Then, choose and execute a command from the menu in the same way: Point to the command name and click the left mouse button.

To cancel a partially completed selection, move the mouse pointer to any area of the screen that is not occupied by a menu and press the left mouse button. You can also move the mouse pointer to the menu name of the pulled-down menu and press the left mouse button again. The right mouse button is never used.

Quitting Learn C

To quit Learn C, press Alt+F to get to the File menu, and select the Exit command to return to MS-DOS. If you're using a mouse, exit by pointing to the File entry in the menu bar and clicking. Then, point to the Exit command in the File menu and click again.

Using Dialog Boxes

Some commands—those followed by an ellipsis (...)—lead to dialog boxes, which are work screens that let you further define your selection or let you choose configuration options. Within a dialog box, use the Tab key or the Backtab key (Shift+Tab) to move to the fields that you need to fill in or select. Descriptive prompts tell you what information is required. After you fill in all applicable fields, press Enter or Spacebar to execute the command.

To see how a dialog box works, let's load a file using the Open command on the File menu. Display the File menu by pressing Alt+F, and then press *O* to execute the Open command. Learn C displays the Open dialog box shown in Figure 1-3.

The Open dialog box contains several fields. The first is the File Name field, an input field called a text box. To identify a file to load, type the name of the file in this text box and press Enter. The filename you type overwrites the **.c* that initially appeared in the text box. You

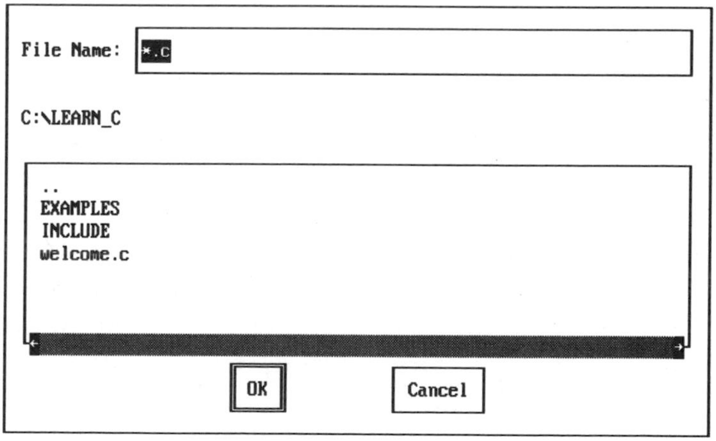

```
File Name: *.c

C:\LEARN_C

 ..
 EXAMPLES
 INCLUDE
 welcome.c

        OK          Cancel
```

FIGURE 1-3. *Choosing the Open command from the File menu displays the Open dialog box.*

can also edit the current name: First, use the direction keys to position the cursor within the text box, and then use the standard editing keys (Backspace, Ins, Del, and so forth) to edit the text.

If you don't want to type the name, or if the file is located in another directory, press the Tab key to move to the second field, which is a list box. The list box contains a columnar listing of all filenames in the current directory that match the pattern given in the first field. The *.c pattern, for example, causes all C source files to be listed. (If you are unfamiliar with the use of MS-DOS wildcard characters [* and ?] to form ambiguous filenames, consult your MS-DOS documentation.) In addition, any subdirectories contained in that directory are listed, including the .. directory, which indicates the directory one level above your current directory. Subdirectory names are displayed in uppercase letters; filenames are displayed in lowercase letters.

Use the direction keys to activate the highlight and move it to the name of the file you want to open or to the directory you want to change to. For now, select the welcome.c file.

At this point, you are ready to execute the command. Notice the word *OK* in the double-line box at the bottom of the dialog box. This is another field, called a command button. The double-line box means that OK is the default button for this dialog box. To execute the current command—in this case, to load the indicated source file—press Enter or the Spacebar or click the mouse on the OK button.

If you decide not to execute a command, either press the Esc key, or press Tab to advance the cursor to the Cancel button and press Enter or the spacebar. Of course, you can also click on the Cancel button with your mouse.

You will encounter two other kinds of fields in dialog boxes, neither of which appears in the Open dialog box. One is called a check box, and the other is called a circular button. The Compile dialog box (shown in Figure 1-5 on p. 16) has these field types.

A check box is a simple on/off toggle associated with some option. It appears on your screen as a pair of square brackets. When the option is turned on or selected, an X appears within the brackets. When the option is off or not selected, the brackets are empty.

Circular buttons are used to indicate that one of a set of related options is selected or turned on. Circular buttons appear as pairs of parentheses. A dot within the circular button indicates that the associated option is turned on or selected. Only one of a set of options can be selected at any time. Therefore, using the Up and Down Arrow keys changes the selection.

If you have not done so already, select welcome.c from the File dialog box and execute the command to load the file. After Learn C reads the file from disk, the screen looks like the one shown in Figure 1-4.

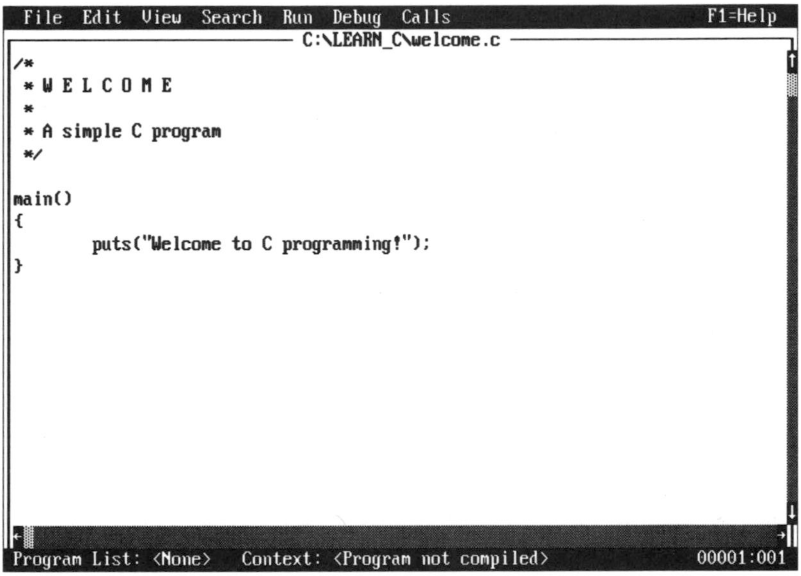

```
 File  Edit  View  Search  Run  Debug  Calls                F1=Help
 ─────────────────── C:\LEARN_C\welcome.c ────────────────────
 /*
  * W E L C O M E
  *
  * A simple C program
  */

 main()
 {
         puts("Welcome to C programming!");
 }




 Program List: <None>   Context: <Program not compiled>      00001:001
```

FIGURE 1-4. *The file welcome.c loaded into the view window.*

Running a Program

The next step is to compile and run the program. Pull down the Run menu by pressing Alt+R, and press *C* to execute the Compile command. You can use the mouse if you prefer. Learn C displays the Compile dialog box, shown in Figure 1-5 on the following page, which lets you set compiler options.

Several fields of the Compile dialog box are of particular interest. Notice that the Current File text field identifies the file you want to run, welcome.c. The compiler warning level is set by choosing a level from the list. This setting tells Learn C how much help you want in checking your program source file for errors or suspicious contents.

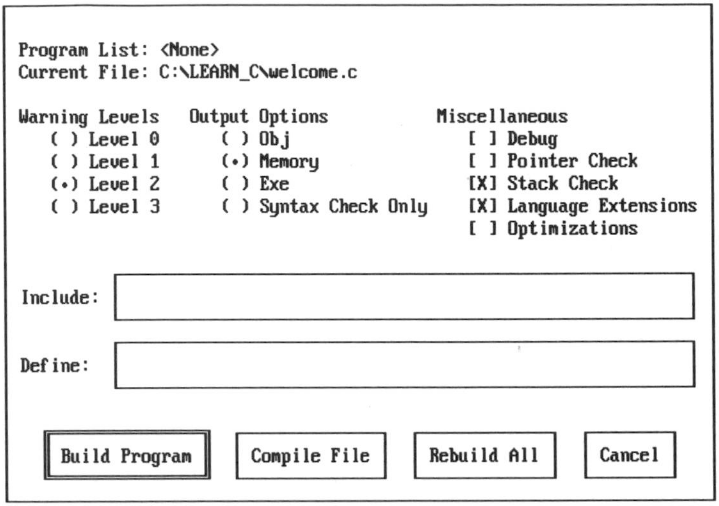

```
Program List: <None>
Current File: C:\LEARN_C\welcome.c

Warning Levels    Output Options        Miscellaneous
   ( ) Level 0       ( ) Obj               [ ] Debug
   ( ) Level 1       (•) Memory            [ ] Pointer Check
   (•) Level 2       ( ) Exe               [X] Stack Check
   ( ) Level 3       ( ) Syntax Check Only [X] Language Extensions
                                           [ ] Optimizations


Include:  [                                                        ]


Define:   [                                                        ]


   [ Build Program ]   [ Compile File ]   [ Rebuild All ]   [ Cancel ]
```

FIGURE 1-5. *The Compile dialog box.*

The default warning level is 2. We need to use warning level 1 for our current work to avoid some warning messages that would serve to confuse rather than help you at this point. Press the Up Arrow key once to choose level 1.

The rest of the fields in the Compile dialog box are set correctly for our current purpose of demonstrating the compiler. Execute the Compile File command by pressing *C*. Learn C compiles the welcome.c program and returns to the edit window.

Now, to run the program, press Alt+R to get to the Run menu, and press *S* to start execution.

When it runs a program, Learn C displays the output of the program on the operating system screen. That screen is actually in a separate area of the computer's memory from the edit window so that you can look at the two alternately on your monitor.

Figure 1-6 shows the output of the welcome.c program. The last line is a message from Learn C that displays the program's return value (which we'll learn about later) and the prompt *Press any key*. Press a key to return to the Learn C edit window. To switch back and forth between the Learn C edit window and the output screen, press F4. (This toggle works only when the edit window is active—meaning that no dialog boxes or menus are displayed.)

```
C:\LEARN_C>lc
Welcome to C programming!

Program returned (0).  Press any key
```

FIGURE 1-6. *Output of the welcome.c program.*

Getting Help and Information

The Learn C environment is designed to pamper you. It does everything possible to help you through the rough spots by using complete command menus and carefully designed dialog boxes, and by offering detailed help at two levels.

You receive complete prompting in all situations that require actions or responses. At any time, you can use the general level of help to get a list of Learn C command keys and some general C language information, or you can display the index to select a C language keyword that you want described in detail.

The On-Line Help System

To display the Learn C Help menu, press Alt+H. The choices on the menu are General, which you can access directly from the edit window by pressing F1; Topic, which you can invoke directly by pressing Shift+F1; and Close Help, which you can also select (to return to the edit window) by pressing the Esc key.

General help is presented as a series of frames that describe Learn C keyboard commands and some C language information. You can page through the frames by pressing *n* (next) and *p* (previous). To switch to the Topic index, press *k* (keywords).

Topic help provides task-specific information that you can select from an index. At this level, you can obtain detailed information about topics you will find discussed in this book—function parameters and return types, C language keywords, and preprocessor directives.

Topic help is "context-sensitive," which means that it can present information that pertains to the location of the cursor in the edit window. To use this timesaving feature, position the cursor on the word that identifies the topic *before* you activate the Help menu. In the file welcome.c, for example, place the cursor anywhere in the word *puts* in your program, press Alt+H, and then press *T*. Alternatively, you can choose the command with a mouse or use the Shift+F1 keyboard shortcut. The on-line help window opens directly below the menu bar and shows you a brief, descriptive entry for *puts()*.

The Learn C Tutorial

In addition to the built-in help system and the information in this book, you can get information from another source. The Learn C on-line tutorial provides an interactive introduction to the Learn C environment and lessons about programming in C. Generally, these tutorial lessons correspond to chapters in the book. The opening page of each book chapter directs you to the parallel information in the tutorial.

To run the Learn C tutorial, you must be at the operating system command level in the directory that contains the tutorial files. Disk #3 of the Learn C distribution set contains the tutorial. You can copy it onto a hard disk if you want. At the MS-DOS prompt, type *learnc*, press Enter, and follow the instructions.

The material covered in the tutorial is divided into individual lessons, each with a set of limited objectives. In general, the lessons explain new terms, analyze fragments of code, and let you check your progress using summary screens and practice exercises. The lessons also refer you to sample programs and explanations in the book that pursue the same objectives as the lesson.

The Learn C Editor

You use the Learn C editor to create and modify source files for your C program. It is a full-screen editor that allows you to view and edit interactively.

Features

The editing commands and basic editing operations of the Learn C editor are WordStar-compatible. The editor produces an ordinary text file—a file that contains only standard ASCII characters such as letters, numbers, and punctuation marks. This is precisely the kind of file the compiler requires.

In the Learn C environment, a C program consists of a single C source file. You can use the Learn C editor to compose and edit C source files, header files, or any other standard text file. A C source file is identified by a .c extension in its name, a header file by a .h extension.

The Learn C editor provides a comprehensive set of commands for positioning the cursor and supports full horizontal and vertical scrolling. In addition, it has a flexible mechanism for selecting text. This mechanism works with the built-in clipboard feature and with the copy, cut, and paste commands to handle even the most sophisticated editing tasks.

Command Summary

The following table shows all Learn C editing commands and the key sequences that invoke them. The table shows both the Learn C and WordStar key sequences. Some commands are available in only one of the key-sequence sets.

Learn C Editing Commands

Command	Learn C Keys	WordStar Keys
Move Cursor...		
Character left	Left Arrow	Ctrl+S
Character right	Right Arrow	Ctrl+D
Word left	Ctrl+Left Arrow	Ctrl+A
Word right	Ctrl+Right Arrow	Ctrl+F
Line up	Up Arrow	Ctrl+E
Line down	Down Arrow	Ctrl+X
Window up	PgUp	Ctrl+R
Window down	PgDn	Ctrl+C
Window left	Ctrl+PgUp	(none)
Window right	Ctrl+PgDn	(none)
Beginning of line	Home	Ctrl+Q S
End of line	End	Ctrl+Q D
Top of window	(none)	Ctrl+Q E
Bottom of window	(none)	Ctrl+Q X
Beginning of file	Ctrl+Home	Ctrl+Q R
End of file	Ctrl+End	Ctrl+Q C

(continued)

Command	Learn C Keys	WordStar Keys
Scroll...		
Up one line	Up Arrow	Ctrl+W
Down one line	Down Arrow	Ctrl+Z
Window up	PgUp	Ctrl+R
Window down	PgDn	Ctrl+C
Window left	Ctrl+PgUp	(none)
Window right	Ctrl+PgDn	(none)
Select...		
Character left	Shift+Left Arrow	(none)
Character right	Shift+Right Arrow	(none)
Word left	Shift+Ctrl+Left Arrow	(none)
Word right	Shift+Ctrl+Right Arrow	(none)
Screen up	Shift+PgUp	(none)
Screen down	Shift+PgDn	(none)
Beginning of file	Shift+Ctrl+Home	(none)
End of file	Shift+Ctrl+End	(none)
Insert...		
Toggle insert mode	Ins	Ctrl+V
Line below	Enter	(none)
Line above	(none)	Ctrl+N
Last deleted line	Shift+Ins	(none)
Tab at cursor	Tab	Ctrl+I
Tab at beginning of each selected line	Tab	Ctrl+I
Delete...		
Current line	Ctrl+Y	(none)
To end of line	(none)	Ctrl+Q Y

(continued)

Command	Learn C Keys	WordStar Keys
Delete...		
Character left	Backspace	Ctrl+H
Current character	Del	Ctrl+G
Word	(none)	Ctrl+T
Selected text	Del	(none)
Cut... (to clipboard)		
Selected text	Shift+Del	(none)
Copy... (to clipboard)		
Selected text	Ctrl+Ins	(none)

Creating and Editing a Source File

Creating a C source file is as simple as typing the text you want to insert. Characters appear in the edit window as you type them. All commands require the use of a special key or key sequence (Ctrl, Shift, or Alt and some other key), so they do not appear as ordinary text.

Be sure to save your work frequently by using the Save command on the File menu. As a general rule, save frequently enough to avoid retyping sizable amounts of text.

Positioning the Cursor and Scrolling

Use the arrow keys to move the cursor locally by lines and columns. To move the cursor word by word, use the Ctrl key in combination with the Right and Left Arrow keys. Alternatively, you can point to a spot with the mouse and click the left button to set the cursor position to the indicated location.

The Home and End keys move the cursor to the beginning and end of the current line, respectively. The PgUp and PgDn keys are used for paging, which scrolls text up and down according to the size of the current edit window. You can move to the beginning or end of the current file by using the Ctrl+Home and Ctrl+End key combinations. To move the cursor the full width of the edit window to the left and right, use the Ctrl+PgUp and Ctrl+PgDn key sequences.

In addition to the keyboard commands, you can use a mouse for scrolling. If the scroll bars are turned on (using the Options dialog box available on the View menu), a small gray rectangle in the vertical scroll bar indicates the current position in the file relative to the beginning and end. Likewise, the horizontal position is indicated in the horizontal scroll bar by a similar rectangle, or scroll box.

To scroll with the mouse, point with the mouse at the scroll box, press the left mouse button and drag the scroll box to the desired position. You can also click in the scroll bar on either side of the scroll box to page up and down or left and right, or you can click on the arrows at either end of the scroll bars to scroll by individual lines or by individual characters.

Selecting Text

To copy, move, or delete a block of text, you must first select the block. As with scrolling, you can use either keyboard commands or the mouse to select text.

To select a block of text beginning at the current cursor location, press and hold the Shift key and use any of the cursor-positioning commands to expand the selected area. Then release the Shift key and issue an editor command. To cancel a selection, release the Shift key and move the cursor in any direction.

With the mouse, selecting is even easier. Simply point to a spot at one extreme of the block, press and hold the left mouse button, and drag the mouse over the block you want to select. Then release the button and issue an editor command.

To help you manipulate blocks of text, Learn C maintains a clipboard, an area of memory into which you can copy or cut text. You can, in turn, paste the text in the clipboard back into the file you are editing. The clipboard lets you copy or move text from one place in a file to another. To copy text, you first select it and choose Copy from the Edit menu. Then you reposition the cursor and choose the Paste command (also on the Edit menu) to copy the text to the new location. Moving text is the same as copying except that you delete the selected text into the clipboard by choosing Cut rather than Copy from the Edit menu.

Searching for and Replacing Text

The Learn C editor provides a helpful search feature that you access from the Search menu. The Find command lets you find the text you specify in a dialog box, which is shown in Figure 1-7. You can also search for the next occurrence of text that you have previously selected in the edit window. You can repeat any search from the menu or by pressing F3.

You can also search for a piece of text and replace it with other text. The Change dialog box gives you the option of prompted replacement (confirmation required) or global replacement. Beware of global replacement. It could become search and *destroy* if you don't specify the search text carefully.

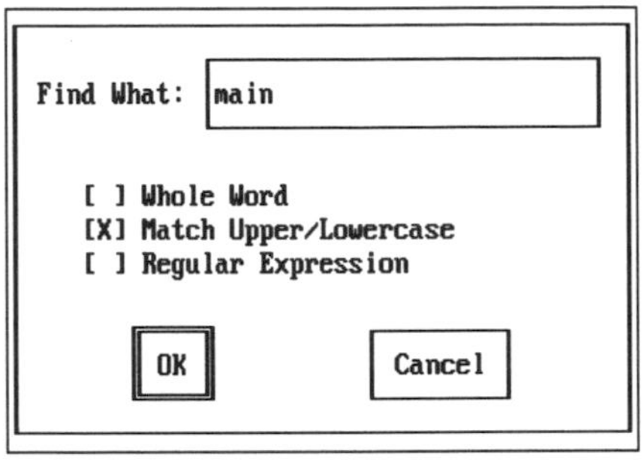

```
Find What: main

       [ ] Whole Word
       [X] Match Upper/Lowercase
       [ ] Regular Expression

       [ OK ]        [ Cancel ]
```

FIGURE 1-7. *The Find dialog box.*

Editing a Sample Program

To get your feet wet, edit the welcome.c file currently displayed in the edit window. First, move the cursor to the left edge of the line that contains *puts("Welcome to C programming!");* and press Shift+Down Arrow. This sequence highlights the entire line. Now, choose Copy from the Edit menu (or use the keyboard shortcut Ctrl+Ins). Next, press the Home key to eliminate the highlighting and keep the cursor on the *p* character. Now, choose Paste from the Edit menu (or use the keyboard shortcut Shift+Ins). You should now have two identical lines on your screen, one directly under the other:

```
puts("Welcome to C programming!");
puts("Welcome to C programming!");
```

Next, edit the line you pasted in. Move the cursor to the quotation mark near the end of the line. Press the Backspace key repeatedly until only the two quotation marks remain within the parentheses. Now type a message of your own, such as *Are we having fun yet?* Figure 1-8 on the following page shows the screen at this point.

```
 File  Edit  View  Search  Run  Debug  Calls                      F1=Help
 ┌───────────────────── C:\LEARN_C\welcome.c ──────────────────────────┐
 /*
  * W E L C O M E
  *
  * A simple C program
  */

 main()
 {
          puts("Welcome to C programming!");
          puts("Are we having fun yet?");
 }




 Program List: <None>    Context: <Program not running>          00010:037
```

FIGURE 1-8. *The WELCOME program with a new line inserted.*

Be sure that your message is enclosed by quotation marks, that both parentheses are in place, and that the line ends in a semicolon—exactly like the message in the preceding line. If one or more of these characters are missing, insert them now.

Now choose Start from the Run menu. When you do, Learn C displays a dialog box that asks whether you want to rebuild the program. Because you made changes to the program, you must rebuild it. Press the Enter key (or use your mouse) to choose Yes. After the program is rebuilt, the results are displayed on the output screen. Press any key to return to the edit window. (If you get an error message, carefully compare your program to the one in Figure 1-8 and make the necessary changes; then choose Start from the Run menu again.)

At this point, you could elect to save the changed welcome.c program on disk under the same name or under a different name. For now, however, discard the changes to the current file. To do so, pull down the File menu, and then choose Exit to quit Learn C or choose New to open a new file. Learn C warns you that your file has changed before it allows you to create a new file or to exit.

Choosing Yes causes Learn C to save the changed contents on disk as welcome.c. The new version overwrites the old one. Because you don't want to do this, press Tab to select the No command button, and then press Enter. Choosing the Cancel button or pressing Esc cancels the operation and returns you to the edit window.

Now that you've seen how easily you can open, edit, and compile programs using Learn C, you're ready to investigate the fundamental concepts of programming and the essential parts of a C program. With this preparation, you'll be able to start creating programs of rapidly increasing sophistication.

2: Introduction to Programming and C

Essential Programming Concepts

An Overview of C

Dissecting a C Program

You are about to learn to program in C. If you have never programmed before, this chapter will teach you the fundamentals of computer programming and then introduce you to C without flooding you with detail. If you are already experienced in another programming language, such as BASIC or Pascal, the material in this chapter will serve both as a review and as an overview of C. The remaining chapters present major aspects of C in appropriate detail for an introductory course in C programming.

For a variety of reasons that will become apparent as you go through this book, C is one of the most popular programming languages. In fact, many software companies have adopted C as their primary development language for most or all of their programs.

Essential Programming Concepts

Regardless of the language you are learning, you need to become familiar with a few fundamental concepts of programming. A program is simply a series of individual instructions to the computer that collectively perform a meaningful task. The way you express these instructions depends on the programming language: To produce the desired result, you must use the appropriate keywords and follow the rules and syntax of the language you are using.

In many programming languages (including C), you begin by writing your program using a text editor or word processor. (If you use a word processor, you must save the program as an unformatted text file, also known as an ASCII file.) The finished product is known as the program source file.

After the program is written, most programming languages require that the source file be processed through a "translator" that transforms the (relatively readable) programming language into a language that the computer can understand. In the case of the C language, this translator is the C compiler. The Learn C compiler performs an additional task, called linking, which adjusts the translated source file so that the program will run. Linking is usually distinct from the compiling process on a machine running MS-DOS.

A program consists mainly of raw information, or data, and a series of instructions that operate on the data. Writing a program boils down to organizing the data items and choosing or creating appropriate sequences of instructions, called algorithms, to manipulate them.

Data

You constantly use data in one form or another:

- What time is it?
- How much gas is left in the tank?
- What is the effect on my car payments if I stretch them out over another year?
- What percentage of total sales was handled by the West Coast office last quarter?

The collection, interpretation, and dissemination of data occupy much of our waking time. Given the importance of these activities, writing a computer program to assist you with them can clearly be useful and timesaving. In a program, different types of data (such as names, interest rates, and telephone numbers) are organized and processed. As you'll learn in later chapters, you can then use these data items to generate summaries or to present the data in a variety of other ways.

Algorithms

A computer program is like a recipe for quiche or the instruction manual for an electronics kit—a series of individual steps that produces a meaningful result. Each step identifies objects (the data items) or describes how they are to be processed and combined (the algorithm) to produce the final product. An algorithm is a series of instructions that performs a specific task, for example, preparing the crust of the quiche or completing a subassembly in the electronics kit. Simple examples of algorithms in computer programs are sets of instructions that convert lowercase letters to uppercase or that find all the prime numbers in a given range. A simple program might contain a single algorithm; a complex program might contain hundreds.

The key to writing good algorithms (and ultimately good programs) is to make them as compact and efficient as possible. You can create and refine your own algorithms, or you can study the algorithms in other people's programs. As a beginning programmer, however, you should concentrate on function rather than form: The first objective is to write algorithms that perform the desired task; striving for efficiency and compactness comes later, as you gain experience.

Generally, algorithms are composed of instructions that establish sequence, decision, and iteration. Let's take a closer look at each of these topics.

Sequence. All programs are based on sequential execution of instructions. Unless you modify this consecutive process, the computer performs instructions one after the other until the set of instructions is exhausted.

An example of a simple sequence is the set of steps you take to prepare firewood from logs.

1. Cut a log to the required length.

2. Place the log vertically on a solid base.

3. Center the wedge on the top of the log.

4. Hit the wedge solidly with a sledgehammer.

5. Stack the resulting pieces.

Decision. The primary way in which you can alter the sequential execution of statements is to insert a decision step. A decision step lets the execution flow in one of two or more directions. In computer programs, this is referred to as branching. Two-way and multiway branches are as common in programs as they are in life.

We can draw from our wood-splitting instructions a situation in which a decision affects flow: Have you run out of logs? If so, pack up your equipment and quit for the day. If not, go back to step 1 and continue working.

In computer programs, decision making is based on the results of tests. These tests can be logical tests (for example, whether a condition is true or false) or numeric comparisons (for example, whether the value of x is greater than the value of y). Thus, the outcome of the tests ultimately controls how the program proceeds after each decision step.

Iteration. Iteration is often called looping. It causes an instruction or a set of instructions to be executed repeatedly. The loop can continue indefinitely, or it can terminate if some condition is met or ceases to be met while the loop is executing.

An example of iteration in the real world is a scanning radio receiver. Such a receiver steps through a set of specified frequencies (channels) that it is designed to monitor and stops at any channel that has communications activity. After the activity on the channel has ceased for some specified amount of time, the scanner resumes its march through the channels until it finds another one that is busy. After scanning all the channels, it continuously repeats the scan until you turn off the power or instruct it to lock onto a particular channel.

Analyzing a Task

A mass mailing campaign provides a good example of programming concepts applied to a real task. It combines sequence, decision, and iteration in the preparation and distribution of information on a large scale. Let's assume that you are trying to sell software by direct mail solicitation and that you are working alone. Your analysis of the task might yield the following procedure:

1. Prepare the cover letter and sales materials.
2. Print address labels.
3. Obtain a supply of envelopes and stamps.
4. Fold all materials to fit into the envelopes.
5. Get an envelope.
6. Insert cover letter and sales materials into the envelope.
7. Close and seal the envelope.
8. Apply a stamp to the envelope.
9. Apply an address label to the envelope.
10. If this is the last letter, go to step 12.
11. Go to step 5.
12. Bundle the letters by ZIP code.
13. Deliver the letters to the post office.

That is the essence of the process. Of course, some steps could be further refined to show detail that has been left out. For example, steps 1 and 2 involve word processing and possibly graphic arts work and printing by third parties under contract. Each might involve iteration, such as revising a draft several times until it is exactly as you want it. And steps 3 and 8 might be altered if you have a postage meter and a bulk mailing permit.

In this sequence of instructions, you find an example of a decision in step 10 and, in step 11, an absolute jump that creates a loop until the condition tested in step 10 is met. This is, of course, only one of many possible procedures that can get the job done successfully.

Thinking out and writing down such a sequence of instructions is a good introduction to writing a computer program. You might try to write out a series of instructions for accomplishing a task, such as changing lanes on a busy freeway.

An Overview of C

You can apply the problem-solving technique described in the preceding example to an infinitely wide range of tasks. Many of these tasks, like preparing a mass mailing, involve problems that lend themselves to computerized solutions. And this is why you need to learn C (or some other computer language) to specify a computer solution.

Features of C

The C language is distinguished by its simultaneous compactness and expressiveness, and it is noted for its applicability to a wide spectrum of programming tasks, from systems programs, such as operating systems, to applications programs, such as word processors, database managers, and spreadsheets.

Compact. C has only 32 standard keywords. Manufacturers of C language compilers are free to use additional keywords if they want. Learn C and other Microsoft C compilers have six additional keywords. (See Appendix A.) C has 40 standard operators; all but one (*sizeof*) are represented by short symbolic sequences, such as + or !=. (See Appendix B.)

Structured. C permits certain portions of a program to have private access to data items stored in the computer's memory, as well as access to data items that are accessible by the rest of the program. It has a set of structured programming statements for decision (*if*, *switch*) and iteration (*for*, *while*, and *do-while*) that permits you to write programs that are organized and easy to comprehend. Structured programming statements discourage you from writing "spaghetti code"—a program that is difficult to read or follow because it jumps around in seemingly arbitrary ways.

Portable. Tasks that require interaction with peripheral devices, such as disk drives or the video display, can be handled by standard library routines, which are not part of the C language itself. Careful programming and the use of the standard libraries make it a fairly easy task to write a program for one type of computer that supports C and then transport it to a totally different type of computer that offers support for similar peripheral devices.

Flexible. C has proved to be suitable for a variety of programming tasks because of its flexible attitude about data. C allows relatively unrestricted conversion of data from one type to another, such as the conversion of a character to its numeric equivalent. Other languages, like Pascal, aren't as flexible. C was designed with the assumption that you, the programmer, know best, so it imposes few restrictions.

Language Elements

The remaining chapters in this book introduce the elements of C in a reasonable sequence. We start with data and operators and then learn how to construct expressions, C statements, control-flow mechanisms, and functions. Next, we cover extensively the important and closely related topics of arrays and pointers. Additional structured data types are then described in the context of solutions to real-world problems. The topic of file input/output wraps up the introduction to C language programming. The last chapter describes the process of writing graphics programs.

Because all elements of the language participate in programs in an interlocking manner, it is impossible to avoid some forward references. We will, for example, use standard library functions before we can fully describe functions and how to write them. Be prepared to take some elements on faith until you arrive at an explanation in the appropriate chapter.

It All Starts with *main()*

A primary programming unit is the function. In C, as in most other modern programming languages, a function is a collection of statements and data items. In BASIC, the equivalent to a C function is the subroutine, although more recent versions of BASIC have introduced true functions into their repertoire.

All C programs begin executing at the *main()* function. Every C program must have one and only one *main()* function. The work done by a program is either in *main()* itself or in other functions called directly or indirectly (through other functions) from *main()*. C functions are covered in detail in Chapter 7.

Dissecting a C Program

The simple WELCOME program shown in Chapter 1, which we used to introduce Learn C, is a very simple C program. Let's examine the program line by line to see what constitutes a C program source file.

```
/*
 * W E L C O M E
 *
 * A simple C program
 */
main()
{
    puts("Welcome to C programming!");
}
```

LISTING 2-1. *The welcome.c program.*

The first five lines of the program form a comment. Comments are simply notes that you can insert into the program to describe what the program is doing at certain points. In this example, the comment gives the name of the program and tells what it will do. Although the C compiler ignores comments, comments are very important to a person who reads the source code because they describe in everyday language what the often cryptic-looking source code does not. Try to get in the habit of using them right from the start.

The character sequence /* begins a comment, and the character sequence */ ends it. Comments can span several lines in the source file. When the compiler sees the /* characters, it assumes that everything that follows is a comment until it encounters the */ characters.

Next comes the required *main()* function, which is the actual beginning of the WELCOME program. The braces (sometimes called curly brackets) delimit, or enclose, the body of the *main()* function. These braces are not optional. The left brace shows where the body of the function begins; the right brace shows where it ends.

The braces must occur in pairs, with the left brace preceding the right; otherwise, the C compiler will generate an error message. The area delimited by the braces contains the actual data and algorithms that are converted by the C compiler into instructions that the machine can understand and execute. In this simple example, the body of *main()* is but a single statement.

The *puts()* function (pronounced "put ess") is the heart of this simple program. It places the characters *Welcome to C programming!* on the user's screen and moves the cursor to the beginning of the next line on the video display.

Looking at WELCOME (and other program listings later in the book), you might wonder why some lines are indented and others are not. The C language has no hard-and-fast rules for indenting program lines, but indenting certain lines makes the program much more readable than one that has no indention.

Generally, a line is indented to show its subordination to a function or to some other significant program line that precedes it. The level, or amount, of indention makes no difference to the compiler; for ease of comprehension, however, use the same amount for all lines that have the same logical level in a program. In the WELCOME program, the single statement in the body is a subordinate element of the *main()* function and is, therefore, indented one level. The easiest way to indent lines—and to maintain consistent indention—is to use the Tab key once for each level of indention.

That's the basic structure of a C program. As you work through the chapters that follow, you will learn much more about the details of designing and writing C programs. But before getting deeply involved in programming per se, you will spend the next two chapters learning about the building blocks of C programs: data, data types, C operators, expressions, and statements.

3: Data and Input/Output

Memory and Objects

Data Output Basics

Data Types

Data Input

Questions and Exercises

C Programming Lesson: *Elements: Data and Input/Output*

Spreadsheets, word processors and text editors, database managers, communications packages, design and presentation graphics products, on-line references—the categories of programs for personal computers continue to increase in number. Within each category are many competing programs, all with a fundamental feature in common: They manipulate data—reading, writing, interpreting, or modifying it.

In this chapter, you will learn to distinguish and use various types of data, and you will come to see the advantages to making these distinctions. Specifically, you will learn about the primary C data types (characters, integers, and floating-point numbers) and type modifiers (unsigned and signed), and you will see how C programs represent data values as constants and variables.

The descriptions of data and data types in this chapter are not complete. An attempt to be rigorous would inundate you with details that would simply obscure the information you need at this stage. In later chapters, we will fill in some of the missing pieces.

Memory and Objects

Memory organization and data types are closely related. A data type indicates to the C compiler the amount of memory that the computer must provide to hold a given item, or "object." In addition, a data type specifies the organization of the storage units set aside, or "allocated," for an object.

❑ NOTE: *The following descriptions are appropriate for the IBM PC architecture but do not apply universally. The proposed ANSI draft standard for C allows many aspects of design and operation to be implementation-specific, that is, applicable to a specific C compiler and to the computer environment for which it is written.*

Bits

The fundamental logical element of computer memory is a single bit. A bit is a binary digit and thus has one of two possible values: 0 or 1. With only two possible values, a single bit contains a severely limited range of information. However, if we use multiple bits to represent a value, we increase the range of possible values. Each time we add a bit, we double the range of values that we can represent. Using two bits, for example, we can store a range of four unique values:

2-bit pattern	Decimal value
00	0
01	1
10	2
11	3

Each bit pattern represents a number in the binary system. As with the familiar decimal system, digits that are farther to the left have a greater "weight" than those to the right. In decimal, for example, the number 26 is effectively 2 tens + 6 units, which is 20 + 6. In this system, the weight of the rightmost digit is one; the next digit to the left has a weight of ten; the next, one hundred; and so on.

To represent binary numbers, the type of numbers that computers understand, we use a similar notational scheme: The rightmost binary digit has a weight of one; the next digit to the left has a weight of two; the next, four; the next, eight; and so on. In the 2-bit table above, for example, the binary pattern 11 represents 1 two + 1 unit, or 2 + 1. The

The Power of 2

To get a feel for how rapidly binary quantities grow each time we add a bit, get an ordinary checkerboard and a (large) pile of pennies. Suppose that the squares on the checkerboard represent bit positions and that the number of pennies on each square represents the binary weight of the corresponding bit position. Begin by placing a single penny on any corner. On the adjacent square in the same row, place two pennies. On the next adjacent square, place four pennies. Continue in this way, moving up the board square by square and row by row.

You will begin to have stacking problems before you get to the end of the first row. And even if you have a direct pipeline to the Denver mint, you'll run out of pennies long before you fill all the squares on the board.

rightmost bit is called the low-order or least significant bit. Conversely, the leftmost bit is the high-order or most significant bit.

As revealed in the sidebar on the previous page, you can represent surprisingly large numbers with a modest number of bits. The fact remains, however, that a binary number is not as compact as its decimal equivalent. The decimal number 824, for example, requires a 10-bit binary number, 1100111000; the decimal number 65,535 is represented by the 16-bit binary number 1111111111111111.

Although individual bits are important, trying to access and manage memory at the bit level would be terribly inefficient, so computers access collections of bits called "bytes" and "words."

Figure 3-1 depicts computer memory of the type found in the IBM PC and compatible machines. The figure shows the relationships among bits, bytes, and words.

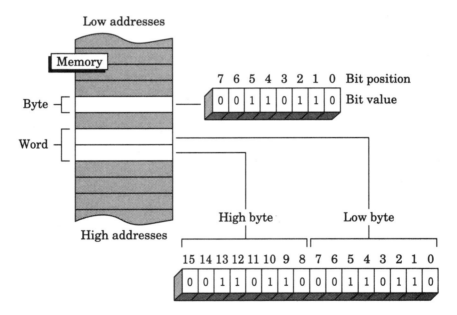

FIGURE 3-1. *A PC memory word is composed of a pair of bytes stored in reverse order.*

Bytes

The smallest collection of bits that you can access directly is called a byte. A byte is composed of eight bits in most modern computer architectures. As you'll learn shortly, a pattern of eight bits can represent a range of 256 unique values.

Although computers are designed to work with binary numbers, you and I are far more comfortable with decimal numbers. For example, would you know offhand that the binary number 10010011 represents a decimal value of 147? Hexadecimal (base 16) numbers represent a compromise between people and computers—not as natural as decimal values but more compact than binary numbers.

The base of a numbering system is derived from the number of unique digits you can use in counting before you have to "carry" a value, or increment the digit to the left. For example, the familiar decimal system provides 10 digits, 0 through 9; to count beyond 9, you have to carry a digit into the tens column. As the table below illustrates, you can use only two binary digits before you have to carry a value—hence, base two. The decimal and hexadecimal numbers are identical from 0 through 9. However, hexadecimal uses the letters A through F, respectively, to represent the numbers between 10 and 15 decimal.

Binary (base 2)	Decimal (base 10)	Hexadecimal (base 16)
0000	0	0
0001	1	1
0010	2	2
0011	3	3
0100	4	4
0101	5	5
0110	6	6
0111	7	7
1000	8	8
1001	9	9
1010	10	A
1011	11	B
1100	12	C
1101	13	D
1110	14	E
1111	15	F

The beauty of hexadecimal numbers is that a single hexadecimal digit represents four binary digits. Therefore, you can represent an 8-bit byte with only two hexadecimal digits. This correlation makes conversion between hexadecimal and binary quite simple.

Conversion from Base to Base. Let's look first at the conversion from binary to hexadecimal. Consider the binary number 10100110. Starting at the right side of the number, group the digits in sets of four: 1010 0110. Looking at the table on the preceding page, we see that 1010 is equivalent to A and 0110 is equivalent to 6 in hexadecimal notation. Thus, binary 10100110 has a hexadecimal value of A6. To convert from hexadecimal to binary, simply reverse the steps: Starting from the right side of the number, convert each hexadecimal digit to its binary equivalent, and then combine the groups of four.

Converting a hexadecimal number to its decimal equivalent is trickier. To make such a conversion, you need to consider the "weight," or place value, of each digit. Let's use the familiar decimal system as an example: The digit in the rightmost column of a whole number, the ones column, has a weight of 10 to the zero power, which is 1. (*Any* number raised to the zero power has a value of 1.) The next column, the tens column, has a value of 10 to the first power, or 10. The next column has a value of 10 to the second power, or 100, and so on. The decimal value 452, therefore, amounts to 4 times 100, plus 5 times 10, plus 2 times 1.

Hexadecimal numbers work the same way, except that we're dealing with powers of 16: The first column has a value of 16 to the zero power (1); the next has a value of 16 to the first power (16); the third column, 16 to the second power (256); and so on. To convert a hexadecimal number to its decimal equivalent, multiply each individual value by its column weight. (Use the decimal equivalent of any hex digits that are A or greater.) Then, add the products together for the result. As an example, consider the hexadecimal value AB9. Using the decimal equivalents of A and B, multiply each individual value by its column weight (10 times 256 equals 2560, 11 times 16 equals 176, and 9 times 1 equals 9). Then add the resulting weighted numbers (2560 plus 176 plus 9) to yield 2745, the decimal equivalent of the hexadecimal value AB9.

The preceding technique applies to conversions from binary to decimal as well. Of course, the column weights in binary numbers correspond to powers of 2, not powers of 16.

To convert a decimal number to its hexadecimal equivalent, you need to perform a series of division steps. The result of each division step provides part of the resulting hexadecimal value. Start by dividing the decimal number by the largest hexadecimal column weight that is still smaller than the decimal value. For example, consider the decimal value 2766. The fourth hexadecimal column weight (16 to the third power, which is 4096) is larger than the decimal number, but the next smaller column weight (16 to the second power, or 256) is not. When you divide 256 into 2766, the result is 10, with a remainder of 206. This quotient, 10, provides us with our leftmost hexadecimal digit: A. The remainder of 206 becomes the dividend for a separate division problem. For the divisor, we drop to the next smaller column weight, which is 16 to the first power, or 16. 16 goes into 206 a total of 12 times, leaving a remainder of 14. The value 12 provides the next digit in our hexadecimal number: C. The remainder of 14 is the dividend for the final division problem. We divide it by the weight of the next column—16 to the zero power, which is 1. Because any number divided by 1 is itself, the final digit of our resulting hexadecimal number is 14, which has the hexadecimal value E. Taken together, then, the decimal value 2766 is equal to the hexadecimal value ACE.

The same procedure works for converting decimal numbers to binary—using powers of 2 rather than 16. Note, however, that it is often easier to convert a decimal value to hexadecimal first and then use the table on page 41 to replace the hex values with their binary equivalents.

Hexadecimal Notation. In C, you must use a prefix to distinguish a hex number from a decimal number. The prefix 0x (or 0X) identifies characters that follow as hexadecimal digits. Thus, the number 0xF is hex notation for 1111 binary, or 15 decimal. In addition, the notation \x (or \X) introduces a hexadecimal number in quoted strings and character constants. (See "Escape Sequences" on p. 48 for details.)

As previously stated, a pair of hex digits conveniently represents the eight bits of a byte. For example, 11101111 binary is \xEF in hex. The obvious advantages of the hexadecimal approach are compactness and uniformity.

❑ NOTE: *You can also represent values in octal (base 8) notation, which was the most commonly used method until fairly recently. The prefix 0 (zero) or \ denotes an octal number. The number 27, for example, is 033 or \33 in octal.*

Words

After bytes, the next smallest group of bits that you can access directly is called a word. In the IBM PC architecture (original IBM PC, XT, AT, and PS/2 models through the Model 60), a word is composed of 16 bits, which is two bytes. Members of the latest breed of personal computers, such as the IBM PS/2 Model 80 and other machines based on the Intel 80386 processor, use a word size of 32 bits, which is four bytes.

A 16-bit word can represent 65,536 unique values. A 32-bit word does significantly better: 4,294,967,296 unique values. (Incidentally, this is the number of pennies you would have to place on a square at the center of the checkerboard. The next square would take twice as many!)

Addresses

An address is a way of keeping track of the location of an object in memory. In effect, a memory address represents an offset, or a relative measurement, into a large array of memory locations, just as a street address indicates a position within a series of buildings along a street. You recall that a byte is the smallest memory element that is directly accessible. Thus, we say that PC memory is byte-addressable, which means that each byte has its own address and can be accessed for reading and writing independently of any other byte in memory.

Figure 3-1 on page 40 depicts a small portion of computer memory. Note that low addresses are shown at the top and high addresses at the bottom. Although this may seem to be upside down, it is more common than its inverse in computer literature. This increase in memory addresses as you move down the page is consistent with the way we read text on a page—top to bottom.

In the IBM PC, a memory word is composed of two adjacent bytes. As with bits, we maintain a notion of significance of bytes within a word. The byte at the lowest address is the least significant byte, and the one at the highest address is the most significant byte.

The address of a word is the address of its first byte in memory, which is its least significant byte. (For this reason, PC memory words are said to be stored in reverse order.)

The fact that words are stored in reverse-byte order on IBM PC–family computers need not concern us here. The important thing to remember is that some objects are stored as single bytes, and others require multiple bytes.

Identifiers

It is inconvenient if not impossible to refer to each object in memory by its physical address. Instead, we use names to identify objects and let the compiler worry about their locations. Names given to functions, variables, and other C objects stored in memory are called "identifiers."

You create identifiers from combinations of uppercase and lower-case letters, digits, and the underscore character. An identifier must begin with either a letter or an underscore. Thus, the identifiers *NumberOfResponses*, *message*, and *_answer* are valid C identifiers. However, *12total*, *total%*, and *one$way* are invalid—note that the identifier *12total* starts with a character other than a letter or underscore; *total%* and *one$way* each contain an illegal character (% and $).

The Learn C compiler regards uppercase and lowercase letters as distinct. It checks as many as 31 characters (starting with the leftmost character) to determine the uniqueness of identifiers. You can, however, use longer names if you want. In this book, we will use long, descriptive identifiers for clarity.

C reserves a small number of identifiers for use as "keywords"; you cannot use these keywords for your identifiers. Most of the 32 keywords are data type specifiers. The others control the flow of execution in your program, and one is an operator. Learn C supports six additional keywords. See Appendix A for a complete list.

Data Output Basics

In the previous chapter, we used *puts()* to display a message on the screen. The *puts()* function is one of several standard library output functions; it's dandy for printing fixed messages, such as *Welcome to C programming!*, but it's not suitable for printing messages that contain variable information.

For example, if you write a program that reads a file from disk and counts the number of characters in the file, you might like the program to print a message that identifies the file being analyzed and states its size in characters:

File *SAMPLE.TXT* contains *3250* characters.

In the preceding sample message, the italic items are the variable elements of the printed message. If you give the program a different file to analyze, it prints the same basic message, but it prints the new filename and the character count determined by the program.

Data Output Using *printf()*

The *printf()* function is a standard library function that prints messages containing variable text. For now, you will learn only enough about *printf()* to display data of various types. Later in this and other chapters, you will learn about some of the more powerful and flexible capabilities of *printf()*.

Like other C functions, *printf()* can take "arguments." An argument is an item or a series of items that you place within the parentheses after a function name. Arguments are the means by which you pass values to a function—in other words, they are the values you want the function to act on when it executes. In some cases, as you'll learn later in the book, arguments can also be used to receive values from a function.

The *printf()* function is unusual among C functions in that it does not take a fixed number of arguments. It does require at least one argument, the control string, which is a sequence of characters enclosed within double quotation marks. If the control string contains only ordinary characters, the *printf()* function simply prints it verbatim.

The following program causes the control string to be printed on the screen:

```
main()
{
        printf("The quick brown fox is hungry. Watch out!");
}
```

To place variable information in a control string, you must put a "format specifier" in the control string at the location of the variable information, and you must add an argument for each variable item. A format specifier is a percent character (%) followed by one or more characters that indicate the type of information represented by the additional argument. When a program runs, *printf()* replaces the format specifier with the value of its companion argument.

Figure 3-2 shows how *printf()* uses the format specifiers in the control string to merge the additional arguments into the control string. The example shows a control string with two format specifiers, followed by two additional arguments: the string *message*, indicated by *%s* in the control string, and the integer *2*, specified by *%d* (for decimal format).

The result of running a program containing the *printf()* shown in Figure 3-2 is as follows:

```
This message contains 2 substitutions.
```

If you provide different values for either the second or third arguments (or both), you get a different output. For example, changing the second argument from *"message"* to *"line"* produces:

```
This line contains 2 substitutions.
```

As you'll learn later, %s and %d are only two of several format specifiers you can use in a *printf()* control string. Each has its own rules and limitations.

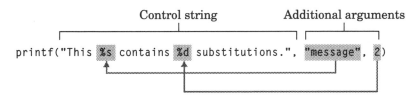

FIGURE 3-2. *The* printf() *parameter list must have a control string and one additional argument for each format specifier in the control string.*

Escape Sequences

An escape sequence is a group of characters that has a special meaning, usually a symbolic representation of something that cannot otherwise be typed at the keyboard or that has no associated displayable graphic symbol. Escape sequences start with the \ character, which escapes (alters) the normal meaning of the subsequent character and gives the character an alternate meaning.

An example of an escape sequence is \n (a backslash followed by the letter n), which symbolizes the newline character. It causes the cursor on a display or the print head of a printer to move to the beginning of the next output line. You can use \n and other escape sequences in strings, and you can use them successively, as the following program demonstrates:

```
main()
{
        printf("This is a line of text.\n");
        printf("This is one more.\n\n");
        printf("The third line is blank; this is line four.");
}
```

The table in Figure 3-3 (a Learn C help screen) lists the escape sequences that Learn C supports and the meaning of each.

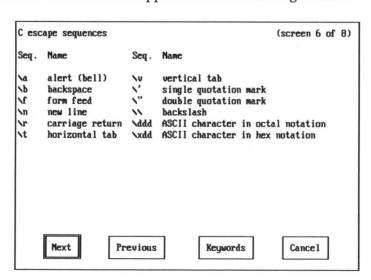

FIGURE 3-3. *Help screen showing escape sequences.*

Notice that you must use escape sequences to print the characters that have special significance within a *printf()* function. To print double quotation marks within the control string, for example, you must precede them with a backslash so that the C compiler doesn't mistake them for the required quotation marks around the control string itself. To print the message:

```
Here is some "quoted text."
```

you must use the escape sequence for the double quotation marks:

```
printf("Here is some \"quoted text.\"");
```

You can show ASCII characters in octal and hexadecimal notation by using the escape sequences \ddd and \xddd, respectively, where ddd is the number whose ASCII value you want to print. These escape sequences come in handy for printing ASCII characters in the range 0 through 31 and character 127, which have special meanings or perform special functions.

For example, the following program will "print" a bell character, causing your computer to emit a tone:

```
main()
{
        printf("\007");
}
```

Try some variations of this simple program. For example, \01 represents the ASCII Ctrl+A, which prints a happy face on IBM PCs.

Data Types

In your programs, you will use constants and variables to represent data. Each constant or variable is introduced with a data type that tells the Learn C compiler how much memory is needed to store the item and how the storage is organized.

A constant is a fixed value, one that does not vary over time. In a C program, you can present a constant literally or symbolically. The number 21, for example, is a literal constant. So is "Welcome to C programming!", which is called a string constant, or string literal. You will learn about symbolic constants in Chapter 6, which introduces the method for creating them.

A variable, on the other hand, is an object whose value can vary during the running of a program. Before you use a variable, you must "declare" it—you must indicate its data type and state its name, which must be a valid identifier. In most cases, a variable must also be explicitly "initialized," or given a value, before you use it.

We can broadly divide data into integral, real, and aggregate types. This chapter focuses on integral and real data types. Aggregate data types, such as arrays and structures (which can mix integral and real data types in various ways), are covered in later chapters.

An integral value is a counting number, a number with no fractional component. You use integers constantly: There are 7 days in a week; a dozen is 12 of something; 100 pennies is equivalent to a dollar.

Numbers that have fractional components are represented as "floating-point" numbers in C. Such numbers are called real numbers. They are used to store data such as physical measurements (lengths, areas, and the like) and averages. For example: An inch is 2.54 centimeters; the hypotenuse of a right triangle that measures 1.0 foot on a side is approximately 1.414 feet long.

An apt comparison of integral and floating-point numbers can be drawn from census data. The number of residents in a specific household is an integral value. However, the average number of children per family is a real number.

Integral Data Types

Although a computer language could conceivably have a single integral data type, C offers several types to permit efficient use of memory. Storing a large number in a small amount of memory produces an overflow problem, which results in the storage of an incorrect value. Conversely, storing a small number in a space reserved for a large one is inefficient. The key is to choose the correct type for the data you want to represent.

C has four primary integral data types, each of which requires a particular amount and arrangement of memory. To specify a data type, you use the appropriate C keyword, as listed in the table that follows.

Type specifier	Description
char	Character
int	Integer
short int	Short integer
long int	Long integer

In addition, you can apply the type modifiers *unsigned* and *signed* to the integral data types. In the Learn C environment, all integral values are signed by default—that is, they can represent either positive or negative numbers. A signed number has a range of values that is split evenly between negative and positive numbers. A value of type *char*, for example, has the range –128 through 127. (0 is considered to be a positive value.) An unsigned number has the same range as its signed counterpart, but is always positive. An *unsigned char* value has the range 0 through 256.

Character. A character is stored in a single byte of memory. For the following declaration:

```
char ch;
```

the type name *char* tells the compiler that variable *ch* is a character.

Characters, like all other items stored in the computer's memory, are represented as numbers. The value stored in a character variable actually corresponds to an element in a table of symbols, called the ASCII character set. (For a complete summary of the ASCII character codes and symbols, display screen 4 of Learn C's on-line help resource or refer to Appendix E of this book.) The number 113, for example, represents the lowercase letter *q*. Placing a character symbol inside single quotation marks creates a character constant, which has the integral value that corresponds to the character. Thus, *'q'* is identical to the integer 113 as far as the computer is concerned. In programs, of course, the *'q'* notation provides a meaning to a reader of the source code that the numeric value itself does not. Figure 3-4 on page 57 summarizes these facts.

The format specifier for a single character in a *printf()* control string is %c. To print the character stored in the variable *ch*, you can use the statements in the program on the next page. (This is admittedly a roundabout way to print a character.)

```
main()
{
        char ch;                /* declare the variable */
        ch = 'N';               /* assign a value to ch */
        printf("%c", ch);       /* print the value of ch */
}
```

❑ NOTE: *Some computers have more than one key for generating single quotation marks. If you have such a keyboard, type only the key with the single quotation mark that you would use as an apostrophe.*

Integer. The keyword *int* identifies an object as an integer. Therefore, the declaration

```
int num;
```

says that the variable *num* is an integer. Integers are signed by default, and in a 16-bit machine environment, the range of values is –32,768 through 32,767.

If the *unsigned* type modifier is applied, as in

```
unsigned int num;
```

the representable range becomes 0 through 65,535. A larger number of bits per word permits a greater range, of course.

The following decimal numbers are all valid integers: 12, 0, 1024, and –102. The number 18,620 is not a valid integer in a C program— the compiler does not permit you to embed spaces, commas, or other non-numeric characters in numbers. Although commas are used in the text of this book to simplify reading, the compiler requires that you represent the previous number in a program as 18620.

The type modifiers *short* and *long* provide for integers that are potentially smaller or larger than the native integer size (the size of a word, as dictated by the hardware). In a 16-bit environment, for example, an *int* and a *short int* are stored in 2-byte words. A *long int* occupies four bytes of memory and offers considerably greater range than an ordinary *int* (–2,147,483,648 to 2,147,483,647). In a 32-bit environment, the *int* and the *long int* have the same size (four bytes). The only fact that is guaranteed in a given C implementation is that

```
short int <= int <= long int
```

If the type modifier *short* or *long* appears in a declaration, the *int* type specifier is assumed. Thus, the following declarations have identical meaning:

```
long int bignum;
long bignum;
```

The same practice applies to the *signed* and *unsigned* type modifiers. Used alone, they are taken to mean *signed int* and *unsigned int*, respectively.

The NUMBERS program (Listing 3-1) shows how to print a message that consists of text and numbers. Note that *n1* and *n2* can both be declared in a single *int* statement, provided they are separated by a comma. The numbers are represented in the control string by the *%d* format specifiers. When you load and run the program, the first *%d* is replaced by the current value of variable *n1*, and the second by the current value of *n2*.

```
/*
 * N U M B E R S
 *
 * Show how to print strings that involve
 * both text and numbers.
 */

main()
{
        int n1, n2;

        n1 = 10;
        n2 = 3;
        printf("The number %d is bigger than the number %d.\n",
                n1, n2);
}
```

LISTING 3-1. *Program source code for numbers.c.*

As an exercise, try modifying the program so that *n1* and *n2* are of type *long* or *short*. To get the correct result, you must modify the format specifiers slightly. Use *%hd* for a *short* and *%ld* for a *long*.

Long Constants. If an integral constant is too big to fit in an integer-size storage location, the compiler stores it as type *long*. But if you want the compiler to store a normal-size integer as a *long*, you must append the letter L to the constant. Thus, you would need to write 100 decimal as 100L. You can also precede the value with a "type cast," which is a data type enclosed in parentheses. These two methods are illustrated in the following statements:

```
printf("Value = %ld", 200L);
printf("Value = %ld", (long)100);
```

Either method of representing a *long* constant ensures that the compiler uses the correct number of bits to represent the value.

If you fail to use either method in a print statement such as the following:

```
printf("Value = %ld", 100);
```

the value printed out will reflect the 100 held in the two low-order bytes, which is fine, but the two high-order bytes, which dominate the value, will contain arbitrary values because they are not explicitly set. To demonstrate this, type in the following program and run it. The output may surprise you.

```
main()
{
        printf("Value = %ld\n", 100L);
        printf("Value = %ld\n", 100);
}
```

Characters as Numbers. The next sample program, CHARS, shows the way C treats characters as numbers. As shown in Listing 3-2, the character variable, *ch*, is given a value of A, and the integer variable, *code*, is assigned a value of 48 decimal. When you compile and run the program, you will see something interesting. The output statements use *printf()* to show that *ch* is printable both as a character, A, and as its associated numeric code, 65.

The numeric code 48 prints as itself (a number) when the format specifier is *%d*, and as a character, 0, when the format specifier is *%c*. Note that the ASCII code 48 is a value that represents the numeral zero, which is graphically displayed as 0. Do not mistake the *character* '0' for the *numeric value* 0. They are 48 entries away from each other in the ASCII table.

```
/*
 * C H A R S
 *
 * Show how to print characters and show the relationship
 * between characters and their internal codes.
 */

main()
{
        /* Declare variables. */
        char ch;
        int code;

        /* Initialize variables. */
        ch = 'A';
        code = 48;

        /* Print the codes and characters. */
        printf("Our PCs use the ASCII character set.\n");
        printf("The ASCII code for the letter %c is %d.\n", ch, ch);
        printf("The ASCII code %d represents the character %c.\n",
                code, code);
}
```

LISTING 3-2. *Program source code for chars.c.*

Real Data Types

Real numbers are important in virtually all scientific and engineering work. Graphics programs also make extensive use of real-number calculations. As mentioned previously, C uses floating-point notation to represent real numbers.

Floating-Point Notation. Recall that a real number is a number that has a decimal point and a fractional component. For example, the real number 105.61 has three digits to the left of the decimal point (the whole-number part) and two digits to the right (the fractional part). The position of the decimal point can shift, however, if you use exponential, or floating-point, notation.

You can, for example, express the number 105.61 as 10.561E+001, 1.0561E+002, 1056.1E–001, or in many other ways. The E, which means "exponential," separates the mantissa, the number to the left of the E, from the exponent, the number to the right of the E. The exponent specifies a power of 10. Thus, 1.0562E+002 represents the same value as $1.0562 * 10^2$.

If you move the decimal point one position to the left, the mantissa is effectively divided by 10. To maintain the same value, you must compensate for the changed mantissa by increasing the value of the exponent by 1, which effectively multiplies the mantissa by 10. Conversely, if you move the decimal point one position to the right, the mantissa is effectively multiplied by 10, and you must compensate by decreasing the exponent by 1. When you apply these rules to change the way a specific number is represented, the decimal point is said to "float" because its position in the mantissa changes. Thus, the values 1.0562E+002, 0.10562E+003, and 1056.2E−001 all represent the same value.

Floating-Point Data Types. As with the integral values, C provides several data types that you can use to declare floating-point numbers, each of which has an associated range. Unlike integral values, floating-point numbers are always signed. Floating-point numbers have another important attribute, precision, which specifies the amount of storage that is devoted to them—numbers with greater precision require greater amounts of memory.

C currently offers two levels of precision in real-number storage: single precision, which requires four bytes of memory, and double precision, which uses eight bytes.

Type specifier	Description
float	Single-precision floating point
double	Double-precision floating point

Use the keyword *float* to declare storage for a single-precision object, and use *double* for a double-precision object.

Figure 3-4 shows a declaration for a *float* variable, *ave*. The chart also compares the memory required to store a *float* with that required for integer and character values.

❑ NOTE: *A third real data type,* long double, *is supported by Microsoft C compilers. It currently has the same range and precision as type* double.

Character values

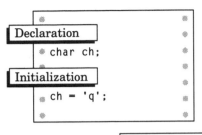
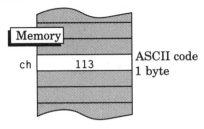

ASCII code
1 byte

Range of values

Signed: -128 through 127
Unsigned: 0 through 255

Integer values

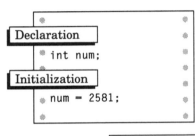
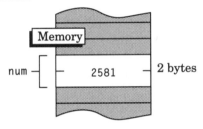

2 bytes

Range of values

Signed: -32768 through 32767
Unsigned: 0 through 65535

Floating-point values

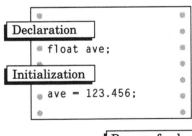
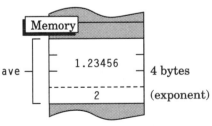

4 bytes

(exponent)

Range of values

10^{-38} through 10^{38}
Precision: ~7 digits

FIGURE 3-4. *Three of the primary C data types.*

Printing Floating-Point Data. You can use the *printf()* function to output floating-point data in a way that is analogous to its use for printing integral data. The format specifier for floating-point data has a number of options, however, which make its use more complicated.

The line at the top of Figure 3-5 shows the general layout of the options available to you for printing floating-point numbers with *printf()*. The first character, %, is required, as is the last item, *format type*; the items in brackets are optional.

Note that not all the format types apply to floating-point numbers; for example, you have already used the *d* and *s* types (decimal and string) for integral values. Before we examine any of the options, such as *flags* and *width,* let's look at the various format type specifiers we can use for floating-point numbers: *f, e* or *E*, and *g* or *G*.

The REALS1 program (Listing 3-3) demonstrates how each of these formats works.

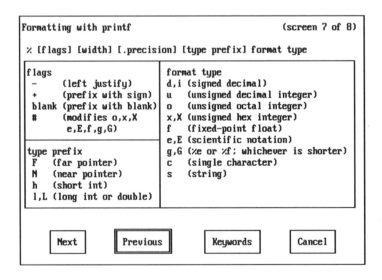

FIGURE 3-5. *Help screen showing format options with* printf().

```
/*
 * R E A L S 1
 *
 * Display a real number in several
 * different formats.
 */

main()
{
        /* Data declaration and initialization. */
        float fv = 1026.75;

        /* Print data in different formats. */
        printf("Variable fv = %f\n", fv);
        printf("Variable fv = %e\n", fv);
        printf("Variable fv = %E\n", fv);
        printf("Variable fv = %g\n", fv);
        printf("Variable fv = %G", fv);
}
```

LISTING 3-3. *Program source code for reals1.c.*

On an IBM PC/AT or compatible, the program displays the following output:

```
Variable fv = 1026.750000
Variable fv = 1.026750e+003
Variable fv = 1.026750E+003
Variable fv = 1026.75
Variable fv = 1026.75
```

The *%f* format specifier displays a floating-point value as a signed number with a fixed number of decimal places to the right of the decimal point—in this case, 6. The *%e* or *%E* format specifier displays a number in scientific notation: a 1-digit whole number, a fixed number of digits to the right of the decimal point (again, in this case, 6), and a 3-digit exponent preceded by a + or − sign (depending on the value). The difference between *%e* and *%E* is that *%e* precedes the exponent with an *e* (lowercase), and *%E* precedes the exponent with an *E*.

The *%g* format displays a value in the *%f* or *%e* format, depending on which of the two is more compact. In REALS1, the *%f* format was used because it was more compact than *%e*. The *%G* format is identical to *%g*, but it uses either the *%f* or *%E* format. Note that *%g* or *%G* does not produce a fixed number of decimal points as do *%f* and *%e* or *%E*.

C offers several formatting options for floating-point numbers (the bracketed items in Figure 3-5). The first optional field, *flags*, accepts the −, +, and blank (spaces) arguments. These options are listed in Figure 3-5 on page 58. The − option indicates that the number will be displayed left-justified; that is, aligned on the leftmost digit. The + option causes the displayed number to be preceded by its sign. The blank-space argument has almost the same effect as the + option: It causes negative numbers to be displayed with a − sign; positive numbers are displayed with a leading blank space rather than a + sign, however. The following program demonstrates the use of the + option:

```
main()
{
        float fv = 12.34;
        printf("The number is %+f", fv);
}
```

The output of this program (on an IBM PC/AT) is as follows:

```
The number is +12.340000
```

Note that the + option caused the number to be preceded by its sign (in this example, +).

The next option, *width*, indicates the *minimum* number of digits you want the *printf()* function to print. Use this option to set field widths to align numbers in columns.

The *.precision* option lets you specify the maximum number of digits to be displayed to the right of the decimal point. The REALS2 program (Listing 3-4) demonstrates the use of this option.

When you compile and run the program, note the formatting of the output values, which appear as follows:

```
Variable fv = 1026.750
Variable fv = 1.0268E+003
Variable fd = 0.000000000008130
Variable fd = 8.13E-012
```

The first *printf()* function used a precision value of 3, which caused *printf()* to display only 3 digits to the right of the decimal point—the value is rounded. The second *printf()* function used exponential notation and a precision value of 4 to print only 4 digits to the right of the

```
/*
 * R E A L S 2
 *
 * Display real data values in several
 * different formats.
 */

main()
{
        /* Data declarations and initializations. */
        float fv = 1026.75;
        double dv = 0.00000000000813;

        /* Print data in different formats. */
        printf("Variable fv = %.3f\n", fv);
        printf("Variable fv = %.4E\n", fv);
        printf("Variable dv = %.15f\n", dv);
        printf("Variable dv = %G\n", dv);
}
```

LISTING 3-4. *Source code for reals2.c.*

decimal point. The third *printf()* statement demonstrates that these formatting techniques work equally well with *double* values, and the last *printf()* function uses the *%G* type to print the more compact version of *dv*, which in this case is exponential.

As an experiment, try changing or adding format specifiers to this program and rerunning it. (The use of *%E* and *%G* as format specifiers, rather than *%e* and *%g*, is a personal preference of mine.)

Storage Requirements and Value Range Summary

Learn C provides a useful help screen, shown in Figure 3-6 on the following page, that summarizes the storage requirements for each of the standard C data types and shows the range of values for each. To display this screen, press F1 and then choose Previous (or press *p*).

❑ NOTE: *The memory required for integer types* int *and* unsigned int *is implementation-specific. In an IBM PC 16-bit environment, they are equivalent to the* short int *types. In a 32-bit environment, they are equivalent to the* long int *types.*

```
C Data Types Range of Values                        (screen 8 of 8)

Type Name       Other Names            Range of Values
char            signed char            -128 to 127
int             signed, signed int     -32,768 to 32,767
short           short int, signed short, -32,768 to 32,767
                signed short int
long            long int, signed long, -2,147,483,648 to
                signed long int        2,147,483,647
unsigned char   none                   0 to 255
unsigned        unsigned int           0 to 65,535
unsigned short  unsigned short int     0 to 65,535
unsigned long   unsigned long int      0 to 4,294,967,295
enum            none                   0 to 65,535
float           none                   3.4E ± 38 (7 digits)
double          none                   1.7E ± 308 (15 digits)
long double     none                   1.7E ± 308 (15 digits)


     [ Next ]      [ Previous ]      [ Keywords ]      [ Cancel ]
```

FIGURE 3-6. *A summary of storage requirements.*

The precision of floating-point values is only approximate because the number of digits needed to express a given decimal value does not correspond uniformly to the number of digits needed to represent its binary equivalent. Single-precision values can be expressed to a precision of 6 or 7 digits, depending upon the actual value. Double-precision values can be expressed to 14-digit or 15-digit precision, again as a function of the actual value.

Data Input

You have already seen a number of examples of data output using *printf()*. A comparable library function, *scanf()*, handles the process of gathering data.

The *scanf()* function uses an argument structure that is similar to *printf()*, but with some important differences. The READNUM program (Listing 3-5) demonstrates some of these differences.

First, we initialize *number* as an integer variable. Next, we use *printf()* to display a message. Note that the \n escape sequence is not used at the end of the control string: This keeps the cursor on the same line as the message so that the user won't get confused.

```
/*
 * R E A D N U M
 *
 * Read a number from the keyboard and print
 * it on the screen.
 */

main()
{
        int number;

        printf("Enter a whole number and press ENTER: ");
        scanf("%d", &number);
        printf("\nThe number you typed is %d.\n", number);
}
```

LISTING 3-5. *Program source code for readnum.c.*

The next line does the actual input work. The *scanf()* function takes two arguments: The first is a format specifier in quotation marks, which tells *scanf()* the type and format of the information it will receive. The second argument, *&number*, specifies a memory location at which *scanf()* is to store the input value. The ampersand (&) that precedes the variable name *number* is an operator that finds the memory location that the compiler reserved for *number*. (The expression &*number* "points to" the location of *number* in memory.)

If you use *scanf()* to obtain a long integer value, you need to use the type prefix *l* or *L* (%ld, for example). Similarly, to read a double-precision floating-point number, use the specifier %lf in the *scanf()* control string. Other type prefixes include *h* for short integers, *F* for far pointers, and *N* for near pointers.

Finally, the last *printf()* statement prints a message into which it inserts the value of *number*. Note that the & symbol is not used here.

Reading an entire string of characters isn't quite as simple. C has no built-in type specifiers for a string, only numbers and single characters. The GREET program (Listing 3-6 on the following page) demonstrates one way to handle a string with the *scanf()* function.

First, the variable *name* is declared as type *char*, with one noticeable difference: the *[40]*. When you declare a variable, any variable, you are actually telling the C compiler, "In this program, I want to use the variable *varname*, and I want you to reserve some memory to hold the value it will represent." The amount of memory it reserves depends on the data type you specify. In the GREET program, we want to reserve enough memory for a series of characters. Because the compiler reserves only one byte for a *char* value—not nearly enough to

```
/*
 * G R E E T
 *
 * Get the user's name and print a personalized greeting.
 */

main()
{
        char name[40];

        /* Prompt for and read the user's first name. */
        printf("Enter your first name and press ENTER: ");
        scanf("%s", &name);

        /* Print the personalized greeting. */
        printf("\nGreetings, %s.  Welcome to C programming!\n",
                name);
}
```

LISTING 3-6. *Program source code for greet.c.*

hold an entire string—we have to indicate the amount of additional memory we want. In this case, we request sufficient memory for 40 *char* values, which should be more than enough to hold someone's first name. We enclose this value in square brackets, immediately following the variable name. No extra spaces are allowed. Technically, what we've created is called an *array,* a topic we will cover in greater detail later in the book.

The fourth line of the program contains the *scanf()* function, which reads the input string. Notice that we've used the *%s* format type, even though *name* was declared with the type *char:* Because *name* was declared as an *array*, we can consider it to be a string when it is subsequently used with *scanf()* and *printf()*.

For its finale, the GREET program employs the name entered by the user to display a message. The last *printf()* function prints a greeting that incorporates the string stored in the *name* array.

Questions and Exercises

1. Manually convert the following numbers from decimal to binary form: 5, 20, 64, 334, 1024, 31025. (Hint: Begin by finding the largest exponential multiple of 2 [2, 4 , 8...] that the decimal number contains.) Now show each of the binary numbers in equivalent hexadecimal form.

2. Which of the following items are not valid C identifiers and why?

_alpha	FLOAT	1_of_many	say_what?
X_	maxValue	howmany	Number
nbytes	pink.floyd	int	string

   Of those that are valid identifiers, which should not be used for other reasons? Explain why.

3. You have learned that a computer represents characters internally as numeric codes. Using the ASCII tables in Appendix E or the pertinent Learn C help screens, convert the following characters and codes to their equivalents. Spell out the name of a character if it has no graphic representation.

Character	Code	Code	Character
'x'	_____	26	_____
^M	_____	0x20	_____
'A'	_____	100	_____
'$'	_____	0x30	_____
'3'	_____	62	_____

4. Which of the following constants are not valid in C? Explain why they are not valid.

562L	0377	99999
.00018	−11.1	0L
0001	+521.6	−88.28
0xFE	0X2C	1.265E−002
\xFE	1234.567	0966
33	0xGA	0xFFFE

5. For each of the following values, show a format specifier that correctly identifies the value in a *printf()* control string.

Value	Format specifier
3000	_____
23.67	_____
"Ah--What's up, Doc?"	_____
'Z'	_____
−205	_____

6. The READNUM program stores the input value as a signed integer, but it does nothing to validate the input. What are the minimum and maximum values that can be correctly displayed on the screen by READNUM? How would you modify the program to guarantee that it would accept numbers up to 2 million above or below 0?

    Run the program before and after modification and observe the results for input values outside the signed 16-bit integer range. Would the machine on which you run the program affect the results? Describe your observations.

7. Write a program that asks the user to type a real number (use a *double* to store the input value) and prints the value in scientific notation with three digits of precision.

4: Operators, Expressions, and Statements

Overview

C Operators

Questions and Exercises

In the previous chapter, you learned about variables and constants, two fundamental elements of C programs. In this chapter, you'll learn how to combine variables and constants with operators to create expressions, and you'll learn how to create statements from expressions.

Overview

First, let's take a high-level view of operators, expressions, and statements. Then we can examine in detail the rich set of operators that makes C a remarkably expressive language.

Operators

You're probably already familiar with operators, such as +, −, and =, that are used in everyday arithmetic. C offers a greatly enhanced set of operators, many of which function like their arithmetic counterparts. For example, these operators let you assign values, perform numeric calculations, and compare values. In C, we refer to the objects (such as values and variable names) that are acted upon by operators as "operands."

The assignment operator is one that we have already used a number of times in this book. It is symbolized by the equal sign (=). Like most other C operators, assignment is a binary operator—that is, it requires two operands. As you will see shortly, C also has several operators that require only one operand, and it even has one that requires three operands.

Expressions

An expression is formed by combining operators and operands in a meaningful way. C has a suite of some 40 operators that you can use with constants, variables, and functions to produce expressions. The purpose of an expression is to perform a calculation and produce a result, or, as we'll learn in later chapters, to cause some action to occur. An expression can be as simple as $a + b$. Simple expressions can be combined to form a more complex expression, such as $(a + b) * (c - d)$.

Statements

A statement is a complete program instruction that can be compiled by the compiler. It can comprise a number of expressions or none at all. In C, a statement can take one of several forms, but essentially it consists of an expression followed by a semicolon. As you learned in earlier chapters, the semicolon is a statement terminator in C; the presence of a semicolon at the end of the line distinguishes a statement from an expression.

Null Statement. The minimum C statement is a single semicolon, which is called a null statement. Although a null statement contains no expressions, it is a perfectly valid C statement that happens to do nothing. Occasionally, you need to use a null statement in the body of a decision or iteration construct. As you will learn in the next chapter, each of these constructs must have at least one valid C statement, even if you have no need for executable code in the statement body.

Compound Statement. A compound statement, often called a block statement, is composed of two or more statements within a single pair of braces. The purpose of a block is to hold together a series of statements as a unit.

An example of a compound statement is a function. We have already dealt with the *main()* function, and most of the programs we used in Chapter 3 were examples of compound statements. Compound statements become important later in the book when we talk about program decision steps and looping.

C Operators

Earlier we classified C operators by their number of operands. Binary operators are the most common. Of the remainder, one operator (the conditional operator) takes three operands and is called a ternary operator. The rest are called unary operators, which take a single operand.

We further classify operators by the types of actions they perform. For the rest of this chapter, operators that perform similar actions are discussed as separate categories. A list of these categories follows.

- Assignment (simple and compound)

- Arithmetic

- *sizeof*

- Relational

- Logical

- Bitwise

- Increment and decrement

- Shift

- Address and indirection

Operator Precedence

When an expression involves more than one operator, ambiguities in the order of evaluation can result. You can always force a required evaluation order by using parentheses to group subexpressions. The expression

```
4 + 5 * 6
```

is potentially ambiguous. Which should the compiler do first: the addition (4 + 5) or the multiplication (5 * 6)? If the compiler performs the addition first, the result is 54; if it does the multiplication first, the result is 34 instead.

C has a built-in set of rules that dictates the order in which operations are performed in an expression. One of the Learn C help screens, shown in Figure 4-1, contains an operator precedence chart. To display the screen within Learn C, press F1 and then page to the third help screen. Don't worry about operators on the chart that are unfamiliar to you—we'll learn about them later in this chapter and in later chapters. Appendix B also provides a handy summary of operators and operator precedence.

Operators with the highest precedence appear at the top of the precedence chart; operators with the lowest precedence are at the bottom. When Learn C evaluates an expression, it acts on operators higher in the chart before it acts on those below.

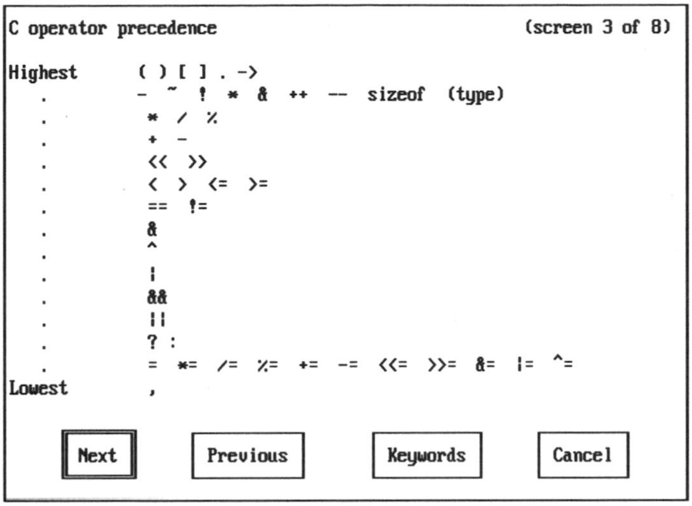

```
C operator precedence                           (screen 3 of 8)

Highest        ( ) [ ] . ->
   .          -  ~  !  *  &  ++  --  sizeof  (type)
   .          *  /  %
   .          +  -
   .          <<  >>
   .          <  >  <=  >=
   .          ==  !=
   .          &
   .          ^
   .          |
   .          &&
   .          ||
   .          ? :
   .          =  *=  /=  %=  +=  -=  <<=  >>=  &=  |=  ^=
Lowest         ,

    ┌────────┐   ┌──────────┐   ┌──────────┐   ┌────────┐
    │  Next  │   │ Previous │   │ Keywords │   │ Cancel │
    └────────┘   └──────────┘   └──────────┘   └────────┘
```

FIGURE 4-1. *Learn C help screen that shows operator precedence.*

If you are uncertain how the compiler will evaluate a given expression, you can use parentheses to dictate the order you require. Using parentheses forces the compiler to evaluate the enclosed expression before it evaluates any other expressions, regardless of their operators. In the ambiguous expression cited in the preceding page, the C compiler's precedence mechanism forces the multiplication to be done before the addition, so the effect is the same as if you had typed the following:

```
4 + (5 * 6)     /* Multiply first (default) */
```

If you want the addition to be done first, force the compiler to do so by parenthesizing the addition:

```
(4 + 5) * 6     /* Add first */
```

In addition to operator precedence, another consideration in expressions is the order of appearance. In an expression that contains several operators at the same precedence level, such as several * signs, the compiler processes them from left to right or from right to left, depending on the particular level. (This secondary order of precedence is shown in Appendix B.)

Simple Assignment Operator

The primary C assignment operator is the equal sign (=). To assign the integer 100 to the variable name *number*, you first declare that *number* will represent an integer and then write an assignment statement:

```
int number;
number = 100;
```

The assignment operator causes the memory location associated with the variable identifier, *number* in this example, to contain the assigned value. Here, the value is obtained directly from a literal constant. The value can also be obtained from the evaluation of an expression or from the return value of a function call. (We'll learn about return values in Chapter 7.)

As you can see on the operator precedence help screen, assignment is low in the precedence hierarchy, so be sure to use parentheses if you have a situation in which ambiguities are possible and evaluation order is important.

Arithmetic Operators

The primary arithmetic operators are the ones you commonly use for simple arithmetic. In C, the symbols × and ÷ are not used because no corresponding keys appear on the keyboard. Instead, the symbol * is used for multiplication, and the symbol / is used for division.

Operator	Description
+	Addition
−	Subtraction
*	Multiplication
/	Division

As shown in Figure 4-2, simple addition obtains the values of the two operands, *value_1* and *value_2*, and adds them together to produce a sum. You can then assign the sum into some other variable or use it immediately in another expression.

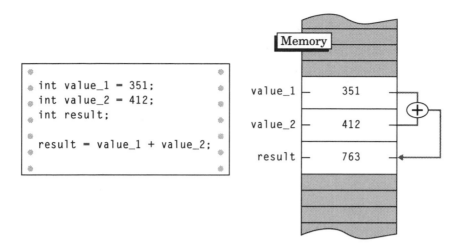

FIGURE 4-2. *An arithmetic calculation.*

In this example, the arithmetic statement

```
result = value_1 + value_2;
```

tells the compiler to assign the sum into the *result* variable.

The TRAP program (Listing 4-1 on the following page) combines three of the arithmetic operators to calculate the area of a trapezoid. To compute this area, you must add the lengths of the top and bottom and multiply the sum by half the height.

After the variables are declared, the program uses a series of *printf()* statements to draw a rough trapezoid on the screen. Note the use of the escape sequences in these *printf()* statements to insert tabs, newline characters, and literal backslash characters.

Next, the program uses three *printf()* and *scanf()* statements to get the trapezoid measurements from the user. Because the rough depiction of the trapezoid appears on the screen when the program is run, the user can see exactly what dimensions are required. This introduces a concept applicable to all computer languages: user friendliness. Basically, a user-friendly program is one that provides clear, meaningful interaction with the user. In this example, the user can see what measurements are required, and the program prompts for each one individually.

```
/*
 * T R A P
 *
 * Calculate the area of a trapezoid.
 */

main()
{
        /* Variable declaration */
        float area, top, base, height;

        /* Get dimensions from the user. */
        printf("\n\tTRAPEZOID AREA CALCULATION\n\n");
        printf("Please enter the following measurements:\n\n");
        printf("                top\n");
        printf("          _____      ____\n");
        printf("         /            \\      ¦\n");
        printf("        /              \\    height\n");
        printf("       /_____\\  __¦__\n");
        printf("              base\n\n");
        printf("Note: Please use numbers only.\n");
        printf("Enter the top measurement of the trapezoid: ");
        scanf("%f", &top);
        printf("Enter the base measurement of the trapezoid: ");
        scanf("%f", &base);
        printf("Enter the height measurement of the trapezoid: ");
        scanf("%f", &height);

        /* Calculate and print the area. */
        area = (top + base) * height / 2;
        printf("The area of the trapezoid is %.2f\n", area);

}
```

LISTING 4-1. *Program source code for trap.c.*

The last lines of the program perform the actual calculation of the trapezoid area and print the result. Note the use of parentheses to force the compiler to perform the addition before the multiplication or division. Using the format specifier *%.2f* in the final *printf()* statement causes the floating-point number *area* to be displayed with only two significant digits in the fractional part. This degree of precision is sufficient for our purpose in this example.

Other Arithmetic Operators. Two other operators are grouped with the four primary arithmetic operators:

Operator	Description
–	Unary minus
%	Modulus (remainder)

The unary minus (–) operator changes the sign of an object without affecting its magnitude. Thus, given a variable x with a value of 6, $-x$ has a value of –6.

The modulus operator (%), also known as the remainder operator, yields the amount that is left after an integer division. As shown in Figure 4-3, the expression 32 % 10 yields a result of 2. (After 10 divides into 32 three times, the remainder is 2.) Modulus operations apply only to integral values.

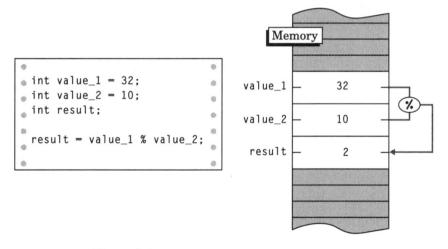

FIGURE 4-3. *The modulus operator returns only the remainder of a division operation.*

Although you might not see its usefulness immediately, the modulus operator is handy in a variety of situations. For example, you can use it to keep a number within a specified range:

```
unsigned int in_range, n;

in_range = n % 256;
```

Whatever the value of n, the expression $n \% 256$ always yields a value in the range 0 through 255. You can also use the modulus operator to test whether a number is even or odd: If the result of $n \% 2$ is 0, then the number n is even.

Data Conversions. You can write expressions that involve operands of differing types, but internally, C must convert operands to a common type before calculating. The following list of arithmetic conversions describes, in order, the steps taken to obtain the required uniformity before a binary operation is actually performed:

1. Operands of *float* type are converted to *double* type.

2. If one operand has *long double* type, the other operand is converted to *long double* type.

3. If one operand has *double* type, the other operand is converted to *double* type.

4. Any operands of *char* or *short* type are converted to *int* type.

5. Any operands of *unsigned char* or *unsigned short* type are converted to *unsigned int* type.

6. If one operand is of *unsigned long* type, the other operand is converted to *unsigned long* type.

7. If one operand is of *long* type, the other operand is converted to *long* type.

8. If one operand is of *unsigned int* type, the other operand is converted to *unsigned int* type.

The CONVERT program shows the effects of implicit (performed by the compiler) and explicit (performed by you) data conversions. A set of declarations reserves storage for a character, two integers, and two floating-point variables. The remainder of the program, shown in Listing 4-2, consists of three sets of assignments and print statements that demonstrate data conversion concepts.

```
/*
 * C O N V E R T
 *
 * Show the effects of both implicit and explicit data
 * conversions in expressions involving different types.
 */

main()
{
        /* Variable declarations and initializations */
        char cv;
        int ivl = 321;
        float fvl, fv2;

        /*
         * Lost precision: Show the effect of storing an
         * integer-size value in a character variable.
         */
        printf("CONVERT:\n\n");
        cv = ivl;
        printf("Integer assigned to character: %d -> %d (%c)\n\n",
                ivl, cv, cv);

        /*
         * Integer arithmetic: Show loss of fractional component
         * when numbers are involved in integer-only expressions
         * and how to retain the fractional component.
         */
        fvl = ivl / 50;
        printf("Integer arithmetic: %d / 50   = %f\n", ivl, fvl);
        fvl = ivl / 50.0;
        printf("   Real arithmetic: %d / 50.0 = %f\n\n", ivl, fvl);

        /*
         * Promotion: In the following example, an integer
         * is promoted to a float before being added to a
         * floating-point variable.
         */
        fvl = 1028.750;
        fv2 = fvl + ivl;
        printf("%f + %d equals %f\n", fvl, ivl, fv2);

        return (0);
}
```

LISTING 4-2. *Program source code for convert.c.*

Loss of Precision. In the CONVERT program, the statement

```
cv = iv1;
```

assigns the value of *iv1*, an integer, to *cv*, a character variable. Precision is lost because the value of *iv1*, 321, is held in two bytes on an IBM PC and *cv* is held in only one byte. Consequently, all but the lowest eight bits are effectively lost, as shown in Figure 4-4, limiting the stored value of *cv* to the range 0 through 255. The program prints the resulting character value both as a decimal number, 65, and as a character, A.

Note that although *cv* is a *char*, it is implicitly widened to *int* when used in the *printf()* statement. The compiler makes this adjustment because the number that is output, specified by the *%d* in the control string, must be an integer.

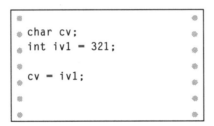

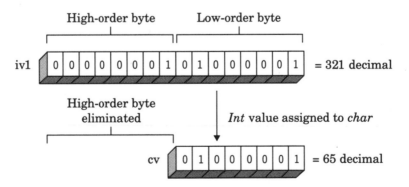

FIGURE 4-4. *Loss of precision when you assign an* int *value to a* char.

Integer Arithmetic. When only integers are involved in an arithmetic calculation, such as the one in the expression *fv1 = iv1 / 50*, any fractional part of the result is truncated, even if the result is assigned to a floating-point variable.

To preserve the fractional component of a calculation, you must coerce the compiler to convert one of the operands to type *float*, either by casting it to type *float* or by expressing the value as a real number. For the second example in the CONVERT program, simply representing the value 50 as a real number (50.0) is sufficient. If the expression involves only variables, at least one operand must be a *float*, or you can use a type cast, such as *(float)iv1*.

Promotion. The last example in the CONVERT program shows a situation in which the compiler promotes a variable to another type when it evaluates an expression. Because the compiler must convert values to a common type before performing a calculation, it promotes the integer *iv1* in the expression

```
fv2 = fv2 + iv1
```

to type *float* before it computes the indicated sum.

The *sizeof* Operator

The *sizeof* operator is the only C operator that is not represented by a cryptic symbol. It is a unary operator, not a function. The value it yields represents the size in bytes of a specified object. The form of a *sizeof* expression is

sizeof *expression*

where *expression* is a variable name or a data type.

The purpose of *sizeof* is to give you a way of determining the sizes of various objects in a machine-independent way. This is useful for writing programs that can be run on other types of computers, whose storage sizes might differ from those of your current machine.

The SIZE program (Listing 4-3 on the following page) shows how to use *sizeof* and tells you something about your system at the same time. It prints a series of messages that tell you how much storage, in bytes, is used for each primary data type.

If you run size.c on a 16-bit system, the program tells you that an integer occupies two bytes. On a 32-bit system, it says that an integer occupies four bytes. Useful information! A program that needs this kind of information can get it easily by using *sizeof*.

```
/*
 * S I Z E
 *
 * Show the sizes in bytes of various data types.
 */

main()
{
        printf("Type    Bytes\n");
        printf("------  -----\n");
        printf("char    %d\n", sizeof (char));
        printf("short   %d\n", sizeof (short));
        printf("int     %d\n", sizeof (int));
        printf("long    %d\n", sizeof (long));
        printf("float   %d\n", sizeof (float));
        printf("double  %d\n", sizeof (double));
}
```

LISTING 4-3. *Program source code for size.c.*

Relational Operators

The relational operators compare operands to yield one of two results:
true (1) or false (0).

Operator	Description
<	Less than
<=	Less than or equal to
==	Equal to
>	Greater than
>=	Greater than or equal to
!=	Not equal to

Consider the variables $a = 2$ and $b = 3$, for example. The relational expressions $a < b$, $a <= b$, and $a != b$ all yield true. For the same variables, the remaining relational operators produce expressions that yield a false result: $a > b$, $a >= b$, and $a == b$.

❑ CAUTION: *Be sure to note that a double equal sign (==) tests for equality. In Pascal, BASIC, and other languages, the single equal sign (=) does this job. Forgetting to use == to test for equality is one of the most frequent C programming errors.*

Logical Operators

Like relational operators, logical operators return a true/false value after evaluating their operands. (See Figure 4-5.) The difference between the two is that logical operators operate exclusively on the logical state (false or true—zero or nonzero) of their operands. The following is a list of the logical operators:

Operator	Description
!	Logical NOT
&&	Logical AND
¦¦	Logical OR

Logical negation is achieved by applying the ! operator. To negate an expression (operand) that yields a certain logical result, precede the expression with the ! operator to produce the opposite result:

```
10      /* Nonzero -- yields a true result */
!10     /* Yields a false (logically opposite) result */
```

Note that the logical NOT operator (!) requires one operand. This operator forces the logical state of an expression or value to its opposite state. It does not change the value of any variable in the expression.

Logical NOT (!)

result = !expression;

Logical AND (&&)

result = expr_1 && expr_2;

Logical OR (¦¦)

result = expr_1 ¦¦ expr_2;

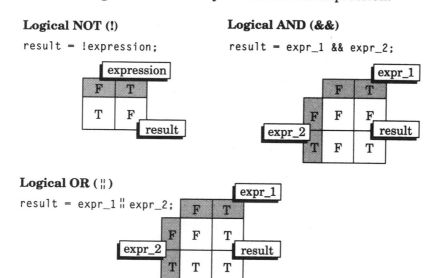

FIGURE 4-5. *Truth tables for the C logical operators.*

The logical AND and logical OR operators, however, require two operands. Therefore, their truth tables in Figure 4-5 have an additional dimension for the second operand. Logical AND produces a true value only when both operands are true, whereas logical OR produces a true value if either of its operands is true or if both are true. The following example demonstrates this:

```
int a = 10, b = 5, c = 0;

a && b          /* True -- both are nonzero */
a && c          /* False -- one operand is zero */
a || c          /* True -- one operand is nonzero */
```

Expressions formed using relational operators described in the previous section can be used as operands with && and || to form compound logical expressions. As you'll notice in the following examples, the logical operators have lower precedence than the relational operators; therefore, the comparisons are performed before the logical connections are tested:

```
int a = 10, b = 5;
int i = 2, j = 9;

a > b && i < j          /* True */
a < b || i > j          /* False */
```

The && operator has a higher precedence than ||. In an expression that involves both, you might need to use parentheses to force the order of evaluation you want. The following expression, evaluated using the preceding variable assignments for *a* and *b*, is shown both with and without parentheses to demonstrate the effect:

```
(a > b || i > j) && a < i          /* False */
a > b || i > j && a < i            /* True */
```

Short-Circuit Evaluation. If the result of a compound expression can be determined before the entire expression is evaluated, the remainder of the expression is not evaluated. Still using the assignments *a = 10* and *b = 5*, the result of the expression

```
a > b || i < j          /* True */
```

is clear as soon as *a > b* is evaluated to be true. The compiler does not evaluate *i < j*. An OR expression yields a true result if either operand is true, so Learn C need not evaluate the second operand if the first is true.

Short-circuit evaluation can cause problems if the unevaluated portions of the expression contain side effects such as assignments or incrementation. Consider, for example, the following expression:

```
a > b !! i < (j - j + 1)
```

Given the previous assignments of *a* and *b*, the variable *j* would not be incremented because the second portion of the expression,

```
i < (j - j + 1)
```

is not evaluated. If *a* were less than or equal to *b*, the incrementation would take place because the first portion would be false, requiring that the second expression be evaluated. Aspects of your program that depend on the evaluation of *j = j + 1* could yield incorrect results, leaving you with a hard-to-find problem.

Bitwise Operators

The bitwise operators work only with integral data types.

Operator	Description
&	Bitwise AND
¦	Bitwise OR
^	Bitwise exclusive OR
~	Bitwise complement

The bitwise operators yield results on a bit-by-bit basis. In any given bit position, the values of the operands are compared. The resulting value depends on the specific operator, as shown in Figure 4-6 on the following page.

If you use operands of different types in a bitwise operation, C converts types, if necessary, and the resulting type is that of the operands after conversion. Therefore, a bitwise AND operation on a character and an integer produces an integer result so that no bits of the wider object are lost.

In the example on the following page, the bitwise AND and bitwise OR are applied to a pair of values. The comments show the binary equivalents of the hexadecimal values. (You can, of course, check the binary values by converting the hexadecimal values yourself, using the method described in Chapter 3.)

```
char result;
char bits1 = \x2A;           /* 00101010 */
char bits2 = \x0F;           /* 00001111 */
result = bits1 & bits2;      /* 00001010 (\x0A) */
result = bits1 ¦ bits2;      /* 00101111 (\x2F) */
result = bits1 ^ bits2;      /* 00100101 (\x25) */
result = ~bits2;             /* 11110000 (\xF0) */
```

Bitwise operators have lower precedence than relational operators, so you must use parentheses in expressions involving both:

```
(bits1 & bits2) != bits2
```

C evaluates the bitwise AND first, producing a value of \x0A (using the value assignments above), which is not equal to \x0F, so the expression yields a true value.

Without the parentheses, the default grouping of operands leads first to the evaluation of *bits2 != bits2*, the result of which is false, numerically 0. Applying the bitwise AND where one operand is 0 produces a result of 0. You can, of course, regard this result as the number 0 or as a logically false condition.

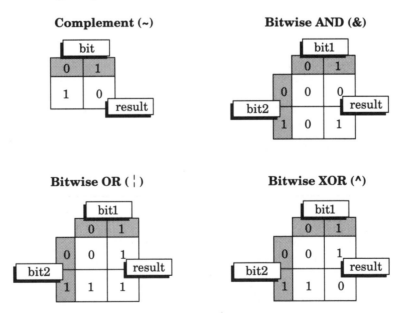

FIGURE 4-6. *Bit-level access using bitwise operators.*

The bitwise complement operator (~) is a unary operator that inverts the sense of each bit in its operand. Given the *char* variable *bits2* with a binary value of 00001111, *~bits2* has a value of 11110000 (as shown in the earlier example).

Shift Operators

The shift operators take two operands. The first is the item to be shifted and the second is the number of bit positions to shift. Both operands must be integral types.

Operator	Description
<<	Shift left
>>	Shift right

Shift operators give C some of the low-level control you would associate with assembly language. They let you get close to the machine in ways that most high-level languages don't permit.

The left-shift operator (<<) shifts bits to the left, filling vacated positions on the right with 0s. Bits shifted off the left end of the data item are lost.

The right-shift operator (>>) slides the bits of an object to the right by the specified number of positions and fills the vacated positions in ways that depend on machine architecture and the type of the data item being shifted.

Most machines, including IBM PCs and compatibles, fill based on the data type of the shifted operand. If the data type is unsigned, 0s are used. Signed operands are filled with 1s if the sign bit (leftmost bit) is 1, and if the sign bit is 0, the fill bits are also 0s. On machines that use arithmetic shift, vacated positions on the left are always filled with 0s.

The second operand, the shift amount, should not be negative: A negative shift amount produces an undefined result. If you are using a variable to control the shift amount, check its value before you use it.

❏ NOTE: *The original operand is not disturbed by a shift operation unless the result of the shift is assigned back into the operand by some other means.*

Compound Assignment Operators

A traditional assignment expression of the form

expr1 = expr1 *op* **expr2**

(where *op* is a bitwise, shift, or arithmetic binary operator) can be represented in C by this shorter form:

expr1 *op*= **expr2**

The obvious advantage of the latter form is that *expr1* need be typed only once. Compare the following identical assignments:

```
i = i + 3;
```

```
i += 3;
```

For this simple expression, the benefit is debatable. But in complex expressions, the notational convenience of compound assignment can be important. In addition, the compound assignment expression is less cluttered, and once you understand the idiom, it's actually easier to read than the traditional form.

The following list offers a summary of the compound assignment operators and their meanings:

Operator	Description
+=	Addition assignment
−=	Subtraction assignment
*=	Multiplication assignment
/=	Division assignment
%=	Remainder assignment
<<=	Left-shift assignment
>>=	Right-shift assignment
&=	Bitwise-AND assignment
¦+	Bitwise-inclusive-OR assignment
^=	Bitwise-exclusive-OR assignment
~=	Bitwise-complement assignment

With a little practice, you'll come to appreciate the notational convenience of this sleight of hand.

Increment and Decrement Operators

Increment and decrement unary operators are technically assignment operators but are singled out here because they cause confusion for some beginning C programmers. Their behavior is rooted closely in the machine language of minicomputers and microcomputers that have increment and decrement operators in their instruction sets.

Operator	Description
++	Increment
--	Decrement

The increment and decrement operators are similar to the compound assignment operators in that they are convenient shorthand notations for common assignment operations. The effect of the ++ operator is to add 1 to its operand; the effect of -- is to subtract 1. The first statement below illustrates the traditional assignment form for incrementation, and the second is the equivalent C incrementing assignment:

```
offset = offset + 1;
++offset;
```

Both statements cause *offset* to have a value 1 greater than it has before the statement executes. The ++ or -- operator can also be placed after the operand, as in the following statement:

```
 offset++;
```

which has exactly the same effect as the preceding examples. (As you'll soon see, placement of the operator can be important.)

The decrement operator works in the same way. The assignments

```
offset = offset - 1;
--offset;
offset--;
```

all cause the value *offset* to be decremented by 1.

A fourth option is to use the += or -= compound assignment operator:

```
offset += 1;
offset -= 1;
```

Again, the result is the same as it was in the foregoing examples.

Prefix and Postfix Notation. In expressions involving other operators and objects, the increment and decrement operators behave differently when placed before (prefix notation) and after (postfix notation) their operands. The prefix form of the increment operator, for example, increments the operand and then uses the resulting value in the rest of the expression. The postfix notation uses the current value of the operand in the overall expression and *then* increments the affected operand.

The PRE&POST program (Listing 4-4) shows some examples:

```
/*
 * P R E & P O S T
 *
 * Demonstrate the uses of prefix and postfix notation
 * in arithmetic expressions.
 */

main()
{
        /* Initialize and declare variables */
        int x = 2, y = 3, result;

        /* Show values before and after expression evaluation. */
        printf("\nSTARTING VALUES: x = %d; y = %d\n", x, y);
        result = ++x + y;
        printf("PREFIX: The result of ++x + y = %d\n", result);
        printf("(After calculation, x = %d and y = %d)\n", x, y);

        x = 2, y = 3;    /* Restore values */
        printf("\nSTARTING VALUES: x = %d; y = %d\n", x, y);
        result = x++ + y;
        printf("POSTFIX: The result of x++ + y = %d\n", result);
        printf("(After calculation, x = %d and y = %d)\n", x, y);
}
```

LISTING 4-4. *Program source code for pre&post.c.*

The program demonstrates the difference between using prefix and postfix notation in calculations. After the variables are declared and initialized, they are printed to verify the starting values. In the next line, x is incremented with prefix notation and added to y, and the sum is placed in *result*. The next two *printf()* statements show the result of the calculation, 6, and the after-calculation values of x and y.

In the next section, x and y are first restored to their original values. Again, the program displays a message to verify the starting values. The next statement calculates *result* again, this time with x incremented using postfix notation. The last two lines print the result of the calculation, 5, and show the after-calculation values.

Be sure to use prefix notation if you want the operand to attain its new value before the calculation is done. Use postfix notation to cause the calculation to be done first, using the original value.

Using increment and decrement operators indiscriminately in expressions is a potentially dangerous practice because of potentially adverse side effects. The results of calculations can be affected in subtle ways that are not immediately obvious.

You can avoid unwanted side effects by not using programming techniques that are designed to make your program appear clever at the expense of clarity and safety. Saving a few lines in a source file while sacrificing clarity and ease of maintenance is just plain foolish.

Address and Indirection Operators

The C language is heavily biased toward the use of "pointers." A pointer is a variable that contains the *address* of a variable or function. Pointers permit indirect manipulation of data and code. C provides two operators to facilitate their use.

Operator	Description
&	Address-of
*	Indirection

The & operator yields the memory address of its operand. The result is a pointer to that object. The * operator provides indirect access to an object through a previously defined pointer to the object. In Chapter 9, we will examine the topic of indirection and the use of pointers in detail.

Sequence Operator

The sequence operator (,) is an enforcer: It sets the order of evaluation of expressions. It is used in critical situations to guarantee that operations are performed in a specific sequence. The sequence operator has the lowest precedence of all the C operators.

For obvious reasons, the sequence operator is often called the comma operator. Do not confuse the sequence operator, however, with the comma that separates entries in a function parameter list.

Questions and Exercises

1. In your own words, describe the terms "operator" and "operand."

2. Describe the difference between an expression and a statement.

3. What is a binary operator? Show the general form of an expression that involves a binary operator.

4. For each of the following, write suitable variable declaration and assignment statements:

   a. An integer with a value of 8000
   b. The letter Z
   c. The average of the numbers 3, 11, 21, and 66
   d. The difference between two integers

5. Write a program that calculates the area of a right triangle. The formula is one half the height multiplied by the base.

6. Given the following variable declarations and assignments, find the value yielded by each expression shown:

   ```
   int a = 1, b = 2, c = 3;

   a < b
   a != c
   b >= c
   a < b && c < b
   a <= c || b > c
   (a += 3) < c
   ```

7. What are the values of n and y after each of the following statements is executed? (Evaluate each expression using the originally assigned values of the variables.)

   ```
   int n, i = 10, j = 20, x = 3, y = 100;

   n = (i > j) && (x < ++y);
   n = (j - i) && (x < y++);
   n = (i < j) || (y += i);
   ```

8. Write a program that gathers a number in the range 0 through 65,535 from the user, inverts all the bits, and prints the decimal value of the modified number. (Hint: Use a variable of type *unsigned short int*.)

5: Controlling Program Flow

Decision

Iteration

The *goto* Statement

Questions and Exercises

C Programming Lessons: *Decision and Iteration*

Controlling the flow of execution is a fundamental aspect of most computer programs. You can perform many simple tasks merely by executing a series of statements in sequence, as we have done in all our programs so far, but significant tasks almost invariably require changes to the execution sequence in response to operating conditions, inputs (such as user commands), and many other factors.

Chapter 2 introduced sequence, decision, and iteration in general terms, independent of any particular computer language. Now let's explore the decision-making and iteration statements that C provides to give us control over the flow of program execution.

Decision

Decision statements let you add branches to the execution flow. To accommodate a range of circumstances, C provides two different decision statements, as well as a conditional operator that is useful in situations where compactness is important.

The *if* Statement

The primary decision-making mechanism in C is the *if* statement. (See Figure 5-1.) An *if* statement has the form

```
if (expression)
statement
```

where *expression* must be enclosed within parentheses. The value yielded by *expression* determines whether *statement* is executed. If *expression* yields a nonzero result, it is considered logically true, and

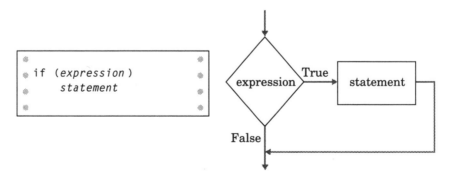

FIGURE 5-1. *In a simple* if *construction,* statement *executes only if* expression *is true.*

statement is executed. If *expression* yields a 0 result, it is logically false, and *statement* is bypassed. The *statement* part can be a single C statement or a block of C statements enclosed in braces.

The INSTRUCT program (Listing 5-1) displays an instruction, which the user can honor or ignore. If the user types the requested letter in response to the prompt, the program prints a commendation message. Otherwise, it lets the user down gently.

```
/*
 * I N S T R U C T
 *
 * This program determines whether its user
 * can follow simple instructions.
 */

main()
{
        char ch;

        printf("Type the letter T and press Enter: ");
        scanf("%1s", &ch);
        if (ch != 'T') {
                printf("Sorry, you don't make the team!\n");
                return (1);
        }
        printf("Excellent!  You're very cooperative.\n");
        return (0);
}
```

LISTING 5-1. *Program source code for instruct.c.*

Notice the use of braces in the INSTRUCT program to enclose the statement body of the *if* statement. The braces are required because the program must bypass both subsequent statements if the user types *T*, and must execute those statements if the user types any other character. The two statements in braces form a block (or compound) statement.

Next, notice that the INSTRUCT program contains two *return* statements. This is perfectly acceptable. The first returns a code of 1 to the operating system, indicating failure. The second returns 0, indicating success. The program executes only one of the return statements.

You might also note that the *scanf()* statement contains the format specifier %1s (for a one-character string) rather than %c, which you could logically expect to see instead. Either is fine for this example, but %c fails in a subtle way in some situations.

Great C Battles

The locations of the opening and closing braces cause considerable debate. As you see in the INSTRUCT program, I choose to place the opening brace at the end of the line that introduces the block and the closing brace directly under the associated keyword (which in this case is *if*). The following are some common bracing methods, using the *if* statement from INSTRUCT as an example.

```
if (ch != 'T') {
        printf("...");
        return (1);
}
```
The technique used in this book

```
if (ch != 'T')
{
        printf("...");
        return (1);
}
```
Braces aligned below keyword

```
if (ch != 'T')
        {
        printf("...");
        return (1);
        }
```
Braces aligned with statement body

```
if (ch != 'T') {
        printf("...");
        return (1);
        }
```
Right brace aligned with statement body

The first method shown (the method used in this book) is based on the standard set by Kernighan and Ritchie in their 1978 book, *The C Programming Language*. In fact, the second method derives from "K & R" as well; however, they use it only for bracing functions. They use the first method for almost every other purpose.

The other methods shown are espoused by various authors in the C programming field. None of these methods has any significant advantage over the others.

As an exercise, remove the braces around the statement body of the *if* statement and run the program again. Without the braces, the only statement that the compiler acts upon exclusively when *expression* is true is the statement immediately following the *if* statement, which in this case is the first *printf()* statement. The *return (1)* statement is no longer part of the statement body; therefore, it always executes. Without the braces to delimit the statement body, the second *printf()* and the following *return (0)* statements never execute.

Explicit Two-Way Branching. The simple *if* statement is a two-way branch, but it provides for only a single action. An *if* statement can have an *else* clause, as shown in Figure 5-2, which provides a distinct alternative action.

```
if (expression)
        statement_1
else
        statement_2
```

The expression-evaluation process works the same as for a simple *if*. If *expression* is true, *statement_1* is executed. Unlike the simple *if* statement, however, if *expression* is false, an alternative statement, *statement_2*, is executed. After one of the statements executes, control passes to the statement following the *if* statement. Also, like a simple *if*

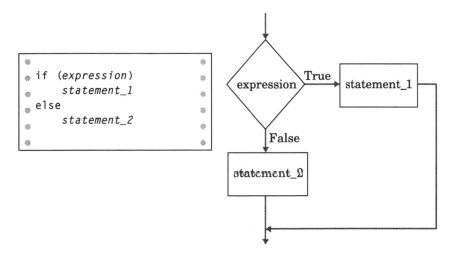

FIGURE 5-2. *Unlike the simple* if *construction, an* if-else *construction supplies a distinct alternative,* statement_2, *which executes only if* expression *is false.*

statement, *statement_1* and *statement_2* can be individual C state-ments or blocks of C statements enclosed in braces.

The MINIMUM program (Listing 5-2) shows how the *if-else* state-ment works. It uses an *if* statement to identify the lesser of two values.

The program prompts the user for two numbers and saves each one in a separate variable. The *expression* part of the *if* statement is *number1 < number2*. If the result of this test is true, the program assigns the value of *number1* to the variable *lesser*. Otherwise, it assigns the value of *number2* to *lesser*. If the two numbers have the same value, it assigns the value of *number2* to *lesser*, which is an acceptable result in the context of this program.

```
/*
 * M I N I M U M
 *
 * This program determines the lesser of two
 * numbers supplied by the user.
 */

main()
{
        int lesser;             /* the result */
        int number1, number2;   /* the input values */

        /*
         * Prompt the user for two numbers and read them.
         */
        printf("Type the first number and press Enter: ");
        scanf("%d", &number1);
        printf("Type the second number and press Enter: ");
        scanf("%d", &number2);

        /*
         * Find the lesser value and report it.
         */
        if (number1 < number2)
                lesser = number1;
        else
                lesser = number2;
        printf("The lesser of %d and %d is %d.\n",
                number1, number2, lesser);

        return (0);
}
```

LISTING 5-2. *Program source code for minimum.c.*

Nested *if* Statements. To nest *if* statements, you insert one *if* statement within a branch of another. The following is an example:

```
int raining;
int window_open;
   .
   .
   .
if (raining == 1)
        if (window_open == 1)
                puts("Close the window.");
```

Nesting lets you establish multiple conditions for the execution of a statement. In this example, the *puts()* statement is executed only if both *if* conditions are true. The second *if* statement is nested—technically, it is the *statement* portion of the first *if* statement and is therefore examined only if the first *condition* is true (in this example, *raining == 1*).

Nesting is certainly legitimate and often necessary, but it is potentially dangerous: You must be careful to associate optional *else* clauses with the appropriate *if* keyword. For instance, if you carelessly add to the preceding fragment an *else* clause that instructs you to take advantage of the nice weather to go for a walk, you would instead be told to walk on a rainy day as long as the window is closed!

```
if (raining == 1)
        if (window_open == 1)
                puts("Close the window.");
else
        puts("Good day for a walk!");
```

The problem here is that the *else* associates itself with the closest previous *if* that doesn't already have an *else* clause. The indention may indicate to you that the *else* is associated with the first *if* statement, but remember that the compiler doesn't care about indention.

To force the correct association, add some braces:

```
if (raining == 1) {
        if (window_open == 1)
                puts("Close the window.");
}
else
        puts("Good day for a walk!");
```

Now the *else* clause is associated with the first *if* statement, and all is right with the world.

RAINING is a complete program (Listing 5-3) that shows the correct version of the nested *if* statement in action. The program prompts the user for the weather conditions and the status of the window, and then it offers friendly advice based on those conditions. If it is raining and the window is already closed, the program quietly terminates.

```
/*
 * R A I N I N G
 *
 * Tell the user what to do based on the weather conditions.
 */

main()
{
        int raining;
        int window_open;

        /*
         * Collect needed data.
         */
        printf("Is it raining outside? (0 - NO, 1 - YES): ");
        scanf("%d", &raining);
        printf("Is the window open? (0 - NO, 1 - YES): ");
        scanf("%d", &window_open);

        /*
         * Give advice based on the conditions.  Offer no
         * advice if it's raining and the window is closed.
         */
        if (raining == 1) {
                if (window_open == 1)
                        puts("Close the window.");
        }
        else
                puts("Good day for a walk!");

        return (0);
}
```

LISTING 5-3. *Program source code for raining.c.*

Multiway Branching with *else if*. Another variation on the theme of nested *if* statements is the use of the *else if* construct to extend the *if* statement for multiway branching. The basic syntax is as follows:

```
if (expression_1)
        statement_1
else if (expression_2)
        statement_2
    .
    .
    .
else if (expression_n)
        statement_n
[else
        statement]
```

❑ NOTE: *Although* else if *might appear to be a C language keyword, it isn't. The* else if *construct is simply a sequence of the* else *and* if *keywords.*

The controlling expressions are evaluated sequentially, beginning with *expression_1* and moving down through *expression_n* (however many you happen to have). When a logically true expression is encountered, the associated statement is executed, and the remaining *else if* (and *else*) statements are ignored. The *statement* in the optional *else* clause is executed if none of the other branches is taken.

The CMD1 program (Listing 5-4 on the following page) demonstrates the use of multiway branching. The program prompts the user for a command without actually saying what the acceptable commands are. To receive a command, CMD1 uses the *getch()* function, part of the run-time library support package that is built into Learn C. It reads a character from the keyboard without displaying it on the screen and returns an integer value that is the ASCII code for the input character. The value is preserved in *key* and is used later in the controlling expressions of the *if* statements.

CMD1 is not a particularly friendly program. The user is forced to press randomly selected keys to see what happens. If the user types the letter *A*, for example, CMD1 displays the message *Unknown command—A*, and quits. The user who types *h* (or *H* or *?*) gets better treatment—CMD1 prints a brief help frame that describes the acceptable commands, and then quits. Only two other commands are supported: Typing *M* or *m* tells CMD1 to print a message, and typing *Q* or *q* requests a graceful exit.

We'll revisit the CMD1 program later to introduce some enhancements and teach it some manners. For now, as an exercise, try adding

```
/*
 * C M D 1
 *
 * Get a command from the user and take the requested action.
 */

main()
{
        int key;

        /*
         * Get a command from the user.  A command is a
         * single key which is acted upon immediately.
         */
        printf("Command: ");
        key = getch();   /* console input */
        if (key == 'q' || key == 'Q')
                puts("Done.");
        else if (key == 'h' || key == 'H' || key == '?') {
                puts("CMD1 understands these commands:");
                puts("h or H or ?: help frame");
                puts("m or M: message");
                puts("q or Q: quit");
        }
        else if (key == 'm' || key == 'M') {
                puts("Here's the message.");
                puts("Pretty disappointing, huh!");
        }
        else
                printf("Unknown command -- %c\n", key);

        return (0);
}
```

LISTING 5-4. *Program source code for cmd1.c.*

some new commands that display new messages. Don't forget to use braces if more than one statement follows your *else if* construct.

The Conditional Operator

The conditional operator is C's ternary operator. It has the following form:

expression_1 ? *expression_2* : *expression_3*

The first of its three operands, *expression_1*, is evaluated to determine if it is logically true or false. If *expression_1* is logically true, *expression_2* is evaluated; if *expression_1* is logically false, *expression_3* is evaluated instead.

The result of the conditional operation is the value yielded by *expression_2* or that yielded by *expression_3*, depending on the result of *expression_1*. In this respect, a conditional operation is identical to an *if-else* statement, as the following example demonstrates:

```
int a = 10, b = 20;
int result;

/* conditional version */
result = a < b ? a : b;

/* if statement version */
if (a < b)
        result = a;
else
        result = b;
```

You may recognize this decision as the heart of our MINIMUM program (Listing 5-2 on p. 96). Admittedly, the conditional expression trades clarity for compactness, but it has its place. You will use it primarily in writing macro definitions (discussed in Chapter 6) and in function return statements (discussed in Chapter 7).

The *switch* Statement

The C *switch* statement is also a multiway branching mechanism. It has the following general form:

```
switch (expression) {
case constant_expression_1:
        statement_body_1
case constant_expression_2:
        statement_body_2

.
.
.

case constant_expression_n:
        statement_body_n
default:
        statement
}
```

A single integer expression is evaluated at the top of a *switch* statement, and this controlling expression is then compared to a series of values, each introduced by the keyword *case*. Each case is defined by a constant or by a constant expression, one that consists entirely of constants or other constant expressions. (The expression 620 / 4, for example, is a constant expression.) If a match for the control expression is found among the cases, the associated statements are executed.

Each *case* label must be unique. If the controlling *expression* does not match any of the labeled cases, the *default* case executes. The *default* case is optional. The cases and the default case can occur in any order.

When control passes to the statement body of a case, execution begins with that statement body and continues until *all* statements in that statement body and in the remaining statement bodies of the *switch* are executed (ignoring the subsequent *case* labels) or until a statement transfers control out of the *switch*. The following fragment illustrates the flow of execution within a *switch* statement:

```
int ch;

printf("Press the letter a, A, or b: ");
scanf("%1s", &ch);

switch (ch) {
case 'a':
case 'A':
        printf("You pressed either A or a.\n");
case 'b':
        printf("You got here for one of two reasons:\n");
        printf("  1) You pressed the letter b or \n");
        printf("  2) You fell through from the previous case.\n");
        break;
default:
        printf("I see you don't follow instructions well!\n");
        break;
}
```

Notice that the behavior of a *switch* lets you arrange labels so that any of a series of cases executes a common statement body. In the fragment above, pressing either *a* or *A* executes the first statement body. Then, because that statement does not transfer control outside the *switch* statement, the next statement body executes, as well. This effect, called "fall-through," is often unanticipated by beginning C programmers. To transfer execution control, use the *return* or *break* statements (as demonstrated in Listing 5-5), or use a function such as *exit()*.

The *break* Statement. The *break* statement causes an immediate exit from an enclosing *switch* statement, or from a loop statement such as *for*, *while*, or *do-while*. (Loop statements are covered later in this chapter.) In the context of a *switch*, it is used to mark the end of a *case* statement body. Consider, for example, the CMD2 program (Listing 5-5), a modification of CMD1. CMD2 employs a *switch* in place of the complicated *if* statement used in CMD1.

The usefulness of fall-through behavior is apparent in CMD2. The first case has an empty body. If the user presses either the lowercase or uppercase letter *Q*, the compiler executes the statement body that follows the second *case* label. Control is then transferred outside the *switch* statement by the *break* statement that ends that body of statements.

The next set of *case* labels selects the help frame, which is simply a series of *puts()* statements that print a brief explanatory message. The user must press *h*, *H*, or *?* to display the help frame. Again, the *break* statement that follows the *puts()* statements guarantees that execution does not fall through to the statements associated with the next case.

You can specify as many *case* statements as you need (as many as 257 for Learn C) to anticipate and react to all expected command keys. The *default* case is used here to respond to any unexpected commands. Note the use of a *break* statement following the *default* case statement body. Because the order of cases is important only if you are depending on fall-through, someone, even you, might add cases after the *default* case at some later time. If that occurs, the *break* statement will be a backstop to prevent unwanted fall-through.

As an exercise, try removing one of the *break* statements and running the program again to observe the fall-through effect.

```
/*
 * C M D 2
 *
 * Get a command from the user and take the requested action.
 * This version demonstrates the use of the switch statement.
 */

main()
{
        int key;
```

LISTING 5-5. *Program source code for cmd2.c.*   *(continued)*

LISTING 5-5. *continued*

```
/*
 * Get a command from the user.  A command is a
 * single key which is acted upon immediately.
 */
printf("Command (? for help): ");
key = getch();  /* console input */
switch (key) {
case 'q':
case 'Q':
        puts("Done.");
        break;
case 'h':
case 'H':
case '?':
        puts("CMD2 understands these commands:");
        puts("h or H or ?: help frame");
        puts("m or M: message");
        puts("q or Q: quit");
        break;
case 'm':
case 'M':
        puts("Here's the message.");
        puts("Pretty disappointing, huh!");
        break;
default:
        printf("Unknown command -- %c\n", key);
        break;
}
return (0);
}
```

Iteration

Iteration is a key component of most programs. In the preceding *switch* example, for instance, the *switch* statement that evaluates user commands could be embedded within a loop that runs indefinitely until the user decides to exit by pressing the designated quit command key.

The *while* Loop

The primary looping construct is the *while* loop. In fact, in most situations the *while* loop is the only loop we need. Its syntax is as follows:

```
while (expression)
        statement
```

As you can see in Figure 5-3, as long as *expression* evaluates to a nonzero value, the *while* loop executes *statement* repeatedly. The loop continues to execute until *expression* evaluates to 0 or until some occurrence within *statement* or some external event terminates the loop.

The statement body can be any valid C statement.

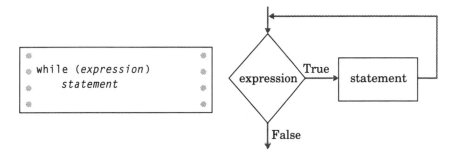

FIGURE 5-3. *A* while *loop executes* statement *as long as the result of the controlling* expression *is true (nonzero).*

The REPEAT program (Listing 5-6) uses a *while* loop to control the repeated displaying of a character.

```
/*
 *  R E P E A T
 *
 * Ask the user for a character and a count.  Display the
 * character the number of times specified by count.
 */

main()
{
        char ch;
        int count;
        printf("Type the character to repeat: ");
        scanf("%1s", &ch);
        printf("Type the repetition count: ");
        scanf("%d", &count);

        while (count > 0) {
                printf("%c", ch);
                --count;
        }
        printf("\n");
        return (0);
}
```

LISTING 5-6. *Program source code for repeat.c.*

The program prompts the user for the character to print, *ch*, and for the value of the repetition counter, *count*. Then, as long as *count* is greater than 0, the loop continues executing the statement body, printing *ch* and reducing *count* by 1 each time it completes a cycle. When *count* reaches 0, the test fails, and the statement body is skipped. Execution then continues with the next statement after the *while* loop, which is a *printf()* that simply displays a newline.

If the program user responds with * and *20*, for example, the output is a string of 20 asterisks. You can use this program to create a "linearity" test for your video display by responding with the letter *E* for the character and a count of *2000*, which is enough to fill the screen in 80-column, 25-line mode. The letter E, because of its straight edges, clearly exposes any waviness or nonlinearity in your video display.

As an exercise, remove the braces around the statement body and run the program again. (Press Ctrl-Break to stop execution.) Note that without the braces, only the *printf()* statement is executed as the statement body of the loop. Because the statement --*count;* is now outside the loop, the value of *count* never changes, so the loop doesn't terminate.

The *for* Loop

The *for* loop has some advantages over the *while* loop, readability being the most obvious. It takes the following form:

```
for ([init_expr]; [cond_expr]; [loop_expr])
      statement
```

In this general form, *init_expr* is the initializing expression, *cond_expr* is the conditional expression (equivalent to *expression* in the *while* loop), and *loop_expr* is the loop expression, generally a statement or function that acts on the value established by *init_expr*. As the square brackets indicate, you can omit any of the expressions, but the semicolons are required.

Figure 5-4 shows a *for* loop graphically. As with the *while* loop, the *for* loop executes *statement* as long as the controlling expression is logically true. Of course, *statement* can represent a single C statement or a block of C statements enclosed in braces. The primary benefit of the *for* loop is that all control information is prominently placed at the top of the loop. An equivalent *while* loop might have the initialization, conditional test, and loop expressions in widely scattered locations.

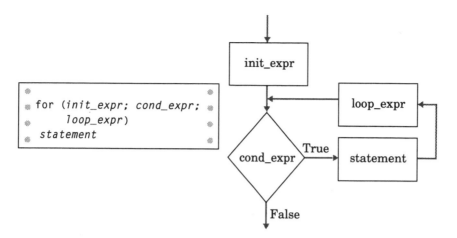

FIGURE 5-4. *The* for *loop is essentially a* while *loop with the initialization and loop expressions all contained within the loop control portion of the construct.*

The PWRTABLE program (Listing 5-7) prints a table of power values for the numbers in the range 0 through 10. The values are calculated by multiplying the base by itself the appropriate number of times.

```c
/*
 * P W R T A B L E
 *
 * Print a table of powers.
 */

main()
{
        int n;                 /* table index */

        /*
         * Label the columns.
         */
        puts("number\t exp2\t exp3\t exp4");
        puts("------\t-----\t-----\t-----");

        /*
         * Print the table of power values.
         */
        for (n = 0; n <= 10; ++n)
                printf("%2d\t%5d\t%5d\t%5d\n",
                        n, n * n,  n * n * n,  n * n * n * n);
        return (0);
}
```

LISTING 5-7. *Program source code for pwrtable.c.*

The *return* statement sends an exit code of 0 to Learn C to indicate that all went well. The program does not return a specific value to indicate an error.

❑ NOTE: *Because C has no exponentiation operator, you must calculate powers by using either repeated multiplications, as shown in* PWRTABLE, *or by calling the standard library function* pow().

Comparing *for* and *while* Loops

You might create the following *for* loop to calculate the "factorial" of a number:

```
main()
{
        int i, number = 6, factorial;

        for (i = number, factorial = 1; i > 1 ; --i) {
                factorial *= i;
        }
        printf("\nFactorial = %d", factorial);
}
```

Compare this *for* loop with the following *while* loop, which performs the same task:

```
main()
{
        int i, number = 6, factorial;

        i = number;
        factorial = 1;
        while (i > 1) {
                factorial *= i;
                --i;
        }
        printf("\nFactorial = %d", factorial);
}
```

The control information for the *while* loop is less compactly presented than in the equivalent *for* loop. If the *while* loop body spans more than a screenful or printed page of code, its control information can become difficult to assimilate.

The Infinite Loop

Many programming situations require that you create a looping operation that continues indefinitely. This is generally accomplished in either of two ways. One common practice is to use a *for* loop with three empty control expressions:

```
for (;;) {
        /* body of loop */
}
```

Another method is to create a *while* loop with a constant nonzero value:

```
while (1) {
        /* body of loop */
}
```

The reason the *for* statement works is that C interprets an empty test expression in a *for* loop as a nonzero (true) value. The *while* loop requires an explicit nonzero value to achieve the same effect. (To my eye, the *while (1)* approach is the more obvious.)

Incidentally, should you find yourself running a program that seems to be caught within an indefinite loop, you can normally break out of it by pressing Ctrl+Break.

Now we can invest our CMD2 program with this new sophistication. The CMD3 program (Listing 5-8) places the *getch()* function and the *switch* statement that processes user commands inside an infinite loop, permitting the user to continue issuing commands until he or she elects to quit.

```
/*
 * C M D 3
 *
 * Get a command from the user and take the requested action.
 * This version demonstrates the use of an infinite loop.
 */

main()
{
        int key;

        /*
         * Loop until the user types the command to quit.
         */
```

LISTING 5-8. *Program source code for cmd3.c.*   *(continued)*

LISTING 5-8. *continued*

```
        printf("Press ? for help.\n");
        while (1) {
                /*
                 * Get a command from the user.
                 */
                printf("Command: ");
                key = getch();  /* console input */

                /*
                 * Analyze and act on the command.
                 */
                switch (key) {
                case 'q':
                case 'Q':
                        puts("Done.");
                        return (0);
                case 'h':
                case 'H':
                case '?':
                        puts("CMD3 understands these commands:");
                        puts("h or H or ?: help frame");
                        puts("m or M: message");
                        puts("q or Q: quit");
                        break;
                case 'm':
                case 'M':
                        puts("Here's the message.");
                        puts("Pretty disappointing, huh!");
                        break;
                default:
                        printf("Unknown command -- %c\n", key);
                        break;
                }
        }
}
```

The comments identifying the function of the *switch* statement and the *while* loop aid readers of the program. Such comments are especially helpful when used with blocks of code that span more than a single page or screen.

Notice that CMD3 is a bit friendlier than its predecessors. Before prompting for input, the program prints the message *Press ? for help*, allowing the inexperienced user a way of getting a list of commands.

The *do* Loop

On occasion, you need to guarantee that the body of a loop executes at least once, even if the test condition fails immediately. The *do* loop, depicted in Figure 5-5, provides this guarantee.

```
do
        statement
while (expression);
```

As it executes the loop, the program first executes *statement* and then tests *expression*. If *expression* yields a 0 (false) result on the first pass, control passes outside the loop. But *statement* has done its job. On the other hand, if *expression* is true, the statement body executes again and continues to execute until *expression* is false. You will find examples of the *do* loop in later chapters.

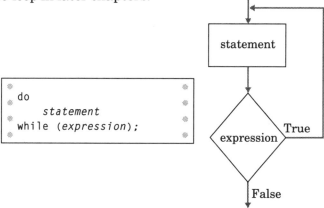

FIGURE 5-5. *The* do *loop executes* statement *at least once because it evaluates* expression *at the bottom of the loop.*

The *continue* Statement

As you have already learned, a *break* statement terminates the *while*, *do*, *for*, or *switch* statement in which it occurs. Another jump statement, *continue*, transfers control to the end of the enclosing iteration statement body. This effectively causes the next iteration of the loop to run unless the loop control expression forces termination of the loop.

A *continue* statement affects only an immediately enclosing loop statement. It has no effect on an enclosing *switch* statement; however, it often appears in a selection statement that is embedded within a loop statement body.

The *goto* Statement

The *goto* statement makes an unconditional jump to a label within the same function. Control immediately transfers to the labeled statement, which can appear either before or after the *goto*, so long as the label is within the current function. The *label* cannot be a reserved C keyword.

```
goto label;
    .
    .
    .
label: statement
```

Although the *goto* statement is appealingly direct (and a virtual requirement in many dialects of BASIC), it is a dangerous and confusing statement that you can easily avoid. The hazard lies in the lack of structure that can result from its use (and misuse). Code that is littered with *goto* statements and labels is needlessly difficult to read and maintain.

Programmers commonly eschew the *goto* in favor of structured control statements such as *while*, *for*, and *do* for looping, and *return*, *continue*, and *break* for transferring execution control. These statements offer all the flexibility you need. Technically, of course, these C statements are little more than *goto* statements in disguise. Their primary virtue is that they encourage a disciplined approach to programming.

Questions and Exercises

1. What is the purpose of statements such as the *if* and *switch* statements, and of the conditional operator (?:)?

2. Write a simple *if* statement that prints what the user types if it is a lowercase letter and does nothing for any other input.

3. Write a program that uses an *if-else* statement to determine whether a digit typed by the user is odd or even and prints a message to tell the user which it was. If the typed input is not a digit, the program should do nothing.

4. Write a program that reads input from a file and counts the number of letters (A–Z and a–z), digits (0–9), and other characters. Use an *if* statement with multiple *else if* clauses to differentiate the input characters.

5. Use a conditional expression instead of an *if-else* statement to handle the odd/even test in Exercise 3.

6. Use a *switch* statement inside a loop to implement a simple menu selection program that has five commands. Execute a command by typing a number from 1 through 5. For testing purposes, each command can simply print its own number. Terminate processing when the user types any character other than 1 through 5.

7. Write a program that prints all the powers of 2, starting with 0 and ending at 2 raised to the power of 8. Use a *while* loop to control the calculations and printing.

8. Rewrite the *while* loop in Exercise 7 in the form of a *for* loop.

9. Use a *do-while* loop to reverse the digits of a number supplied by the user.

10. Explain the difference between a *break* statement and a *continue* statement in a loop. Why would you use *continue* instead of *break*?

11. Rewrite the following code to eliminate the unnecessary *goto* statements:

```
int ch;

read_input:
        ch = getchar();
        if (ch == 'q')
                goto end_read;
        putchar(ch);
        goto read_input;
end_read:
```

6: The C Preprocessor

The *#include* Directive
The *#define* Directive
Questions and Exercises

One task of a C compiler is to examine source files for special instructions, called directives, that are not actually part of the C language itself. Directives are intended for the preprocessor, a part of the C compiler system that performs preliminary work in the overall compilation process. The preprocessor accomplishes its work before the C compiler compiles the actual source file.

This chapter introduces two preprocessor directives and gives an overview of their uses. Later chapters present further examples and additional information about the preprocessor as the need arises.

The *#include* Directive

We have already used the *#include* directive without saying much about it. When the preprocessor encounters an *#include* line, it replaces the line with the text of a named file, called a header file, in the current C source file. Then, when the file is compiled, the Learn C compiler effectively "sees" the text of that header file as if it were part of the source file. All you see in your program source file, however, is the *#include* directive.

A header file is so named because it is usually included at the top of a C source file, although the *#include* directive can actually be placed anywhere in the source file. The location of the *#include* directive does, however, affect the extent of the header file's visibility in the source file. The compiler can only be "aware" of the contents of the header file from the point at which the file is included in the source code through the end of that source file. Hence, the usual position of an *#include* directive is at or near the top of the source file.

The *#include* directive helps reduce the amount of work (typing) you have to do. You (or someone else) can prepare a header file that contains often-used information, and you can then use the file in many programs by adding a single line in any source file that needs that information.

Local Header Files

A "local" header file is one that resides in the current directory, along with the program source file that includes it, or in a directory that you name explicitly using a full or relative pathname. For example, to include a file named *myfile.h* that is located in the *WORK* directory in drive C, you would use the line:

```
#include "c:\work\myfile.h"
```

The pair of double quotation marks signifies that the enclosed string is a hard-coded pathname—that is, the full name and location of the file.

System Header Files

Learn C comes equipped with a set of "system" header files that were prepared for you by Microsoft. These are standard header files that contain information needed to meet common programming needs, such as creating graphics or getting data input from the keyboard.

When you set up Learn C on your computer, you used an MS-DOS environment variable to tell the compiler where system header files reside. Consequently, you can include a system header file in one of your programs by adding a line to your C source file of the following form:

```
#include <filename.ext>
```

The angle brackets indicate that Learn C will first look for *filename.ext* in the system include directory. If the system include directory does not exist or does not contain the specified header file, Learn C looks for *filename.ext* in the current directory. If the file is not found there, the compiler displays an error message.

File-naming Conventions

The usual header file extension is *h* (for "header"). However, this extension is not required. You can use any legal filename extension. For example, you might create a file of standard error messages to be used in your programs. You might appropriately call such a file message.h, but you could also use a more descriptive name such as error.msg.

One of the most commonly used system header files is stdio.h, the standard I/O header file. To include it in a program, place the following line near the top of your program source file:

```
#include <stdio.h>
```

Several other system header files, such as stdlib.h, ctype.h, and string.h, are frequent participants in the programs in this book.

❑ NOTE: *Unlike MS-DOS, most operating systems that support C programming are case sensitive, and it is customary to use only lowercase letters in filenames. This book uses lowercase letters in all filenames that are not specific to MS-DOS (such as AUTOEXEC.BAT). Although this adherence to lowercase isn't required, learn to do it this way in case you program in C on another type of machine someday.*

The #*define* Directive

The #*define* directive has two primary uses. The first is to define symbolic constants. The second is to create macros, which are essentially abbreviations. Symbolic constants and macros, if used correctly, contribute significantly to the clarity of C program source code.

Symbolic Constants

As a rule, the use of raw numbers in program source code is bad form. The reason is that a number is only a number: It conveys no meaning in the context of a given program beyond specifying its value. A source file that incorporates raw numbers becomes difficult, at best, to read and understand.

Experienced programmers disparagingly call literal numbers in program source code "magic" numbers because they are cloaked in mystery. You can save yourself a lot of grief by avoiding them (magic numbers).

Consider the following example:

```
for (n = 0; n <= 10; ++n)
        total += n;
```

This code fragment tells you that a value of n exceeding *10* is cause for terminating a loop (the test $n <= 10$), but it doesn't offer a clue as to why. If you define a symbolic constant *MAXROW* and give it a value of 10, the code fragment becomes the following:

```
#define MAXROW 10
.
.
.
for (n = 0; n <= MAXROW; ++n)
        total += n;
```

Now a reader of the program knows at least that *n* relates to the number of a row in a list or table of some kind. (Changing the variable name from *n* to a more descriptive identifier, such as *row*, also makes the code more readable at the expense of only a few keystrokes.)

A definition of a symbolic constant has three components: the *#define* preprocessor directive, the symbolic name, and the defining value. Use spaces or tabs to separate the components. Choose as the symbolic name any valid identifier (not a keyword) that tells a reader what the constant represents. It is customary to type symbolic names in uppercase to make them highly visible in program source text.

❏ NOTE: *When you use the symbolic name in your program, it must have the exact capitalization and spelling as the name in the* #define *directive; otherwise, the Learn C compiler generates an error message.*

Another advantage of using symbolic constants instead of magic numbers (beyond the readability of the code) is that you can change multiple occurrences of the value by making a single change in the *#define* directive. If, for example, the maximum row value occurs a dozen times in your program, you can laboriously locate them all and change each literal value individually, or you can change a single *#define* directive.

In addition, if two constants happen to have the same value, using symbolic constants lets you keep them distinct.

Consider the following directives, for example, which define symbolic constants for, say, the maximum number of rows and the maximum number of commands your program accepts:

```
#define MAXROW 10
#define NUM_CMDS 10
```

After you state these definitions, you can easily change all occurrences that refer to the maximum number of rows to another value without having to search for all the places in the source file where this value appears (and where it refers to the number of rows rather than the number of commands). To change the maximum number of rows from 10 to 20, for example, simply change the *MAXROW* definition:

```
#define MAXROW 20
```

Simple and trouble free.

Where constants are needed in your program source code, use symbolic constants. The traditional exceptions are the obvious logical uses of 0 and 1 to signify false and true respectively and the use of 0 as an initial value. I suggest that you even use the symbolic constant names TRUE and FALSE (defining them to have the values 1 and 0, respectively) to show clearly the Boolean nature of the values.

Macros

A macro is essentially an abbreviation. There is nothing mysterious about macros, except possibly the term itself! You can refer to a person named Jane Doe by her initials, JD. JD is effectively a macro that stands for Jane Doe.

A macro consists of a name (identifier) and an associated definition. When the C preprocessor reads a source file and sees an identifier that has been defined previously, it substitutes the definition for the identifier. This process is called macro expansion. In Jane's case, JD is the macro name, and Jane Doe is the definition, or expansion text.

Macros fall into one of two major categories: those that lack parameters and those that require them. A macro that lacks parameters produces nothing more than a simple text-replacement operation. Suppose you state the following definitions:

```
#define STD_OUT 1
#define PROGNAME "ViewFile"
```

The preprocessor expands the *STD_OUT* and *PROGNAME* identifiers as shown in the following code fragments:

```
write(STD_OUT, PROGNAME, sizeof PROGNAME);  ——— Before substitutions



write(1, "ViewFile", sizeof "ViewFile");  ——— After substitutions
```

The symbolic name *PROGNAME* is replaced by the defined value *"ViewFile"*, as *STD_OUT* is replaced by the number *1* in the example.

As you probably observed, a symbolic constant is simply a parameterless macro. The other type of macro, a "parametized" macro, is one that accepts one or more parameters. Parameters provide a means of getting information into a macro. An example is the following macro, which calculates the square of a number:

```
#define SQR(x) ((x) * (x))
```

SQR is the macro name, *x* is the parameter, and the remainder of the line, *((x) * (x))*, is the macro definition. Notice the parentheses immediately following *SQR*. Whatever lies between that set of parentheses is the parameter; the remainder of the line, the macro definition, shows how the parameter is to be acted upon when the macro occurs later in the program.

To use a macro in a program, simply use the macro name followed immediately by a set of parentheses enclosing the value you want the macro to act upon. When you run the program, the preprocessor replaces the macro name and its associated parentheses with the macro definition, using the value you put in parentheses next to the macro name. Thus, the following code fragment:

```
#define SQR(x) ((x) * (x))

int n;
.
.
.
n = SQR(7);
```

is expanded during precompilation to become:

```
#define SQR(x) ((x) * (x))

int n;
.
.
.
n = ((7) * (7));
```

The variable *n* is, therefore, assigned the value 49.

If you need to extend a definition beyond a single physical line, type \ before you press the Enter key. This sequence, called an "escaped newline," hides the newline character from the compiler. Thus, the effect of the following two-line sequence during compilation is the same as that of a single continuous source line:

```
#define MESSAGE \
        "Congratulations! Now press Enter to begin the next lesson."
```

Using this technique, you can extend definitions to span any number of lines as long as all but the last newline are escaped (preceded by a \).

Power Table Revisited. Let's modify the PWRTABLE program presented in Chapter 5 so that it uses header files, parametized macros, and symbolic constants. First, we need to create a local header file called macros.h (Listing 6-1). The file contains three macro definitions.

```
/*
 * macros.h
 *
 * A collection of useful macro definitions.
 */

#define SQR(x)  ((x) * (x))
#define CUBE(x) ((x) * (x) * (x))
#define QUAD(x) ((x) * (x) * (x) * (x))
```

LISTING 6-1. *Source code for the macros.h header file.*

The three macros each take a single argument, x, which is the value to be raised to a power. As their names suggest, *SQR(x)* squares the value of x, *CUBE(x)* raises it to the third power, and *QUAD(x)* raises it to the fourth power.

The PWRTBL2 program (Listing 6-2) uses the macros to produce a cleaner-looking program, one that is much easier to read than the original. The line *#include "macros.h"* makes the macros defined in macros.h available to this program. Any other program that needs the macros can include them in the same way (assuming that you modify the path or copy the header file if necessary).

In PWRTBL2 the symbolic constant *MAXN* is defined to have a value of *10*. *MAXN* is used in the *for* loop control expression instead of the literal number 10 to tell the reader what the significance of the number is.

As you can see, using macros in the *printf()* statement makes it more readable than one containing a mass of repeated multiplication expressions. In addition, the statement with macros is more compact, and, let's face it, easier to type.

To summarize macro operation, let's see how these files are processed when you tell Learn C to run pwrtbl2.c. The preprocessor first brings in the lines of text from the included header file. Next, it replaces *MAXN* with the number *10*, the *printf()* argument *SQR(n)* with *((n) * (n))*, and so on. Finally, Learn C translates the preprocessed source file into an executable "program image" in memory.

```
/*
 * P W R T B L 2
 *
 * Print a table of powers.
 */

#include "macros.h"
#define MAXN 10

main()
{
        int n;
        /*
         * Label the columns.
         */
        puts("number\t exp2\t exp3\t exp4");
        puts("------\t----- \t -----\t-----");
        /*
         * Print the table of power values.
         */
        for (n = 0; n <= MAXN; ++n)
                printf("%2d\t%5d\t%5d\t%5d\n",
                        n, SQR(n), CUBE(n), QUAD(n));
        return (0);
}
```

LISTING 6-2. *Program source code for pwrtbl2.c*

Multiple Parameters. Macros can have more than one parameter. For example, a macro that yields the lesser of two values takes two parameters. As you recall from Chapter 5, you can use the C conditional operator in the macro definition:

#define MIN(x, y) ((x) < (y) ? (x) : (y))

The definition says that if the x parameter is less than y, the value passed as x becomes the value of the expression. Otherwise, the expression yields the value of the y parameter.

> ❑ NOTE: *Recall that the left parenthesis for the parameter list must be immediately adjacent to the macro name. Any intervening white space would be interpreted as the separation between the macro name and its definition text. You can, however, leave white space between parameters and within the definition text.*

Watch Out for Side Effects

What looks like an overkill of parentheses in the *SQR* macro definition is a necessary precaution against adverse "side effects." A side effect in an expression is a result that is secondary to a primary purpose of the expression. For example, the primary purpose of the assignment

```
y = n++;
```

is to assign the value of *n* to the variable *y*. The side effect is to increment the value of *n* after the assignment.

In the *SQR* macro, an expression involving several variables could be used for *x* instead of the literal value 7. Because of the way C handles text replacement, an expression is first substituted and then evaluated. Let's reexamine our *SQR* macro to see the effect of the parentheses within a macro definition. Our original macro was:

```
#define SQR(x) ((x) * (x))
```

If you use the expression *a* + *b* in your program instead of the value 7, the result of the macro expansion is:

```
((a + b) * (a + b))
```

Note that *x* is replaced by the value used in the program—all other items in the macro definition, such as operators and parentheses, are included when expansion occurs.

Suppose you define the macro without the inner sets of parentheses (as most beginning C programmers will do at least once):

```
#define SQR(x) (x * x)
```

If you use the expression *SQR(a + b)* in your program, the result of the macro expansion is:

```
(a + b * a + b)
```

Because of operator precedence (summarized on Learn C help screen 3 of 8), the result of this calculation is probably not what you intended, given that multiplication is performed before addition.

For example, assume *a = 3* and *b = 4*. In this case, the expanded macro is *3 + 4 * 3 + 4*, which evaluates to *19*. However, if parentheses are used as they were in the previous example, the macro expands to *(3 + 4) * (3 + 4)*, yielding the correct result of 49.

The moral here is to use parentheses regardless of how forbidding they make the code look (and despite the additional typing). They will save you a lot of debugging effort and anguish during your career as a C programmer.

C offers several other preprocessor directives that we do not cover here. They are intended for advanced programming tasks, such as conditional compilation, which are outside the scope of this book. You can learn more about them by exploring "Preprocessor directives" in Learn C's Topic help resource.

Questions and Exercises

1. The file string.h is one of the standard header files provided with Learn C. Where should this file be located? How do you include this file in your program using a preprocessor directive?

    STEP 1 (location of file): _____

    STEP 2 (preprocessor directive): _____

2. Name the three required components of a statement that creates a symbolic constant or macro.

    a. _____

    b. _____

    c. _____

3. What's in a name? If a name is chosen well, it conveys a lot of information about the item—a constant or macro, for instance—that it identifies. Try your hand at choosing descriptive names for the following items:

    a. The number of days in a year: _____

    b. A very large number: _____

    c. A very small difference between two real numbers: _____

    d. The number of screen rows: _____

    e. A macro that yields the larger of two values: _____

4. Suppose the following macro definition is given:

    ```
    #define DATA(x) 2 * x + 3
    ```

    a. Write a program that creates a table of x and y values where $y = DATA(x)$ for x between 0 and 9.

    b. What needs to be done to the $DATA(x)$ macro definition to prevent incorrect results for values of x that contain side effects?

5. The absolute value of a signed number is that number with its sign information removed. (For example, the absolute value of −4 is 4.) Write a macro, *ABS(x)*, that yields the absolute value of *x*. Use the conditional operator in the definition and be sure to parenthesize the definition fully.

6. Write a macro that yields the minimum value from a set of three input values, *MIN3(x, y, z)*. (Hint: Conditional expressions can be nested.)

7: Functions

C Programming Lessons: Building Blocks: Functions

You are now at a major milestone in your trek toward becoming a C programmer. Thus far, this book has emphasized programs that consist of a *main()* function and calls to a limited set of standard library functions, such as *printf()* and *scanf()*.

Now you are ready to become a producer of functions rather than simply a consumer of them. In the course of this chapter, you'll learn how to create your own functions and how to use them in designing and constructing programs.

What Are Functions and Why Use Them?

Functions are essentially building blocks, subprograms that you combine in meaningful ways to build programs. As shown in Figure 7-1, a function takes zero or more inputs, performs some task, and (optionally) produces an output called a return value.

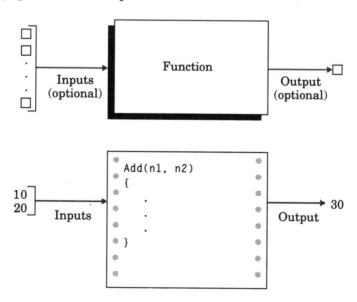

FIGURE 7-1. *Functions are the building blocks of C programs.*

Your first thought might be that a function with neither inputs nor output is not particularly useful, but this is not the case. We might create a function called *ClearScreen()*, for example, that takes no inputs and produces no return value but which performs the useful task of clearing the user's screen.

The block diagram of the sample function *Add()* shown in Figure 7-1 has a pair of inputs and an output. The output is the sum of the two inputs. Thus, a call to *Add()* with the values 10 and 20 as inputs produces an output of 30.

Other functions lack either input or output. A function that produces a random number as an output does not necessarily need an input. A function that moves the cursor to a particular position on the screen takes a row number and a column number as inputs and performs the positioning action. It need not produce a return value.

Modularization

C functions are analogous to electronic subsystems that engineers use to build electronic devices. Each subsystem usually performs a specific task or set of tasks. Certain fundamental subsystems are versatile enough to be used in a variety of electronic devices—everything from stereos to satellites.

One primary purpose of using functions is to help organize a program into manageable units. Although you can write a large program as a single *main()* function, that approach is neither necessary nor recommended. Instead, divide the overall program into a set of separate functions, each designed to do a single task. Designers call this design approach the "divide and conquer" method.

Functions in C programs give you leverage by letting you focus on the small, individual tasks that accomplish the overall objective. Of course, at least one function, typically *main()* itself, has to know "the big picture" and orchestrate the work of other functions.

Recall the discussion of task analysis in Chapter 2. When you divide a problem—there we analyzed a mass mailing—into its component tasks, you are doing a "functional decomposition." You can express a functional decomposition in numerous ways. One method is to use "pseudocode," a merging of C and English language descriptions. The pseudocode lists the operations in sequence and shows how they relate to each other. As with your C source statements, indention level shows subordination.

For example, the pseudocode description of the REPEAT program in Chapter 5 (on p. 105) looks like this:

```
prompt for a character
read the character
prompt for a repetition count
read the count
while count is not 0
        print the character
        decrement the count
print a newline
```

After you outline the logic and flow of the program, it is a relatively easy task to write a working program in C or any other computer language. Indeed, the hardest part of programming is analyzing the problem and designing a solution. Writing the actual program statements in a particular computer language is usually the easy part.

A function should be designed to do one job as well as it can be done. In this way, it is analogous to a subsystem in an electronic device. By carefully crafting sets of specialized and general-purpose functions, programmers can have the same advantages in program design as engineers have in their fields with off-the-shelf and custom electronic and mechanical subsystems.

Memory Conservation

The use of functions also saves space. If a program has two or more instances of the same sequence of instructions, whether with the same or different data, you can save space in memory by packaging the instructions in a function.

The BANNER program (Listing 7-1) demonstrates the use of functions to handle repetitive tasks. The banner generated by this program is a message surrounded by a large border of asterisks (*). The top and bottom edges of the border consist of 73 asterisks. Because these edges are identical, a single function called *Line()* is called from *main()* to draw each of them. The sides of the banner are generated by repeatedly printing a single asterisk, 9 tab characters, and then another asterisk character. You can use a single function named *Sides()* to perform that task—for all but the line containing the message. The *printf()* statement used to print the message is unique and is therefore included in the *main()* function.

```
/*
 * B A N N E R
 *
 * Print a message surrounded by a border. Use
 * functions to draw the elements of the border.
 */

#include <stdio.h>

#define WIDTH   72
#define ROWS    4

Line()
{
        int x;

        for (x = 0; x <= WIDTH; ++x)
                putchar('*');
        putchar('\n');
}

Sides()
{
        int y;

        for (y = 0; y <= ROWS; ++y)
                printf("*\t\t\t\t\t\t\t\t\t*\n");
}

main()
{
        Line();
        Sides();
        printf("*\t\t\t    (your ad here)\t\t\t\t*\n");
        Sides();
        Line();

        return 0;
}
```

LISTING 7-1. *Program source code for banner.c.*

The space-saving characteristic of a function results from the fact that the instructions it represents need appear only once in the executable program. C's function call mechanism permits a single copy of the instructions to serve any number of calls to the function.

For example, the *main()* function in BANNER contains two calls to *Line()*, the first for the top border and the second for the bottom border.

Even though *Line()* contains only a short loop and a single *putchar()* statement, you can see that duplicating the same sequence of statements in *main()* would add length and complexity to the program. The same is true for the *Sides()* function.

BANNER is merely a brief introduction to the power and flexibility of functions, but consider a program containing dozens or even hundreds of repetitive statements. When you consider programs of such magnitude, which are, incidentally, quite common in practice, the savings in memory space, program length and complexity, and, yes, typing, become significant.

Information Hiding

Another purpose of functions is to hide information. To minimize the chance that data will become corrupted, you should make it available only to those parts of a program that require it.

Data items are considered either "local" or "global," depending on the extent to which they are available to a program. Local data items are visible (accessible) only within a restricted range of program statements, typically within a block of statements or a function. Global data items, on the other hand, are usually visible throughout a program.

You can generally avoid using global data in your programs. If you need to supply data outside a given function, the preferred programming practice is to use local data and to pass copies of the data to other functions that have a legitimate need for access. (You'll learn about passing data later in this chapter.)

Program Size *vs* Speed

In Chapter 6 you looked at macros as a means of abbreviating complex actions as single words. Because functions offer that same capability, let's stop to consider the benefits of each method.

Macros generally produce fast-running, in-line code. They also provide a degree of independence from considerations of data type. The primary drawbacks to macros are code size and safety. They tend to increase the ultimate code size because the preprocessor replaces each use of a macro name with the full text of its definition. And macros can be dangerous when they produce unforeseen side effects.

Functions, on the other hand, tend to shrink code size because a single instance of the code serves all callers. But each call to a function involves a transfer of data (additional overhead), slowing overall program execution somewhat. In addition, functions are sensitive to the type of data they operate on. A function designed for integers, for example, cannot handle real numbers.

The ADD program (Listing 7-2) uses functions to add values together. The program contains one function, *AddIntegers()*, that adds

```
/*
 * A D D
 *
 * This program demonstrates the use of functions
 * to perform calculations.  A separate function is
 * needed for each data type.
 */


/*
 * AddIntegers()
 *
 * This function takes two integer arguments
 * and returns their sum in a long integer.
 */
long
AddIntegers(int number1, int number2)
{
        long total;
        total = (long)number1 + (long)number2;
        return (total);
}


/*
 * AddReals()
 *
 * This function takes two float arguments
 * and returns their sum in a double.
 */
double
AddReals(float number1, float number2)
{
        double total;
        total = (double)number1 + (double)number2;
        return (total);
}
```

LISTING 7-2. *Program source code for add.c.*   *(continued)*

LISTING 7-2. *continued*

```
int
main(void){
        int n1 = 20, n2 = 25;
        float f1 = 12.34, f2 = 56.78;

        /* Add two integers. */
        printf("%d + %d = %ld\n", n1, n2, AddIntegers(n1, n2));

        /* Add two real numbers. */
        printf("%f + %f = %f\n", f1, f2, AddReals(f1, f2));

        return (0);
}
```

two integers together and returns a *long* integer result. The program also contains a function called *AddReals()* that adds two values of type *float* and returns a *double* result.

The program specifies a *long* integer as the return type of *AddIntegers()* so that either or both of the input values can be large values. If the return type were also *int*, the program could not return a correct result if the sum exceeded the range of an *int*. Similarly, *AddReals()* accepts two *float* values and returns a *double* to guarantee adequate range in the result.

To avoid the need for separate integer and real addition functions, you can write a simple macro that can perform any addition operation:

```
#define ADD(a, b) ((a) + (b))
```

Using this directive, you can rewrite the ADD program to eliminate the use of functions. The ADD_ANY program (Listing 7-3) shows one possible result.

As you can see, the ADD macro can add a pair of integers, a pair of real numbers, or even a combination of integer and real values. Provided you use the correct format specifiers in the *printf()* statements, the values are printed correctly. The program using the macro requires less source code, and it runs a bit faster because it incurs little function call overhead.

You have to analyze the performance of your program to determine whether functions or macros are better in a given set of circumstances. Usually, the best approach is to code with functions first and then tweak performance of critical sections of your program with macros.

```
/*
 * A D D _ A N Y
 *
 * Add values without regard to data type.  This program uses
 * a macro to do the calculation instead of using a separate
 * function for each data type.
 */

#include <stdio.h>
#include <stdlib.h>

#define ADD(a, b) ((a) + (b))

int
main()
{
        int n1 = 20, n2 = 25;
        float f1 = 12.34, f2 = 56.78;

        /*
         * Use the ADD macro to add a pair of integers.
         */
        printf("%d + %d = %d\n", n1, n2, ADD(n1, n2));

        /*
         * Use the ADD macro to add a pair of reals.
         */
        printf("%f + %f = %f\n", f1, f2, ADD(f1, f2));

        /*
         * We can even use the ADD macro with
         * operands of mixed data types.
         */
        printf("%d + %f = %f\n", n1, f1, ADD(n1, f1));

        return (0);
}
```

LISTING 7-3. *Program source code for add_any.c.*

Function Definitions and Declarations

As shown in Figure 7-2, a C function definition consists of a function header and a function body. The definition of a function must occur only once in a program.

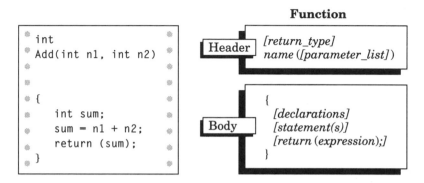

FIGURE 7-2. *Each function definition has a header and a body of statements.*

The following lines show a generic function definition. The first two lines form the header. The items in the block between the braces form the function body.

```
return_type
name([parameter_list])
{
        /* data declarations and definitions */

        /* executable code */
        statement(s)

        /* optional return statement */
        return [expression];
}
```

Before you use a function within a program, you must declare it. A function declaration consists of only the header part of the function definition, which provides information to the compiler about a function's name, its parameters, and its return type.

If a function definition occurs in a program source file before the function is ever called, it does double duty, serving as both the definition and the declaration.

```
/* Declare and define */
int
Add(int n1, int n2)
{
        .
        .
        .
}

int
main(void)
{
        .
        .
        .
        z = Add(x, y);          /* Call already-declared function */
}
```

However, if the program calls a function before the compiler encounters its definition—the more likely situation in practice—you must provide a forward declaration, or "prototype," to tell the compiler what to expect when the function is later called. The prototype is essentially the header part of the function definition, separated from the body of the definition. Notice that it ends with a semicolon.

```
/* Declare function using function header */
int Add(int, int);

int
main(void)
{
        .
        .
        .
        z = Add(x, y);       /* call */
}
/* Define full function */
int
Add(int n1, int n2)
{
        .
        .
        .
}
```

Actually, the declaration of the *Add()* function before its first use is optional because *Add()* returns an integer. When the program does not declare a return type, Learn C assumes a return value of type *int*. If you fail to declare the return type of a function that returns something other than an *int*, Learn C prints an error message at compile time.

Function Header

As you've noticed in the preceding examples, a function header consists of a return type, the function name, and an optional parameter list. These elements of the header declare to the compiler what argument types a caller must pass to the function and what return type to expect from it.

Function Name (and Parameter List). In a C program, you need only include a function name and its optional parameter list in a statement to execute the function:

```
FunctionName();
```

If the function requires no parameters, you must still type the parentheses—they are one of the distinguishing characteristics of a function. The semicolon is also required, of course, to terminate the statement.

If a function does require parameters, the compiler must know in advance (from the declaration) how many parameters are involved and what their data types are.

When listed in function declarations and definitions, parameters are called "formal" parameters. They are effectively placeholders for the actual arguments. The actual arguments are the expressions and values that are passed by the caller at runtime and substituted into the places reserved by the formal parameters.

Learn C currently supports two different parameter list formats. The traditional format has a separate list of parameters and type specifiers. The following header uses this format to declare a function that takes two *float* values and returns their product as a *double*:

```
double Fproduct(value1, value2)
float value1;
float value2;
```

The proposed ANSI format combines parameter names and their data types, resulting in a more compact, easier-to-read function header:

```
double Fproduct(float value1, float value2)
```

The proposed ANSI standard will eventually cause the traditional format to be dropped in favor of the newer combined format. With Learn C, you can use either. If portability to older C environments is a concern, use the traditional format for quite a while longer because many C compilers do not yet support the ANSI format. In this book, however, I will favor the new ANSI format.

Return Type. The declared return type must match the type of the data being returned. If a function provides no return value, identify the function as being *void*. The *void* keyword means that the function does not return a value and therefore has no return type. If the function returns an integer, you can leave off the type specifier. But even if you work mostly with functions that return integers, showing a return type is a good habit to fall into. Doing so forces you to think about the function and to assure yourself that the return value is indeed an integer and not some other item that happens to fit in integer-size storage on a given machine.

Function Body

A function header does not show how the function does its job. That is the purpose of the function body. A C function body is a block of statements enclosed in braces. It can contain data declarations and definitions, executable statements, and a return statement. Each of these items is optional, but the braces must be used even if the block contains only a single statement.

Variable Declarations and Definitions. Variable declarations and definitions must appear at the top of a block. Unless you specify otherwise, all the variables you declare inside the body of a function are "automatic" and are, therefore, local to the function. They come into existence when control passes to the function, and they are destroyed when the function relinquishes control.

In the ADD program (Listing 7-2 beginning on p. 135), for example, the *AddIntegers()* function creates an automatic variable, *total*. Initially undefined, it receives a value from the assignment statement. The *return* statement passes that value to the caller. Following the return statement, *total* no longer exists.

Variables declared with the keyword *static* inside a function are also visible only within the function, but they exist before, during, and after execution of the function. Thus, a *static* variable retains its value between function calls.

Statements. The executable statements are the heart and soul of a function. They do the work. Functions without statements are valid, but they do nothing. (Bodiless functions, called "stubs," are often used during development to test programs incrementally.)

The number and complexity of the statements in a function body depend on the task. The statements can include calls to other functions, which can in turn call other functions, and so forth. In fact, a function can also contain calls to itself—a behavior known as recursion. Recursion is a suitable way to solve some classes of problems, such as calculating the factorial of a number.

The *return* Statement. The *return* statement is used to terminate processing within a function by transferring control back to the calling function. The syntax of a *return* statement for a function that returns a value is as follows:

```
return [expression];
```

The optional element *expression* must yield a result of the type specified in the function declaration.

Void functions can have *return* statements, too. With no *expression* component, however, such statements simply return execution control to the caller. Of course, if no *return* statement occurs, falling off the end of a function at its closing brace provides an implicit return to the calling statement.

A function can have a number of *return* statements, if necessary. For example, you might use additional *return* statements to handle error conditions. The program fragment on the following page uses a *return* statement to skip processing if certain parameters are out of range.

```
void
ClearRectangle(int r0, int r1, int c0, int c1)
{
        if (r0 < 0 || r1 >= MAXROW)
                return;
        .
        .
        .
}
```

In this example, the *return* statement causes the function to terminate harmlessly if either the *r0* or *r1* argument is out of the expected range. If both values are within the expected range, the other statements execute, and then the function returns to its caller.

You could add statements to the function so that it returns an integer value of 0 if *ClearRectangle()* completes its job successfully and a nonzero value if it fails to achieve its goal. Then the caller can monitor the return value and take corrective action if *ClearRectangle()* fails.

Using Function Prototypes

The more information the compiler has about a function, the more help it can be in detecting errors early. A common problem in C programs is calling a function with too many or too few arguments or using incorrect argument types. In older C environments, the compiler did little or nothing to detect this condition, which led to marathon debugging sessions (programmers aided by piles of Snickers bars and six-packs of Jolt, trying to find out why things didn't work "quite right").

The Learn C compiler checks function parameters and return values by default if you provide that information using a function prototype. Function prototypes are simply function headers that show all data types for formal parameters and return values. If you activate the appropriate checking mechanisms (by choosing a higher Warning Level in the Compile dialog box), the compiler can quickly point out arguments and return values that are used incorrectly or suspiciously.

Many of the standard header files provided with Learn C, such as stdio.h and stdlib.h, contain function prototypes. In your C programs, always include the header files that are appropriate for standard library functions you use. To find out which header files to include, use the Learn C help resource. Simply place the cursor on the function name in the edit window and press Shift+F1.

How Functions Communicate

The function call/return mechanism is a central feature of C programs. The AREA program (Listing 7-4) demonstrates all the elements of a function call, including the use of parameters to pass data values into called functions and to pass the results back to the caller.

AREA calculates and prints a table of surface areas for circles and spheres for a fixed range of radii. Rather than clutter *main()* with the details for finding the areas of various objects, the program uses two functions, *CircleArea()* and *SphereArea(),* to do the calculations. The calls from within *main()* pass the radius of the object to the function, and each function returns the computed area. Figure 7-3 illustrates this use of the call/return mechanism.

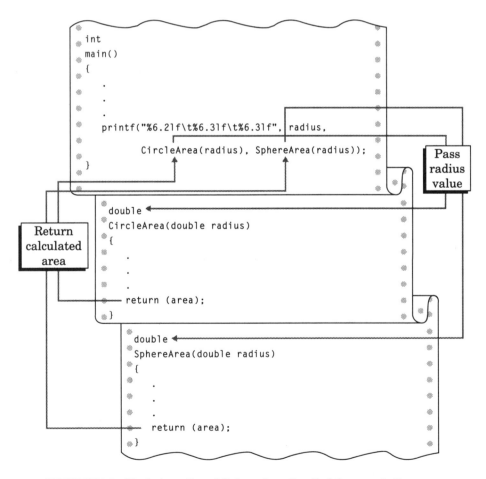

FIGURE 7-3. CircleArea() *and* SphereArea() *called from* main().

```
/*
 * A R E A
 *
 * Print a table of circle and sphere areas for
 * radii in the range of 0 through 2 in 0.2 increments.
 */

#include <float.h>
#include <math.h>

#define MAX_RADIUS      2.0
#define PI              3.141592

/*
 * Function prototypes.
 */
double CircleArea(double);
double SphereArea(double);

int
main(void)
{
        double radius;

        /*
         * Print the banner, column titles, and bars.
         */
        puts("=== Table of Areas ===");
        puts("Radius\tCircle\tSphere");
        puts("------\t------\t------");
        /*
         * For each value of radius, print the radius and
         * surface areas for the resulting circle and sphere.
         */
        for (radius = 0.0; radius <= (double)MAX_RADIUS;
            radius += 0.2)
                printf("%6.2lf\t%6.3lf\t%6.3lf\n", radius,
                        CircleArea(radius), SphereArea(radius));

        return (0);
}

/*
 * CircleArea()
 *
 * Calculate the area of a circle for the specified radius.
 */
```

LISTING 7-4. *Program source code for area.c.*　　　　　　*(continued)*

145

LISTING 7-4. *continued*

```
double
CircleArea(double radius)
{
        double area;
        area = PI * (radius * radius);
        return (area);
}

/*
 * SphereArea()
 *
 * Calculate the surface area of a sphere for the specified radius.
 */

double
SphereArea(double radius)
{
        double area;
        area = 4.0 * PI * (radius * radius);
        return (area);
}
```

Function prototypes near the top of the program provide forward declarations for both area functions because *main()* contains calls to them before they are defined. In addition, the prototypes tell the compiler how many arguments to expect and what their types are.

The *main()* function first declares the variable *radius*, and then it prints the table header. A *for* loop is set up to control the calculations. Because we relegated the details for computing area to separate functions, all we need in the *for* loop is a *printf()* statement that contains calls to the calculation functions with the appropriate argument.

Both *CircleArea()* and *SphereArea()* are homegrown functions that demonstrate floating-point calculations. The area formulas require the square of the radius, so the passed value is multiplied by itself. Note the use of parentheses to force this multiplication to occur before any other operation in the formula.

After each area calculation, the *return* statement at the end of each function returns the calculated value to *main()*. The function calls evaluate to the returned values, which are printed by the *printf()* statements to generate a table of areas.

Parameter-passing Considerations

As you have already learned, values are passed to functions by means of parameters. The default mechanism for passing parameters, the one used in the AREA program, is known as the "call-by-value" method, which passes copies of data. Parameter passing can also be achieved by using the "call-by-reference" mechanism, which passes the *locations* of data items, not their values.

Call-by-Value. Call-by-value means that the values passed are copies of the arguments provided in the function call. No changes to the data copies that occur within the function affect the original variables from which the copies were made.

The calling function is left to make any changes to the variables it controls. In this way, the caller maintains control over the call/return process while using the services of the called function in a safe and dependable way.

Call-by-Reference. The alternative means of passing data to a function permits a called function to access variables directly, bypassing the protection mechanisms offered by the call-by-value method. Call-by-reference also permits a function to "return" more than one value to its caller. Under normal circumstances, a function can return only a single value to its caller through a *return* statement.

To understand call-by-reference parameter passing, you must have knowledge of pointers and indirection. It is the mechanism that permits *scanf()* to work by passing the addresses of input buffers that are set aside for expected values. The topics of indirection and call-by-reference are covered in detail in Chapters 9 and 10.

Questions and Exercises

1. Describe in your own words what a function is and why functions are an important aspect of C programming.

2. What is the difference between a formal parameter and an actual argument?

3. Given that the formula for the volume of a sphere is 4 times pi times the cube of the radius, write a program that prints the volume for various radii between 0 and 4.0 units at increments of 0.2 units. Use a separate function to calculate the volume.

4. Write another version of the program described in Exercise 3, but this time use a macro to do the calculation.

5. Write a function *ClearScreen()* that clears the screen by emitting a series of newline characters, the number of which is determined by an integer parameter, *n*. Write a *main()* function that calls *ClearScreen()* with the number of lines needed to clear your screen. You will need at least 25 newlines, more on large-screen systems.

8: Arrays

Arrays in C
Character Strings
Multidimensional Arrays
Questions and Exercises

An array is a collection of objects arranged contiguously. Arrays are hardly mysterious. You encounter them every day, as the following examples suggest:

- P.O. boxes in a post office
- A group of parking spots in a lot
- The pages in a magazine or book
- A calendar
- The squares of a chessboard
- The set of holes in a belt
- The table of logarithms

Some of these arrays, such as the belt holes and printed pages, typify one-dimensional, or linear, arrays. The chessboard and the parking lot typify multidimensional arrays.

This chapter introduces arrays in C. You will learn the C notation for arrays, the proper technique for declaring and initializing them, and a few ways to use them in your programs. You will also learn about the "string," which is, in C, a special use of an array.

Arrays in C

In C, as in other computer languages, an array is a set of variables of the same data type. A component of an array is called an "element." The elements are stored in consecutive locations in memory.

An array declaration has the following form:

type name[size];

where *type* specifies the data type of each and every element in the array, *name* is the identifier by which you access the array, and *size* is the number of elements in the array.

Compare the following program statements:

```
int n;
int number[5];
```

The first statement is the familiar declaration for an integer variable; the second creates an array variable *number* that stores five integers.

The brackets indicate that *number* is an array, and the 5 specifies that the array contains five elements.

Each element in an array has an associated index number, just as each page of a book has an associated page number. The first element in a C array always has an index of 0. The next element has an index of 1. Each element occupies the same amount of memory—the amount needed to store an item of the array's data type. The address of element 1 is thus greater than the address of element 0 by the size of an array element.

Figure 8-1 shows the memory organization that results from the declaration of *number*. The compiler allocates five adjacent integer-size locations in memory. The first array element, the one at the lowest memory address, has an index of 0. The last element in the array has an index of 4. Initially, the value of each element is undefined. Elements have the values, if any, that were previously stored in memory at those locations.

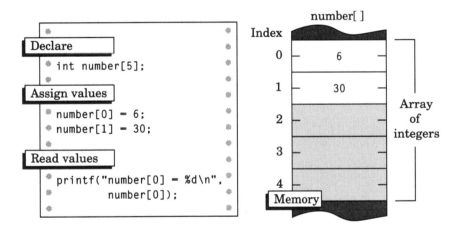

FIGURE 8-1. *The array is one of the aggregate data types.*

Array Access

To access an element of an array, combine the array name with an index. To specify the first element of the array *number*, for example, type *number[0]*. You might find it odd that the first element of the array carries an index of 0, but you'll simply have to get used to it.

Unlike the size of an array (which you specify in its declarations), the index represents an offset. Each element of an array is located at some offset from the array's starting location. Therefore, the first element is at offset 0 because it coincides with the starting location of the array. To avoid confusion, we refer in text to the first element as element 0. Similarly, we refer to the third element of the *number* array, *number[2],* as element 2.

❑ CAUTION: *One of the most common errors in a C program is incorrect indexing of an array. Because C is defined as it is, the compiler does not warn you if you use an index that is out of the declared range.*

As you can see in Figure 8-1 on the preceding page, you assign values to array elements just as you would assign values to ordinary variables. The only difference is that the array reference must have a bracketed index to indicate which element of the array is the target of the assignment. The two assignments presented in the figure,

```
number[0] = 6;
number[1] = 30;
```

set element 0 to the value 6 and element 1 to 30. The other elements are still undefined because we have made no assignments.

If you attempt to read values from the *number* array, you can retrieve meaningful values from only the first two elements. Thus, the statement

```
printf("number[0] = %d\n", number[0]);
```

prints the following line on the screen:

```
number[0] = 6
```

Printing the values of elements 2 through 4 results in meaningless output until you assign values to those array elements.

The ALPHA program (Listing 8-1) is an example of an array used as a table of values. A table is usually an ordered list that enables you to look up a value if you know its index or its relationship to other values in the table.

Examining the alpha.c source file, you see that the program declares an array of integers, called *alpha*, with 26 elements. The number of elements is specified by the symbolic constant *NLETTERS*. This array is large enough to hold all the values for the letters of the alphabet.

```
/*
 * A L P H A
 *
 * Create an integer array that holds the ASCII codes
 * for the letters of the alphabet.  Then print out
 * the contents of the array in numeric order.
 */

#include <stdio.h>

#define NLETTERS 26

int
main(void)
{
        int alpha[NLETTERS];
        int i, length;

        /*
         * Assign values to the array.  This loop assigns
         * the letters of the alphabet to the array.
         */
        for (i = 0; i < NLETTERS; ++i)
                alpha[i] = i + 'A';
        /*
         * Print out the contents of the array.
         */
        for (i = 0; i < NLETTERS; ++i)
                putchar(alpha[i]);
        putchar('\n');

        return (0);
}
```

LISTING 8-1. *Program source code for alpha.c.*

The first *for* loop in the program assigns a value, the numeric code of a capital letter, to each element of the array. The loop index, *i*, starts at 0 and is incremented each time the loop executes until its value reaches 26. The value of *i* is used as an index in the subsequent assignment statement, resulting in assignments to the array elements with offsets of 0 through 25. Notice that no element of array *alpha* has an index of 26—the condition in the *for* loop will fail when *i* exceeds 25.

The value assigned to a given element is its index value (the current value of *i*) added to the code for the letter A. The *'A'* component of the expression *i* + *'A'* is a character constant, which yields the numeric

(ASCII) code of the character (A = 65). The first time through the loop, *i* is 0, so the value 65 (the result of the expression 0 + 65) is assigned to the element *alpha[0]*. Element *alpha[1]* gets a value of 66 (1 + 65, corresponding to the letter B), and so on.

The second *for* loop in the program cycles through the *alpha* array and prints the value of each element as a character. The *putchar()* macro is defined in the stdio.h header file. It has the same effect as a *printf()* function call with a format specifier of *%c*. The output of the ALPHA program is the following, concluded by a single newline character:

```
ABCDEFGHIJKLMNOPQRSTUVWXYZ
```

The ALPHA program demonstrates how you declare an array, assign values to array elements, and read values from array elements. But this is not the whole story. You can assign values to array elements at the time you declare the array. Before tackling this initialization technique, however, you need to learn about storage class.

Storage Class

The discussion of functions in the preceding chapter touches briefly on the subject of storage class. The storage class of a C variable defines its lifetime and scope. The lifetime of a variable is its storage duration, which can be either transient or permanent. A transient variable is one that endures only for the time that the function or block in which the variable is defined is executing. A permanent variable is one that exists throughout the running of a program.

A variable's scope describes its accessibility for writing and reading at various locations in a program. You have access to a local variable only within the function or block in which it is defined. By contrast, a global variable is, by definition, accessible anywhere in a program.

Transient Variables. Variables declared within a function or statement block are transient, which means they exist only during the time that your program is executing within that function or block. Transient variables are afforded a category of storage called "automatic storage." You can use an explicit *auto* keyword to declare automatic storage, but *auto* is the default if you don't specify a storage class. The *auto* keyword is rarely used.

Consider a program that consists of several functions. Within one of the functions, you declare a variable *index* as follows.

```
void
FunctionA()
{
        int index;
        .
        .
        .

}
```

When program execution control passes to *FunctionA()*, *index* is allocated space on the stack. The stack, which is a special range of locations in the memory occupied by your program, contains transient values. The *index* variable serves its purpose while *FunctionA()* is running. Then, when *FunctionA()* concludes its work, *index* is effectively removed from the stack. It no longer exists.

Permanent Variables. A variable that is declared outside any function or statement block has permanent storage duration. Permanent variables exist throughout the execution of the program. In addition, a variable declared within a function or statement block can be made permanent if you so specify by using the keyword *static*.

The following function uses both global and local static variables:

```
int Verbose = 0;        /* global variable */

void
FunctionB()
{
        static int first = 1;   /* permanent local variable */
        if (first) {
                /* Do some initialization task one time only. */
                .
                .
                .
                first = 0;
                if (Verbose)
                        printf("Initialized configuration data\n");
        }
        /* Do some routine FunctionB() tasks. */
        .
        .
        .
        if (Verbose)
                printf ("Processing data\n")
        .
        .
        .

}
```

Static variables retain their most recently assigned values. Consequently, they are handy for functions that remember values from one call to the next, such as *FunctionB()* in the preceding example. The variable *first* is initialized to 1 when the program is run. The first time *FunctionB()* executes, *first* has a nonzero value, so the code block is executed and a value of 0 is assigned to *first*. On subsequent calls to *FunctionB()*, the function does not reinitialize the value of *first*.

The global variable *Verbose* controls the printing of messages in *FunctionB()*. *Verbose* receives an initial value of 0, so the program runs without being "chatty." If some other part of the program sets *Verbose* to a nonzero value, the program gets talkative and prints messages that tell you what it is doing.

The global variable *Verbose* is accessible to any part of the program, so its value is both readable and writable by other functions. The static variable *first*, on the other hand, is a local variable. Although the *static* keyword endows it with a permanent lifetime, it is accessible only from within *FunctionB()*.

External Variables. The *extern* keyword applied to a variable declaration indicates that the variable accessed in the current file is defined in another file. Learn C requires that all source code for a program fit in a single file, so we won't be using external declarations for variables. Nevertheless, you need to know what *extern* means if you read C programs written for other environments.

Register Storage for Variables. You can apply the register storage class to variables declared as integral types of size *int* or smaller. The *register* keyword is a request that the variable be placed in a machine register for speedy access. If the compiler can comply, it will. If the machine cannot supply enough registers to satisfy the request, the compiler provides ordinary automatic storage to the variable. The listings in this book do not explore the use of the register storage class, but you are likely to encounter it as you progress to more sophisticated programming.

Initializing an Array

Initializing an array means that you give values to some or all of its elements at the time you declare the array. You can initialize an array only if you declare it globally or declare it locally as a *static* array.

The form of an array initialization is as follows:

```
type name[size] = { init-list };
```

where *init-list* is a set of initial values of the appropriate type. The initializer list can contain values for all the elements of the array or for some number less than that. An incomplete list initializes as many elements as there are initializers. Any remaining elements are automatically initialized to 0.

If you provide a full set of initializers, you can leave out the *size* specifier because the C compiler figures out the number of elements from the values you provide.

The following statement creates an array of integer values that specifies the number of days in each month of the year:

```
static int days[] = {
    31, 28, 31, 30, 31, 30,
    31, 31, 30, 31, 30, 31
};
```

Notice a couple of things about this declaration. First, it declares no *size* specifier because it provides a full set of initializers. You could put a *12* inside the square brackets, but it is not necessary. Second, the initializer list spans several lines. Because C requires no particular form, the number of lines you use is of no consequence. Third, the comma between initializers is a separator, so you need no comma after the last initializer. And last, notice that element 0 represents January. (Remember, the indexing of array elements always starts with 0.) In any program that uses this array, you need to index the months from 0 through 11, not 1 through 12.

To create the array using an alternate design, you might declare the *days* array with 13 elements and assign a dummy value (0 will do) to element 0. Elements 1 through 12 would provide valid numbers to your program, which correspond directly to the months of the year. Of course, any loops that access the array would need to use a starting index of 1 instead of 0.

The MINMAX program (Listing 8-2 on the following page) shows how you can find the maximum and minimum values in a set of numbers. The program uses a *static* array of arbitrary numbers as input and two macros, MIN and MAX, to compare pairs of values read from the array. MIN yields the minimum and MAX yields the maximum of

```
/*
 * M I N M A X
 *
 * Demonstrate the use of a static array.  The
 * program checks a set of numbers and reports
 * the minimum and maximum values found.
 */

#define MIN(a, b)  (((a) < (b)) ? (a) : (b))
#define MAX(a, b)  (((a) > (b)) ? (a) : (b))

#define NVALUES 20

int
main(void)
{
        int i;
        int minval, maxval;
        static int value[] = {
                20, 11, 13, 19, 55, 99, 87, 30, 62, 15,
                36, 76, 18, 94, 86, 22,  7, 12, 88, 47
        };

        /*
         * Find the minimum and maximum values in the list.
         */
        minval = maxval = value[0];
        for (i = 1; i < NVALUES; ++i) {
                minval = MIN(minval, value[i]);
                maxval = MAX(maxval, value[i]);
        }

        /*
         * Report the results.
         */
        printf("Minimum value = %d;  Maximum value = %d\n",
                minval, maxval);

        return (0);
}
```

LISTING 8-2. *Program source code for minmax.c.*

the two values. The macros use the C conditional operator to compare the input values and choose the correct one.

The variables *minval* and *maxval* are initially set to the value of the first element of the array (*value[0]*). Next, a *for* loop causes all remaining values in the array to be read one at a time. If the value currently being read is less than the current value of *minval*, MINMAX saves the new minimum value in *minval*. If the value currently being read is greater than the current value of *maxval*, MINMAX saves the new maximum value in *maxval*. After reading all the values from the array, MINMAX reports the minimum and maximum values of the array by printing the current values of *minval* and *maxval*.

To make the MINMAX program more flexible, you can use a variable to specify the size of the array. The hard-coded value of NVALUES, 20, limits you to an array of 20 values. If you declare another integer variable, for example *size*, you can get the program to tell you how big the array is, eliminating the need for the NVALUES constant in the program. After the declaration and initialization of the value *array*, the following statement tells the program how many elements were initialized:

```
size = sizeof (value) / sizeof (int);
```

The *sizeof* keyword is the C operator that gives the size of an object or a data type in bytes. In the above example, *sizeof (value)* is the size of the array, and *sizeof (int)* is the size of an *int* value for the machine you're using. Thus, the size of the array in bytes divided by the size of an *int* value in bytes is the number of elements in the integer array.

This calculation accounts not only for the number of initializers, but also for the possibility of different sizes of integers on different machines. If portability is important, do not hard code a value of 2 in place of the *sizeof (int)* expression. On a 32-bit computer, C treats an integer as a 4-byte object.

Figure 8-2 and the HEXDEMO program (Listing 8-3) on the following pages show how you can use an array as a conversion table. The hexdemo.c listing consists of a *main()* function that handles all input and output and a function, *DecToHex()*, that handles the conversion task. The program prompts the user for a number in the range 0 through 15 and then prints both the decimal and hexadecimal representations on the screen.

The array, *hextab*, contains 16 elements. The values in the first 10 elements of the array match their offsets. The values of the remaining 6 elements are the hexadecimal equivalents of the decimal numbers 10 through 15. This array implements a simple conversion table between the decimal array offset and its equivalent hexadecimal digit. As you learned earlier, hexadecimal notation provides a compact single-digit code for each value that can be represented by a 4-bit number.

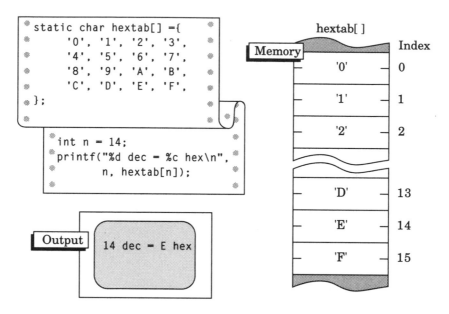

FIGURE 8-2. *An array can function as a translation table.*

Notice that *DecToHex()* keeps the input value within a single-digit range by calculating the modulus of *digit* for a base of 16. The result is used as the array index. This precaution prevents a user from specifying an out-of-range value to the conversion table.

```
/*
 * H E X D E M O
 *
 * Demonstrate the conversion of decimal numbers to
 * hexadecimal presentation.
 */

char DecToHex(int);

int
main(void)
{
        int number;

        /*
         * Prompt the user for a number and read it.  Then
         * convert the number to hex and print it.
         */
        printf("Enter a decimal number (0 through 15): ");
```

LISTING 8-3 *Program source code for hexdemo.c.* *(continued)*

LISTING 8-3. *continued*

```
        scanf("%d", &number);
        printf("%d -> %c hex\n", number, DecToHex(number));

        return (0);
}

/*
 * DecToHex()
 *
 * Convert a number from decimal to hexadecimal.
 */

char
DecToHex(int digit)
{
        char hexchar;
        static char hextab[] = {
                '0', '1', '2', '3', '4', '5', '6', '7',
                '8', '9', 'A', 'B', 'C', 'D', 'E', 'F'
        };

        /*
         * Guarantee that the digit is in range (modulo 16) and
         * look up the equivalent hex digit in the conversion table.
         */
        hexchar = hextab[digit % 16];

        return (hexchar);
}
```

Character Strings

Unlike BASIC and Pascal, C lacks a string data type. In C, a string is simply an array of characters that concludes with a byte of zeros (ASCII NUL character). The NUL byte is called a "sentinel" because it "stands watch" at the end of the array of characters. C uses this sentinel to determine where the array of characters ends.

This approach to strings has good and bad aspects. An advantage is that a string can be arbitrarily large. In BASIC and Pascal, the length of a string is contained within the string itself, limiting the string to some fixed size.

A disadvantage of the C approach to strings is that a programmer can create an array of characters and forget to provide the terminating NUL byte. It is then possible for programs that try to read or write the string to go beyond the end of the array and return an invalid value or clobber some other area of memory. Such problems provide real debugging challenges to even experienced C programmers.

You create strings in C in one of several ways. Because a string is an array of characters, you can declare a character array and initialize it a character at a time:

```
static char prompt[] = {
        'C', 'o', 'm', 'm', 'a', 'n', 'd', ':', ' ', '\0'
};
```

Notice the '\0' that initializes the last array element; '\0' is the character constant that specifies the NUL character.

This method of initializing a character string is tedious. You have to type four or five characters for every one in the string. Predictably, C provides a shortcut: To produce the same result as the preceding initialization, simply type the text of the string surrounded by double quotation marks:

```
static char prompt[] = { "Command: " };
```

Not only does this method result in less typing, it also eliminates the need for you to type a terminating NUL byte—Learn C automatically appends one when it compiles the source file.

The STRINGS program (Listing 8-4) shows how to declare a couple of strings and print them in different ways. Note that the *static* declarations are necessary (with nonglobal arrays) for initialization.

```
/*
 * S T R I N G S
 *
 * Show how to print character strings that
 * involve various kinds of substitutions.
 */

int main(void)
{
        static char word1[] = { "basket" };
        static char word2[] = { 'b', 'a', 'l', 'l', '\0' };
```

LISTING 8-4. *Program source code for strings.c.*   *(continued)*

LISTING 8-4. *continued*

```
        printf("The goal in %s%s is to put the %s in the %s.\n",
            word1, word2, word2, word1);

        return 0;
}
```

The *printf()* statement in this program concatenates the strings in one instance, pasting them end to end, and prints them separately in another, producing the output

```
The goal in basketball is to put the ball in the basket.
```

The SUBSTR program (Listing 8-5) goes beyond STRINGS to show a more complicated use of strings and array indexes. The program

```
/*
 * S U B S T R
 *
 * Extract a substring from a source string.
 */

void CopySubstring(char [], int, int, char []);

#define MAXSTR   100

int
main(void)
{
        char str1[MAXSTR];      /* input buffer */
        char str2[MAXSTR];      /* substring buffer */
        int i;                  /* array index */
        int spos;               /* starting index */
        int len;                /* requested length */

        /*
         * Get the user's input.
         */
        printf("Enter the source string: ");
        gets(str1);
        printf("Enter starting index: ");
        scanf("%d", &spos);
        printf("Enter substring length: ");
        scanf("%d", &len);
```

LISTING 8-5. *Program source code for substr.c.*   *(continued)*

LISTING 8-5. *continued*

```
        /*
         * Extract the substring.
         */
        CopySubstring(str1, spos, len, str2);

        /*
         * Display the result.
         */
        if (strlen(str2) > 0)
                printf("Substring = %s\n", str2);
        else
                puts("Empty substring--check your input values");

        return (0);
}


/*
 * CopySubstring()
 *
 * Extract a substring out of a source string.  Copy from the
 * specified starting point until the requested number of characters
 * is copied or the end of the source string is reached.
 */

void
CopySubstring(char source[], int start, int count, char result[])
{
        int i;                  /* index */

        /*
         * If the starting point is within the string, copy
         * characters from the source string to the result string.
         */
        if (start >= 0 && strlen(source) > start)
            for (i = 0; i < count && source[start + i] != '\0'; ++i)
                result[i] = source[start + i];

        /*
         * Apply a string termination. Also supplies
         * bounds check for invalid input.
         */
        result[i] = '\0';
}
```

prompts the user for a string of text, a starting index, and a length. It then attempts to extract a substring with the specified starting index and length from the string provided by the user.

The two character arrays, *str1* and *str2*, are "string buffers," reservoirs where characters will be collected. The arrays are not declared static because they are not initialized. Values are copied into *str1* by the *scanf()* statement that reads the source string or into *str2* by direct assignment in the *CopySubstring()* function.

Figure 8-3 shows what happens in the *CopySubstring()* function. In essence, the function begins at the specified starting location (*spos*) in the source string (*str1*), copies the specified number of characters (*len*) from the source string to the result string (*str2*), and provides a proper termination for the result string.

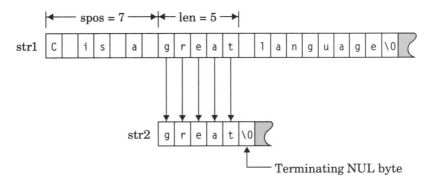

FIGURE 8-3. CopySubstring() *extracts a substring from a string.*

CopySubstring() introduces a new topic: passing an array to a function. Passing an ordinary variable to a function in C normally means passing a copy of the variable. This is call-by-value parameter passing, described in Chapter 7. Passing an array, however, involves call-by-reference, which gives the function direct access to the array. The function header *CopySubstring()* contains the following parameter declaration for the source string:

```
char source[]
```

When the compiler passes this parameter, it passes the address of the array—its location in memory. The function can therefore access directly any element of the array in memory. The *result* array works the same way.

An important aspect of programming is making sure that a program operates correctly at its limits. For example, if someone using the SUBSTR program purposely or accidentally specifies a starting location that is beyond the end of the string, or a negative value, the program has to defend itself. The bounds check in *CopySubstring()* provides a terminating NUL byte for the destination string, which creates an empty string.

CopySubstring() uses the standard library function *strlen()* to verify that the starting location falls within the source string. The *strlen()* function takes a NUL-terminated string as an argument and returns its length in bytes. (The NUL byte is not counted in the length.) If the source string length is greater than the offset to the starting location, the function begins to copy characters. However, another check is made to assure that the function does not copy beyond the end of the source string. If the length request would require copying more characters than remain in the source string, the copying loop terminates early, stopping when it reaches the end of the source string.

Multidimensional Arrays

As noted at the beginning of this chapter, arrays can have more than a single dimension. The chessboard is an example of an ordinary object that has two dimensions. A Rubik's Cube has three dimensions. Many scientific problems require modeling in four or more dimensions.

C permits you to create multidimensional arrays by declaring an array whose elements are themselves arrays. Adding another dimension to a C array is as easy as adding another subscript:

```
array[dim1][dim2]...[dimN]
```

Figure 8-4 shows how a 4×2 array of integers is stored in memory. As you can see, the two-dimensional array is actually a 4-element one-dimensional array in which each element is a 2-element array. The array declaration reserves the required storage and initializes the entire array. Note that the braces around each pair of values are not required, but add significantly to the clarity. If we look upon the data array as a collection of rows and columns, the first (leftmost) subscript of the declaration tells how many rows the array contains, and the second specifies the number of columns, which is effectively the number of array elements per row.

To access elements of a two-dimensional array, you must give two subscripts—the first to indicate the row containing the element, the second to indicate the column. To print the values of the entire *data* array, the 2DARRAY program (Listing 8-6 on the following page) uses two loops, one to control each subscript.

The next chapter introduces pointers, one of the most important aspects of C language. The close relationship between arrays and pointers enables you to handle easily many tasks that are difficult or impossible in other languages.

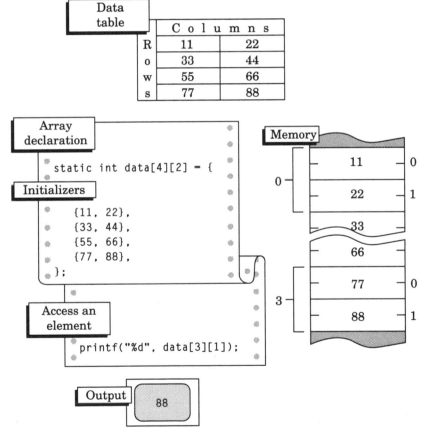

FIGURE 8-4. *A 4 × 2 array is stored as a 4-element array, each element of which is a 2-element array.*

```
/*
 * 2 D A R R A Y
 *
 * Create a two-dimensional array, initialize it,
 * and then print all its element values.
 */

#define ROWS    4
#define COLS    2

int
main(void)
{
        int row, col;

        static int data[4][2] = {
                { 11, 22 },
                { 33, 44 },
                { 55, 66 },
                { 77, 88 }
        };

        /*
         * Print the contents of the array.
         */
        for (row = 0; row < ROWS; ++row)
                for (col = 0; col < COLS; ++col)
                        printf("data[%d][%d] = %d\n",
                                row, col, data[row][col]);

        return (0);
}
```

LISTING 8-6. *Program source code for 2darray.c.*

Questions and Exercises

1. In your own words, describe what an array is and suggest five uses of arrays in programs.

2. Strike out any incorrect statements from the following list:

    a. The squares on a chessboard form a two-dimensional array.

    b. The first element of an array has an index of 1.

    c. You must always provide a size specification in an array declaration.

    d. Attempting to index past the end of an array results in undefined behavior.

    e. All elements of an array must have the same data type.

3. Under what conditions can an array be initialized? Write the declaration for a 10-character array, *letters*, and initialize it with the first 10 lowercase letters of the alphabet. Make the array local to a function.

4. Is anything about the following source code fragment suspicious? If so, say what and why.

```
#define MAXITEMS   10
   .
   .
   .
int i, value[MAXITEMS];
for (i = 0; i <= MAXITEMS; ++i)
        value[i] = i;
```

5. C has no string data type. So what is a string in C and how do you create one?

6. An integer array is initialized with the following element values: 12, 34, 56, 78. Write a program that contains this array, sums the array elements, and calculates the average value. Print the sum and the average.

7. True or False: You can pass the values of array elements to a function, but you cannot pass an entire array to a function.

8. What is the easiest way to initialize all the elements of an integer array to 0? To 100? Write code fragments to show each of these cases for a 10-element array called *numbers*.

9. The standard library function *strlen()* returns the number of characters in a string, excluding the terminating NUL byte. Write your own *StringLength()* function to do this job.

10. You are given this array declaration:

```
int array[] = {
        10, 20, 30, 40, 50, 60
};
```

Write a program that uses a loop to exchange the outermost pair of element values, then the next interior pair, and finally, the innermost pair. Write the program so that it is not sensitive to the number of elements in the array and test it on an integer array that contains nine elements.

9: Pointers

C Programming Lessons: *Pointers and Indirection*

We now come to an aspect of C programming that is at once the most important and the most confusing—the use of pointers. Pointers are the addresses of objects. You use pointers to provide indirect access to objects in much the same way that your home or business address provides correspondents with indirect access to you.

This chapter introduces C pointers in the simple but useful context of accessing individual items such as numbers or characters. It then shows the use of pointers as a means of manipulating strings and explores the close relationship between pointers and arrays.

Addresses, Pointers, and Indirection

Whether you realize it or not, you deal with addresses and pointers frequently when you read a book. Each page of a book has a page number, which can be regarded as an address. Accordingly, the index of this book, which presents a list of topics with associated page numbers, is comparable to an array of symbolic names and their associated memory addresses. The page numbers "point to" locations in the text in the same way that pointers in C specify physical addresses in memory. Both offer a convenient and coherent way of finding information.

Using Addresses

All objects in a program, except those that are maintained inside the microprocessor itself, reside at specific memory addresses. Normally, you refer to objects by their names, not by their addresses. The following program fragment, for example, manipulates variables by name— the method we have used thus far in the book:

```
int number1, number2, sum;
number1 = 5;
number2 = 7;
sum = number1 + number2;
```

In the addition statement, the values of the variables *number1* and *number2* are added together, and the result of the addition is stored in the variable *sum*. You need not worry about the locations of the variables. The computer program knows where they are, and that's sufficient.

To understand pointers, you must first understand what is actually happening in the computer's memory during this sample addition

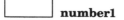 **number1**

172

process. Let's begin with a simple exercise. Notice the small box beside the page number on the preceding page and each of the next few even-numbered pages. The boxes represent the storage space at the memory location (page number). The labels beside the boxes are identifiers that correspond to the allocated memory units—the space allocated when the variables were initialized. You play the part of the computer. Grab a pencil and do what the following "program" statements tell you to do:

Source Code	Action You Take
`number1 = 5`	Write the value *5* in the box labeled *number1*.
`number2 = 7`	Write the value *7* in the box labeled *number2*.
`sum = number1 + number2`	Add *number1* to *number2* and write the result in the box labeled *sum*.

To perform this simple operation, your brain acted as the circuits of a computer: It fetched a value from one memory location and stored it in an "accumulator" (that is, you remembered it). Then it fetched a value from another memory location, added it to the value already in the accumulator, and then stored that sum in yet another memory location.

Notice that your brain/processor dealt with the physical addresses of the variables. To retrieve and save values for variables, you turn to their locations on different pages. But the program is written in a way that is independent of addresses—it uses only symbolic names. If the storage boxes were scattered elsewhere in the book, how would you know where to retrieve and save values?

For a compiler, the solution is to create a "symbol table," a look-up table that relates every variable name to its corresponding memory address. Sounds a lot like a book index, doesn't it? By the time you run a program, the names of variables and all other symbolic information, which are in the code primarily for your benefit, are gone. The executable program uses only the memory addresses and data values.

Creating Pointers

Having seen how values are stored and manipulated when you perform a calculation using variable names, let's look now at the use of pointers as an alternative, eventually constructing the same simple addition calculation with pointers.

Most modern computer languages employ some notion of a pointer, a variable that holds the address of another variable. The amount of storage occupied by a pointer is dependent upon the computer's architecture, the design of the compiler, and in the case of the IBM PC, the way you choose to declare the pointer.

You have used pointers already in the *scanf()* function, where the first parameter is the formatted control string, and any additional parameters are pointers to establish memory locations. When you write an expression that involves *scanf()*, you must provide actual arguments in the form of addresses:

```
int  i;
.

.

.
scanf("%d", &i);
```

The & preceding the variable name *i* tells the compiler to store the integer entered by the user at the address of *i*, the address established when *i* was initialized.

In the case of *scanf()*, the memory location to which &*i* points has been established by a variable declaration earlier in the program. To create your own pointers, you simply establish a memory location for a familiar object, such as an integer, and then you declare a new kind of object, a pointer, to store the address of that integer.

To create a pointer, you must write a declaration that gives the name of the pointer and the data type of the object to which it points. The general form of a pointer declaration is thus:

type *name;

The * operator distinguishes this statement from the declaration of an ordinary variable. You can read this declaration in either of two ways:

- *name* is a pointer to an object of type *type*.

- **name* is an object of type *type*.

Either interpretation of the preceding pointer declaration is correct. The first applies in expressions that use the address itself. The second applies in expressions that involve the value stored at the address.

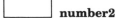

❑ NOTE: *The * character has several uses in C. These uses are not in conflict. The * operator in a pointer declaration is a unary operator. By contrast, when it signifies multiplication, (even in the *= form), * is a binary operator. The C compiler knows which operation to perform from the context of the expression. Recall as well that the character shows up in the symbols that open and close comments, /* and */, but those symbols also have no bearing on pointers.*

To put this discussion into a familiar context, let's revisit the addition operation we coded earlier. To declare a pointer to the *sum* variable, you need to type:

```
int *sp;
```

Read this declaration from right to left as "The variable *sp* is a pointer to an integer." Similarly, the following statement:

```
int *np1, *np2;
```

declares *np1* and *np2* as pointers to integers. Notice that each variable name must be accompanied by the * operator. If you write the following declaration:

```
int *np1, np2;
```

you are declaring one pointer to an integer and one simple integer. Without exception, you must declare a pointer with a preceding asterisk.

Now you have allocated storage to some variables that are the right size to hold addresses. Next you need to put some addresses in them. As you learned in Chapter 3, & is a unary operator that yields the address of its operand. Thus, &*sum* is the address of the variable *sum*. To store this value in the pointer variable *sp*, use the following simple assignment statement:

```
sp = &sum;              /* make sp point to the address of sum */
```

In the same way, you can set pointers to the two number variables:

```
np1 = &number1;         /* make np1 point to number1 */
np2 = &number2;         /* make np2 point to number2 */
```

Now that you know where the values are stored, your next step is to use the locations stored in the pointers to put values into the variables so that you can read values out of them later. The * operator comes to the rescue; it lets you access the value in the memory location identified by a pointer. Thus, the value of *np1 is the value stored in the variable *number1*. The following assignment:

```
*np1 = 5;
```

has the identical effect as the assignment:

```
number1 = 5;
```

The variable name *number1* and the expression *np1 both identify the value stored at the location in memory that is identified by the pointer variable *np1*.

Now let's revise the addition exercise by doing the entire job with pointers. In the following table, the left column presents program statements that put the required values in the pointer variables and then perform the calculation. The right column contains parallel instructions that let you imitate the activity of the compiler. As in the previous example, write the specified numbers in the appropriately labeled boxes in this chapter (at the foot of even-numbered pages). Erase and reuse the boxes from the previous exercise.

Source Code	Action You Take
np1 = &number1	Write the address (page number) of *number1* into the box for the pointer variable *np1*.
np2 = &number2	Write the address (page number) of *number2* in the box for *np2*.
sp = &sum	Write the address (page number) of *sum* in the box for *sp*.
*np1 = 5	Write the value *5* in the box pointed to by *np1*.
*np2 = 7	Write the value *7* in the box pointed to by *np2*.
*sp = *np1 + *np2	Add the value stored in the box pointed to by *np1* to the value in the box pointed to by *np2*, and write the result in the box pointed to by *sp*.

Figure 9-1 illustrates the procedure you completed. It shows the relationship between objects and their addresses, and it demonstrates the meaning of "pointing" as the term applies to C.

 **sum**

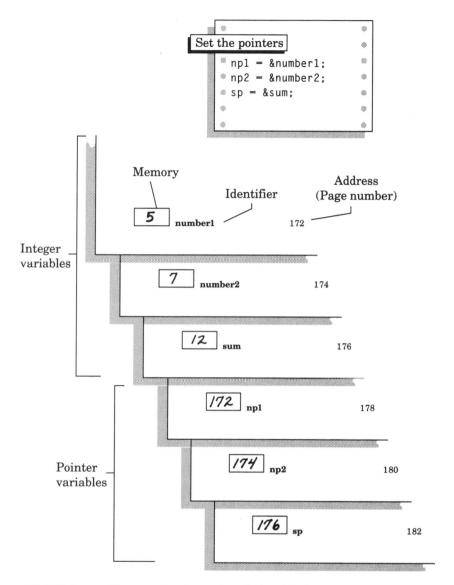

FIGURE 9-1. *The exercise shows the relationship between memory objects and addresses.*

The ADD_PTR program (Listing 9-1 on the following page) takes the obvious next step: employing the addition operation you have analyzed in a simple executable program. ADD_PTR also prints a table of variable names, addresses, and values to demonstrate the various pointer concepts.

```
/*
 * A D D _ P T R
 *
 * Demonstrate declaration and use of pointers.
 */

int
main(void)
{
        int number1, number2, sum;     /* declare variable names */
        int *np1, *np2, *sp;           /* declare pointers        */

        /*
         * Load pointers with addresses of the declared variables.
         */
        np1 = &number1;
        np2 = &number2;
        sp = &sum;

        /*
         * Put values into memory locations pointed to
         * by the pointers.
         */
        *np1 = 5;
        *np2 = 7;
        *sp = *np1 + *np2;

        /*
         * Print out the addresses of the variables
         * and their contents.
         */
        printf("\nName\tAddress\tValue\n");
        printf("----\t-------\t-----\n");
        printf("%s\t%u\t%d\n", "number1", &number1, *np1);
        printf("%s\t%u\t%d\n", "number2", &number2, *np2);
        printf("%s\t%u\t%d\n", "sum", &sum, *sp);
        printf("%s\t%u\t%u\n", "*np1", &np1, np1);
        printf("%s\t%u\t%u\n", "*np2", &np2, np2);
        printf("%s\t%u\t%u\n", "*sp", &sp, sp);

        return (0);
}
```

LISTING 9-1. *Program source code for add_ptr.c.*

The first two lines declare a total of six integer-size items—three ordinary *int* variables and three pointer variables. Then the *addresses* of the memory locations reserved for the three ordinary variables are

npl

placed into the memory locations reserved for the three pointers. The next statement places values into the memory locations to which the pointers refer—in this program, the values go in the memory locations reserved for the three ordinary variables. Finally, the program uses several *printf()* statements to display a table of the variable names, their addresses in memory, and their values.

Incidentally, the *printf()* statements show how to display the address of a variable. They use the %u format specifier, which represents the associated value as an unsigned integer. Note, however, that this technique for displaying the address of a variable is valid only on a 16-bit machine, such as an IBM PC. It fails in subtle ways on machines with a different native word size. Also, the address is not an absolute address; rather, it is an offsct into the current data segment. An explanation of "segmented architecture" lies outside the scope of this book.

❑ NOTE: *For the IBM PC, a variable of type* int *and a pointer variable are stored in memory locations of identical size. They are, however, fundamentally different types and can have widely different storage allocations in other environments. A pointer is not an integer!*

I believe that it is important to learn about and use pointers early in your career as a C programmer, just as I believe that parents should talk to their children using real words instead of baby talk. The concepts may seem impenetrable at first, but you'll progress more rapidly and exploit C far more effectively than you would otherwise.

"Why bother with pointers at all?" you might ask. It's a good question. There are several reasons. First, pointers let you access sequential array elements more simply and efficiently. They also let you pass the locations of arrays and structures rather than passing copies of entire aggregate objects. And pointers are useful as parameters in functions that must provide multiple "return" values.

When your expertise in C programming grows, you will be able to tackle programs that involve complex arrangements of data in which objects refer to one another as members of various types of interrelated lists. Once again, pointers offer the easiest method for creating these references, or "links."

Using a Character Pointer

Lest you think that pointers relate only to integer variables, let's look at an example of pointers to characters. The CHAR_PTR program (Listing 9-2) demonstrates the use of a character pointer. The program compares direct and indirect access to a character variable.

```c
/*
 * C H A R _ P T R
 *
 * This program shows how to use a character pointer
 * to access a character variable indirectly.
 */

int
main(void)
{
        char ch;                /* character variable */
        char *cp;               /* character pointer  */

        /*
         * Store the address of the character variable,
         * ch, in the character pointer variable, cp.
         */
        cp = &ch;       /* & is the "address of" operator */

        /*
         * Assign the letter 'A' to ch directly and
         * print it out for the world to see.
         */
        ch = 'A';
        printf("ch = %c\n", ch);        /* ch accessed directly */

        /*
         * Assign the letter 'A' into ch via indirection
         * through the pointer cp.  Then print out the values
         * of ch, *cp, and cp.
         */
        *cp = 'A';                      /* indirect assignment */
        printf("ch = %c\n", ch);        /* ch read directly */
        printf("*cp = %c\n", *cp);      /* ch read indirectly */
        printf("cp = %u\n", cp);        /* the address of ch */

        return (0);
}
```

LISTING 9-2. *Program source code for char_ptr.c.*

As shown in Figure 9-2, the program declares a simple character variable and a character pointer variable and sets the pointer. The figure shows the process of accessing a character variable indirectly. The physical addresses are not shown because you really have no need to know what they are. Your only concern is that the pointer variable *cp* points to character variable *ch*.

The first assignment of a value into *ch* uses the direct method to set *ch* to the letter *'A'*. The second method assigns the value *'A'* to *ch* by the indirect route. Note that *∗cp* is as much a character object as *ch* is.

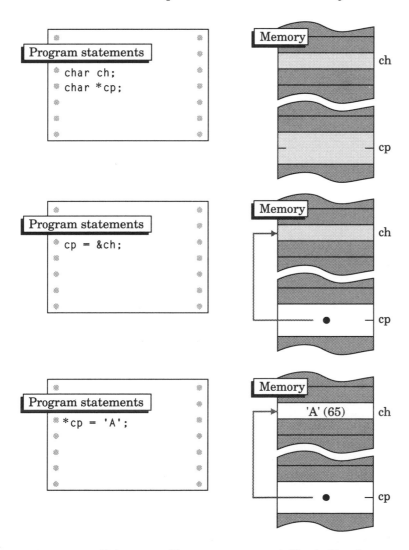

FIGURE 9-2. *Pointers enable you to access variables indirectly.*

Pointers as Function Arguments

As mentioned earlier, one reason for passing a pointer to a function instead of passing a copy of the variable's value is to save time and space. Passing a copy of a large aggregate variable, such as an array or a complex data structure, requires significant amounts of stack space and time. To improve the performance of a program, you can pass the address of such a variable and let the function access its elements through a pointer.

Another reason for using pointers as parameters is to permit functions to return more than a single value. You know already that a function can return a single value by way of its *return* statement. By using pointer parameters, however, you can give a function access to—and thus the ability to change—the values of variables in a calling function. The calling function must cooperate by passing an actual argument as an address rather than as a value.

Swapping Values

As you learned in Chapter 7, passing parameters using the call-by-value method is the C language default. At that time, we couldn't investigate call-by-reference parameter passing (which is address-based) because that method requires a knowledge of pointers. The SWAP program (Listing 9-3) shows how both types of parameter passing work and points out the primary differences.

The program consists of a *main()* function and two other functions, *SwapByValue()* and *SwapByReference()*. The *main()* function sets up two integer variables and then calls *SwapByValue()* with the two variable names as parameters. Because the call-by-value method of parameter passing hands copies of the value to the function, the function call has no effect on the original values. The *SwapByValue()* function can perform any operation you define with the copies it was passed, but the variables in *main()* are safe.

To affect a variable in *main()*, you must either return a value from the called function and then assign it to the variable or call a function from *main()* that uses call-by-reference parameter passing.

SwapByReference() is such a function, as its name suggests. Its two arguments are declared as pointers to integers. In *main()*, the function

```
/*
 * S W A P
 *
 * Exchange values in storage by using "call-by-value" and
 * "call-by-reference" parameter-passing methods to show
 * the fundamental differences between the methods.
 */

#include <stdio.h>

int
main(void)
{
        int val1, val2;          /* integer values */

        /*
         * Function prototypes.
         */
        void SwapByValue(int, int);          /* uses variables */
        void SwapByReference(int *, int *); /* uses pointers */

        /*
         * Initialize variables.
         */
        val1 = 10;
        val2 = 20;
        puts("Parameter-passing test\n");
        printf("Starting values:\n\tval1 = %d;  val2 = %d\n",
               val1, val2);

        /*
         * Pass parameters by value.
         */
        puts("After call-by-value attempt:");
        SwapByValue(val1, val2);
        printf("\tval1 = %d;  val2 = %d\n", val1, val2);

        /*
         * Pass parameters by reference.
         */
        puts("After call-by-reference attempt:");
        SwapByReference(&val1, &val2);
        printf("\tval1 = %d;  val2 = %d\n", val1, val2);

        return (0);
}
```

LISTING 9-3. *Program source code for swap.c.*   *(continued)*

LISTING 9-3. *continued*

```
/*
 * SwapByValue()
 *
 * Attempt to swap two variables in memory by using
 * call-by-value parameter passing.
 */

void
SwapByValue(int v1, int v2)
{
        int tmp;          /* temporary variable for use in swap */

        /*
         * Swap the values of v1 and v2.  Because v1 and v2
         * are copies of the actual arguments, the variables
         * in main() are unaffected by this action.
         */
        tmp = v1;
        v1 = v2;
        v2 = tmp;
}


/*
 * SwapByReference()
 *
 * Attempt to swap two variables in memory by using
 * call-by-reference parameter passing.
 */

void
SwapByReference(int *vp1, int *vp2)
{
        int tmp;          /* temporary variable for use in swap */

        /*
         * Swap the values in the variables pointed to by
         * vp1 and vp2.  Because vp1 and vp2 are addresses of
         * the actual arguments, the values in main() are
         * changed by this action.
         */
        tmp = *vp1;
        *vp1 = *vp2;
        *vp2 = tmp;
}
```

call passes the addresses, *&var1* and *&var2*—precisely the sort of arguments you need. Operations that occur within *SwapByReference()*, which use pointers instead of copies of values, can therefore affect the values of *var1* and *var2* in *main()*.

Notice that *SwapByValue()* and *SwapByReference()* don't have return values, hence the *void* return types.

Pointers and Arrays

As you learned in the previous chapter, an array is a collection of objects with the same date type. You can access an element by using its index, of course, but now you have an alternative. You can declare a pointer, set it to the beginning of the array, and then use it for indirect access to array elements. Let's begin with the variable declarations:

```
#define NITEMS 16
    .
    .
    .
long lnum[NITEMS];
long *lp;
```

Notice that the pointer *lp* has the same type as the elements in the array. Now you have to set the pointer to the beginning of the array. Remember the & operator? It works with arrays too. The address of an array is the address of its first element. To establish the required pointer for the variable declared above, you need to make the following assignment:

```
lp = &lnum[0];
```

Figure 9-3 on the following page depicts the allocation of memory after you assign a value to the pointer in this manner.

To give element 0 of the *lnum* array a value of 1000L, you can use the index in the assignment, as follows:

```
lnum[0] = 1000L;
```

You can also make this assignment using a pointer to the appropriate element. Because you set the pointer *lp* to the first element of *lnum*, you can assign the value of element 0 with the following statement:

```
*lp = 1000L;
```

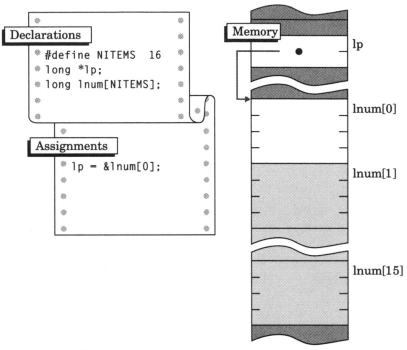

FIGURE 9-3. *Setting a pointer to an array.*

To assign the value 92000L to element 2 of the *lnum* array, you have the same options. You can use either of the following assignments:

```
lnum[2] = 92000L;
```

```
*(1p + 2) = 92000L;
```

The second method works because pointer references are scaled to the data type of the object to which they point. Thus, the offset of 2 in the expression *(lp + 2)* identifies element 2 of the array. The offset specifies the number of elements, not the number of bytes, to add to the base address to arrive at the destination. (Note that the asterisk is *outside* the parentheses. It operates on the result of the expression in parentheses, not on *lp* alone.) In this case, using *long* data, the number of bytes is 8 because each element occupies 4 bytes. Figure 9-4 illustrates this use of offsets with pointers.

The assignment statement that uses pointer *lp* does not change the value of *lp*. The pointer still specifies the base of the array after

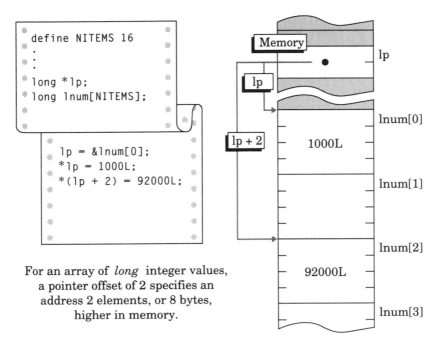

```
define NITEMS 16
    :
    :
long *lp;
long lnum[NITEMS];
```

```
lp = &lnum[0];
*lp = 1000L;
*(lp + 2) = 92000L;
```

For an array of *long* integer values, a pointer offset of 2 specifies an address 2 elements, or 8 bytes, higher in memory.

FIGURE 9-4. *Specifying an array element by incrementing a pointer.*

the assignment. If you want the pointer to designate a different element, you can assign it a new value:

```
lp = &lnum[15];      /* points to element 15 */
```

You can also perform a limited range of arithmetic operations with pointers. If *lp* points to the base of the array, you can make it point to element 15 by assigning the pointer a new value relative to the old one:

```
lp += 15;       /* add 15 longs to the pointer */
```

By either method—reassignment or "address arithmetic"—you change the value of *lp* so that it no longer points to the start of the array. You'll learn more about address arithmetic in the next chapter.

Constant Pointer

Because programmers frequently pass the address of an array as a function parameter and assign the base of an array to a pointer variable, C treats the name of an array as a constant pointer to the base of the array. An unadorned array name is identical to the address of the array's first element. Therefore, the following assignments have identical results:

```
lp = &lnum[0];
lp = lnum;
```

Each statement sets *lp* to the starting address of the array.

Pointers and Strings

The close relationship between pointers and strings in C is a consequence of the relationship between pointers and arrays. After all, a string is merely a special case of an array—an array of characters that concludes with a NUL termination character. The NUL character is important because it lets you create strings of arbitrary size and scan them with pointers.

Printing Strings

The PRINTSTR program (Listing 9-4) compares three ways of printing text strings. The first way is to pass the string to *printf()*. The second way is to loop through the string with an index. The third is to scan the string with a character pointer.

The first step is to declare the string and initialize it. Recall that you can initialize an array only if you declare it either as a global object or as a static variable within a function.

String Argument Method. The second *printf()* function expects a single argument beyond the control string, *"%s"*, because %s is the only format specifier. The argument is the constant pointer represented by the array name *string*. You could also use *&string[0]* as the argument to emphasize that it is an address.

Indexed-Array Access Method. Another method is to use *putchar()* (rather than *printf()*) to print the string one character at a time. The printing occurs within a *for* loop that increments the array index *i*. To determine when to stop the loop, the program uses the standard library function *strlen()*, which returns the number of characters in the string, excluding the NUL byte. The string in PRINTSTR is 54 characters, so the loop executes from element 0 through element 53. Recall that the maximum index is one less than the size of the array.

```
/*
 * P R I N T S T R
 *
 * Compare the printing of strings using several
 * methods, including indirect access via a pointer.
 */

#include <stdio.h>
#include <string.h>

int
main(void)
{
        int i;          /* loop index */
        int len;        /* string length */
        char *cp;       /* character pointer */

        static char string[] = {
          "What goes up must come down.  Ask a market analyst!\n"
        };

        /*
         * Print the string by using the printf() library function.
         */
        printf("Using printf(): ");
        printf("%s", string);

        /*
         * Print the string by using array indexing.
         */
        printf("Using an array index: ");
        len = strlen(string);   /* length of string */
        for (i = 0; i < len; ++i)
                putchar(string[i]);

        /*
         * Print the string by using a character pointer.
         */
        printf("Using a character pointer: ");
        cp = string;                    /* beginning of string */
        while (*cp) {
                putchar(*cp);
                ++cp;
        }

        return (0);
}
```

LISTING 9-4. *Program source code for printstr.c.*

Pointer Access Method. The pointer method is easier to implement than the indexed-array version, and it executes faster to boot. You set the character pointer to the beginning of the string (*cp* = *string*) and then loop as long as the value of *cp* is not NUL ('\0'). The controlling expression in the *while* loop implies a comparison of the value yielded by *cp* with 0. As long as the expression evaluates to a nonzero value, the loop continues running.

You can combine the two lines in the body of the loop into a single statement if you can tolerate the following cryptic-looking expression:

```
while (*cp)
        putchar(*cp++);
```

In this compact form, the incrementing of the pointer variable, because of the postfix notation, takes place after *putchar()* prints the character to which *cp* is currently pointing. I doubt that the loss in clarity is repaid by any increase in efficiency of the executable code. Nevertheless, you should recognize the code in either form.

Note that compactness can lead to subtle problems if you're not careful. As an exercise, replace the body of the *while* loop with the compact version above and rerun the program. Then, try changing *putchar(*cp++);* to *putchar(*++cp);* and running the program again.

Shorthand Declaration and Initialization

The following statements declare a string and a pointer variable and initialize them:

```
static char string[] = { "This is a string." };
char *str = string;
```

Because this action is such a common one, C permits the following shorthand that combines pointer declaration and initialization:

```
char *str = { "This is a string." };
```

If you declare the pointer this way, you need no intermediate character array declaration.

❑ NOTE: *Following this shorthand compile-time assignment,* str *points to the start of the string. Subsequent changes to* str *cause the pointer to lose the address of the string with no way to recover the information. If you need to point to other parts of the string, declare and use an auxiliary pointer.*

Questions and Exercises

1. Explain the connection between a pointer and an address.

2. Cite three reasons for using pointers in your programs.

3. A program contains the following lines. What does it print?

```
char ch = 'M', *cp;
cp = &ch;
*cp = 'Z';
putchar(ch);
```

4. Because a pointer and an integer can be stored in memory areas of the same size, you can use them interchangeably. True or False?

5. Explain the differences between call-by-value and call-by-reference parameter passing. What are the benefits and drawbacks of each?

6. Write a program that prints the value of each element in the following array, one value per line of output. Use a pointer, not an array index, to access array elements, and calculate the array size rather than using a defined constant.

```
static int number[] = {
        0, 1, 2, 3, 4, 5, 6, 7, 8, 9
        };
```

7. What is wrong with the following string declaration?

```
*str = { "Aim for zero defects!" };
```

10: More on Pointers

Functions That Return Pointers
Pointer Arithmetic
Sorting an Array
Debugging Programs
Questions and Exercises

C Programming Lessons: *Pointers and Indirection*
The Learn C Compiler: *Debugging a Program*

You now have a taste for pointers and what they can do for you. This chapter extends the coverage of pointers by looking at functions that return pointer values, functions that format and manipulate strings, pointer arithmetic, and sorting. It also gives you a chance to use the Learn C debugging feature to diagnose and fix pointer problems.

Functions That Return Pointers

You know that the default return type from a function is *int*. If you design a function that returns anything else, you need to specify the data type of the return value.

It is good practice to indicate the return type with a specifier even if the return type is *int*. As you have seen several times, functions that return nothing should have a return type specifier of *void*.

By providing function argument and return type information in the form of function prototypes and complete function definitions, you help the C compiler detect and report type mismatches that could cause problems (such as a disagreement between the return type of a function and the type of data in a *return* statement). The compiler can help you avoid problems, but only if you give it enough information.

We now turn our attention an important topic—functions that return pointers. The solutions to many programming problems are best expressed by functions that return pointers. Let's start with a program that shows how to format strings in various ways.

String Formatting

The STRCASE program (Listing 10-1) alters the format of a string typed by the user. It prints the text of the string first in all uppercase letters, then in all lowercase, and then with an initial capital letter.

```
/*
 * S T R C A S E
 *
 * Display a string in each of several presentation formats:
 *      - all uppercase
 *      - all lowercase
 *      - initial capital letter
 */
```

LISTING 10-1. *Program source code for strcase.c.*   *(continued)*

LISTING 10-1. *continued*

```c
#include <stdio.h>
#include <ctype.h>      /* for conversion macros */

/*
 * Function prototypes
 */
char *StringUpper(char *);
char *StringLower(char *);
char *StringCapitalize(char *);

#define MAXSTRING 20

int
main(void)
{
        char buffer[MAXSTRING + 1];      /* add 1 for NUL byte */

        /*
         * Prompt the user for a string and read
         * it into the input buffer.
         */
        printf("Type a string (%d characters max.) + ENTER: ",
                MAXSTRING);
        gets(buffer);

        /*
         * Convert and display the string (three ways).
         */
        printf("%s\n", StringUpper(buffer));
        printf("%s\n", StringLower(buffer));
        printf("%s\n", StringCapitalize(buffer));

        return (0);
}

/*
 * StringUpper()
 *
 * Convert all the alphabetic characters in a string
 * to uppercase.  Nonalpha characters are unaffected.
 */
```

(continued)

LISTING 10-1. *continued*

```
char *
StringUpper(char *string)
{
        char *cp;

        cp = string;
        while (*cp != '\0') {
                *cp = toupper(*cp);
                ++cp;
        }

        return (string);
}

/*
 * StringLower()
 *
 * Convert all the alphabetic characters in a string
 * to lowercase.  Nonalpha characters are unaffected.
 * /

char *
StringLower(char *string)
{
        char *cp;

        cp = string;
        while (*cp != '\0') {
                *cp = tolower(*cp);
                ++cp;
        }

        return (string);
}

/*
 * StringCapitalize()
 *
 * Convert the first character in a string to uppercase and
 * the rest to lowercase.  Nonalpha characters are unaffected.
 */
```

(continued)

LISTING 10-1. *continued*

```
char *
StringCapitalize(char *string)
{
        char *cp;

        cp = string;
        *cp = toupper(*cp);
        ++cp;
        while (*cp != '\0') {
                *cp = tolower(*cp);
                ++cp;
        }

        return (string);
}
```

If the user types *thIS is A tEsT!*, the program responds as follows:

```
THIS IS A TEST!
this is a test!
This is a test!
```

Three functions perform the conversion tasks. Each function takes a pointer to a character as an argument, converts the string to the requested format, and returns a pointer to the beginning of the converted string. Therefore, each function has the return type *char* *.

Notice what is happening. Because each function receives a pointer to the input buffer *buffer* rather than a copy of its contents, each is also free to alter the string itself. The functions return a pointer so that you can use the function concisely in assignments such as the ones shown in the three *printf()* statements in *main()*.

Pointer Arithmetic

You have already seen examples of pointer arithmetic—pointer increment and decrement operators and expressions involving offsets, such as *ptr + 4*. You can also take the difference between two pointer values, and you can compare pointers for equality.

You cannot, however, add pointer values together, multiply or divide them, or use them in any other kind of arithmetic expressions as you would with ordinary variables. Such expressions could easily yield pointer values that are outside the valid addressable range of your program.

The following are examples of valid expressions involving integer pointers *pa* and *pb*:

```
pb - pa          /* subtract one pointer from another */
++pa;            /* increment a pointer */
pa += 3;         /* add-assign a pointer */
pa + i           /* add an integer value to a pointer */
pa < pb          /* compare pointers */
```

Note that the increment and add-assignment expressions alter the value of the pointer. None of the others affect the pointer values.

The following operations involving the same pointers are strictly forbidden:

```
pa * pb          /* ILLEGAL: multiply pointers */
pa + pb          /* ILLEGAL: add pointers together */
pa >> 8          /* ILLEGAL: shift a pointer */
```

Reversing a String

The REVERSE program (Listing 10-2) prompts the user for a string and reverses it. The program demonstrates the use of pointer arithmetic—incrementing, decrementing, and comparing pointer values. It also introduces the concept and implementation of the NULL pointer.

```
/*
 * R E V E R S E
 *
 * Reverse a string in memory.
 */

#include <stdio.h>
#include <stdlib.h>

#define NBYTES   80

/*
 * Function prototypes
 */
char *GetString(char *);
char *ReverseString(char *);
```

LISTING 10-2. *Program source code for reverse.c.*   *(continued)*

LISTING 10-2. *continued*

```
int
main(void)
{
        char buf[NBYTES + 1];          /* input buffer */

        /*
         * Get a string from the user, reverse
         * it, and display the reversed string.
         */
        if (GetString(buf) == NULL) {
                fprintf(stderr, "ERROR: Cannot get input string\n");
                exit (1);
        }
        if (ReverseString(buf) == NULL) {
                fprintf(stderr, "ERROR: Empty string\n");
                exit (2);
        }
        printf("Reversed string: %s\n", buf);

        return (0);
}


/*
 * GetString()
 *
 * Prompt the user for a string and save the reply
 * in the specified input buffer.  Return a pointer to
 * the string buffer or NULL if a read error occurs.
 */

char *
GetString(str)
char *str;
{
        fputs("Input string: ", stdout);
        if (gets(str) == NULL)
                return NULL;

        return (str);
}
```

(continued)

LISTING 10-2. *continued*

```
/*
 * ReverseString()
 *
 * Reverse a string in place.
 */

char *
ReverseString(char *str)
{
        char *p, *q;    /* character pointers */
        char temp;      /* swap buffer */

        /*
         * Point to the ends of the string.  Report an
         * empty string if the first character is NUL.
         */
        p = str;                    /* first character */
        if (*p == '\0')             /* if NUL, string is empty */
                return NULL;

        q = str;
        while(*q != '\0')
                ++q;
        --q;                        /* last character */

        /*
         * Reverse the string and return a pointer to
         * the beginning of the modified string buffer.
         */
        while (p < q) {
                temp = *p;          /* swap characters */
                *p = *q;
                *q = temp;
                ++p;                /* adjust pointers */
                --q;
        }

        return (str);
}
```

The *main()* function in reverse.c sets up an input buffer, *buf*, and calls *GetString()* to prompt the user for a text string and read it into the input buffer. Then it calls *ReverseString()* to reverse the order of the characters in the string. Both functions return a pointer to a character, usually the beginning of the input buffer. If an error occurs in one of the functions, however, the function returns a special value called NULL.

The NULL Pointer

NULL is a pointer constant that has a value of 0. When you assign the value NULL to a pointer, the pointer is guaranteed by the C system to point at "nothing." The "NULL pointer," as it is called, is defined in the standard header file stdio.h as a symbolic constant with a value of 0. NULL is not the same as the ASCII NUL character, '\0', although they both have a numeric value of 0. NULL is a pointer constant and NUL is a character constant.

As a pointer value, NULL usually implies an error condition or the end of an array of pointers. Many standard library functions return NULL if they are unable to perform a requested action, such as opening a file or reading a string from the keyboard.

In the REVERSE program, *GetString()* attempts to read a string by calling the standard library routine *gets()*. If *gets()* cannot read the string for some reason, it returns NULL, which *GetString()* passes back to its caller.

Scanning a String with Pointers

The *ReverseString()* function, which is illustrated in Figure 10-1 on the following page, uses two character pointers, *p* and *q*, to scan the input string. Both pointers are initially set to the beginning of the string. The loop containing only the pointer *q* scans to the end of the string:

```
while (*q != '\0')
        ++q;
--q;
```

The loop finds the end by comparing the value of *q* with the character it is pointing at to see if it is the NUL character. When it reaches the NUL byte, the loop terminates, and the pointer *q* is moved back one position so that it points to the last text character.

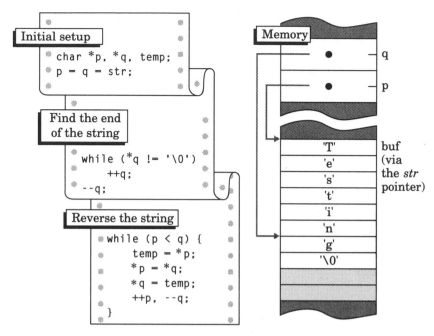

FIGURE 10-1. *The* ReverseString() *function uses pointers to manipulate a string.*

The second loop involves both character pointers. At the start of this loop, pointer p points to the beginning of the string and pointer q to the end. The loop continues to run as long as the address contained in p is less than the one in q. Each time it executes, the loop exchanges a pair of characters using the temporary variable *temp*, increments p, and decrements q. The effect is that the pointers scan from opposite ends of the string and meet in the middle. The result is a reversed string.

Sorting an Array

A frequently performed operation in computer programs is the sorting of data into ascending or descending order. Many useful algorithms for sorting have survived the test of time. These methods include the Bubble sort, various Exchange sorts, the Shell sort, and the Quick sort, among many others. While all have their advantages and disadvantages, we'll examine a simple Exchange sort because its performance and complexity fall somewhere between those of the other methods.

This Exchange sort algorithm loops through the data, comparing values and exchanging pairs that are not in the desired order. To sort elements into ascending order, you compare the first element of the data array to the next element. If the first element has a greater value than the second, exchange the values. Then compare the first element to the third and exchange the values if necessary. Continue comparing the first element to successively higher elements until none remain.

Next, compare the second array element to each succeeding element, and continue in this manner until you can make no further comparisons. At that point, the elements are all in ascending order.

The XSORT program (Listing 10-3) demonstrates an Exchange sort. It operates on a series of integers held in a static array within *main()*. As you read the program for the first time, ignore the *SHOWME* definition and lines contained within the *#if defined (SHOWME)* preprocessor blocks. The *ExchangeSort()* function does the bulk of the work in the XSORT program. It receives two parameters: a pointer to the data array (*array*), and an unsigned integer (*nelem*) that specifies (as a number of elements) the portion of the array to sort.

```
/*
 * X S O R T
 *
 * Sort an array of numbers by using a simple exchange sort.
 */

#define SHOWME

#include <stdio.h>

void ExchangeSort(int *, unsigned int);

int
main(void)
{
        int n;          /* loop control variable */
        int *ptr;       /* integer pointer */
        int size;       /* calculated array size in elements */

        /* array data */
        static int numbers[] = {
                82, 30, 12, 1, -6
        };
```

LISTING 10-3. *Program source code for xsort.c.*   *(continued)*

LISTING 10-3. *continued*

```
        /*
         * Calculate the array size and display the
         * array in its initial condition.
         */
        size = sizeof numbers / sizeof (int);
        puts("Array before sorting:");
        for (n = size, ptr = numbers; n-- > 0; ++ptr)
                printf("%5d  ", *ptr);
        putchar('\n');
        putchar('\n');

        /*
         * Sort the array
         */
        ExchangeSort(numbers, size);

        /*
         * Display the array after sorting
         */
        puts("\nArray after sorting:");
        for (n = size, ptr = numbers; n-- > 0; ++ptr)
                printf("%5d  ", *ptr);
        putchar('\n');

        return (0);
}

/*
 * ExchangeSort()
 *
 * A simple exchange sort function
 */

void
ExchangeSort(int *array, unsigned int nelem)
{
        int *p, *q;      /* array indexes */
        int temp;        /* buffer for exchanges */
#if defined (SHOWME)
        int loopcount = 0;
        int *ptr;
#endif

        for (p = array; p < array + nelem - 1; ++p) {
```

(continued)

LISTING 10-3. *continued*

```
#if defined (SHOWME)
                printf("Loop %d:\n", ++loopcount);
#endif
                for (q = p + 1; q < array + nelem; ++q) {
                    if (*p > *q) {
                            temp = *p;
                            *p = *q;
                            *q = temp;
                    }
#if defined (SHOWME)
                    /*
                     * Show partially sorted array after each
                     * pass of the inner loop.
                     */
                    for (ptr = array; ptr < array + nelem; ++ptr)
                            printf("%5d   ", *ptr);
                    putchar('\n');
#endif
                }
        }
}
```

You need a pair of nested loops to implement this Exchange sort. The outer loop sets a pointer to the beginning of the array and loops through all but the last element. The inner loop starts at the element immediately after the one to which the outer loop is pointing. It compares each remaining element to the element to which the outer loop is pointing; the elements are swapped if they are out of order.

The additional source code in the conditional blocks lets you see how the elements are arranged after each pass through the sorting loops. It also introduces the topic of conditional compilation.

Conditional Compilation

In Chapter 6 you learned how to define symbolic constants by using the *#define* preprocessor directive. You can also use *#define* to define a name without giving it a value. The following line, which comes near the beginning of the XSORT source file, defines the name *SHOWME*:

#define SHOWME

The name is added to the program's symbol table.

The *#if defined* directive checks the symbol table to determine whether a specified symbol is defined. If the symbol is not defined, the compiler skips all lines in the source file through the closing *#endif*. If the symbol is defined, the enclosed statements become part of the source file seen by the rest of the C compiler passes.

To see how this Exchange sort works, compile and run the program as it is provided on the source disk. Examine the output and observe the way values are exchanged. Also notice that as the outer loop moves to higher addresses in the data array, the inner loop has fewer elements to access.

To disable the statements that reveal the intermediate steps of the Exchange sort, delete the line *#define SHOWME* and recompile the program.

Debugging Programs

As you write programs, you might be astounded by the number of things that can go wrong and by the frequency with which they do. Simple typing mistakes account for many errors. Fortunately, Learn C is able to detect and warn you about such errors, which usually arise as syntax errors.

Syntax errors result from typing constant, variable, and function names incorrectly, or from using unrecognized symbols for operators, or from forgetting semicolons or parentheses—the list could go on. The compiler faithfully reports syntax errors and helps you to locate them.

Another kind of error is usually not detected by the compiler. Semantic errors, which result from logical mistakes, do not affect the compilation process. Your program compiles without comment, but it fails to run, or perhaps it runs but produces incorrect results.

Before errors of this kind drive you to consider a different career, take a look at the Learn C debugging feature. It can save you a considerable amount of time and effort (and give you renewed hope). The built-in debugger is one of several Learn C (and QuickC) features that distinguish the product from others in the field.

Let's deliberately create a semantic error in the REVERSE program (Listing 10-2 on p. 198) and use the debugger to diagnose it. Of course, the debugger cannot do everything for you. You still have to tell it where to look and what to look for, but it relieves you of the burden of managing a great number of details. It also lets you debug at the source code level—a far easier task than debugging at the machine code level, which has traditionally been the only available procedure.

Start Learn C and open the reverse.c file. Scroll through the file until you find the first occurrence of the line *−−q;* in the *ReverseString()* function and delete it by pressing Ctrl+Y. Doing this simulates a common "off-by-one" error, which can produce some unexpected results. Save the file and then recompile it with the Debug and Pointer Check options set. (An X appears in the corresponding locations in the Compile dialog box.)

Compiling with the Debug option turned on forces Learn C to save special debugging information in the executable memory image of your program. Using the Pointer Check option is a precaution that I recommend to programmers who are new to C in all programs that make use of pointers. It adds run-time code that checks for possible pointer mistakes, such as using a pointer before it has been initialized. Because this additional pointer-checking code can slow program execution considerably, turn it off after you completely debug your program.

When you run the modified REVERSE program, it correctly gathers the input string, but the output is an empty string. Because you know where the error is, you can probably see what is wrong. But pretend for now that you don't know what is wrong. How would you go about locating the problem?

A good place to start is in *main()*. You can examine the value of the *buf* variable before and after the string is reversed. To do this, you could put in some extra *printf()* statements that would show you the values as the program runs, but doing so is unnecessary and inconvenient.

Use Learn C "watch expressions" and "breakpoints" instead. A watch expression is an expression that you want to be able to observe in a special watch window at the top of the screen. It might be a simple variable, an expression consisting of variables in combination, or an array or structure in its entirety. A breakpoint is a line in the program at which you want execution to stop temporarily.

Adding Watch Expressions

To add a watch expression, type Alt+D to activate the Debug menu, and then select Add Watch from the menu. In the resulting dialog box, enter the expression you want to observe. For this example, type *buf* and press Enter to conclude the entry. A one-line window opens above the edit window and displays the following information, which shows that *buf* does not contain a meaningful value:

```
buf: <>
```

This shows that *buf* contains nothing of value yet.

If you add more watch expressions, Learn C devotes more screen area to the watch window.

Setting Breakpoints

The best places in the REVERSE program to examine the contents of the *buf* array are the following lines, both of which occur in *main()*:

```
if (ReverseString(buf) == NULL ) {
```

and

```
printf("reversed string:  %s\n", buf);
```

The first line contains the string as it was input and the second should contain the reversed string. Note that a breakpoint stops execution before the specified statement is executed; thus, you see the value of the variable before it is passed to the function.

To set a breakpoint at a given line, move to the line and press F9. This function key is a toggle command. The first press on a given line turns the breakpoint on; the next press on the same line turns it off.

After you set the watch expression and the breakpoints, your screen should resemble the one shown in Figure 10-2. Run the program by pressing Shift+F5. When prompted for input, type *12345* followed by Enter. The program stops executing on the line containing the first breakpoint, and the watch window shows you the current value of *buf*.

The array is 81 characters long, and at the first breakpoint it contains the value *12345\0* followed by a potentially intimidating series of characters. Those other characters are artifacts of earlier code or data in those memory locations, but they are meaningless now. The *\0*

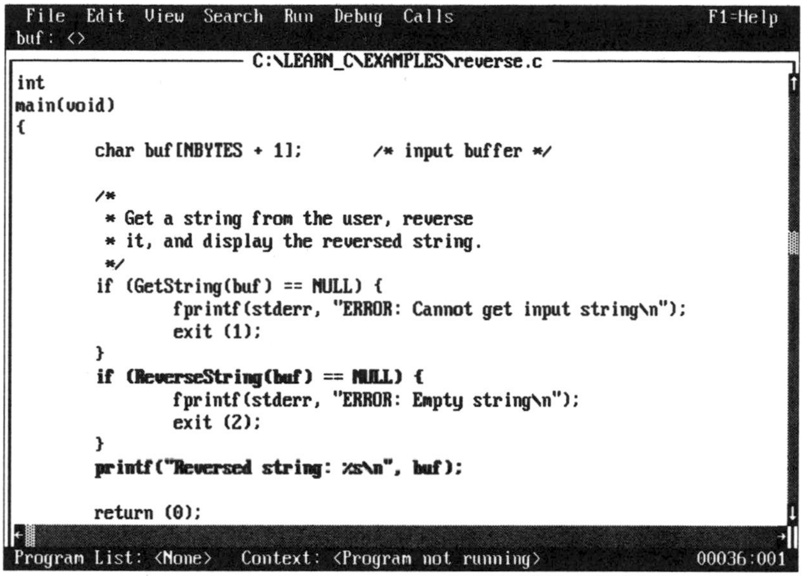

```
 File  Edit  View  Search  Run  Debug  Calls            F1=Help
buf: <>
┌─────────────────── C:\LEARN_C\EXAMPLES\reverse.c ───────────────────┐
│int                                                                  ↑│
│main(void)                                                            │
│{                                                                     │
│        char buf[NBYTES + 1];        /* input buffer */               │
│                                                                      │
│                                                                      │
│        /*                                                            │
│         * Get a string from the user, reverse                        │
│         * it, and display the reversed string.                       │
│         */                                                           │
│        if (GetString(buf) == NULL) {                                 │
│                fprintf(stderr, "ERROR: Cannot get input string\n");  │
│                exit (1);                                             │
│        }                                                             │
│        if (ReverseString(buf) == NULL) {                             │
│                fprintf(stderr, "ERROR: Empty string\n");             │
│                exit (2);                                             │
│        }                                                             │
│        printf("Reversed string: %s\n", buf);                         │
│                                                                      │
│        return (0);                                                  ↓│
│←                                                                    →│
│Program List: <None>   Context: <Program not running>    00036:001   │
└──────────────────────────────────────────────────────────────────────┘
```

FIGURE 10-2. *The Learn C debugging facility highlights breakpoints and displays watch variables in a window above the edit window.*

(NUL) following the *5* terminates the string currently stored in *buf*. Nothing beyond that point is of any consequence to the REVERSE program.

So far everything is as it should be. To continue, press F5 to resume program execution. The *ReverseString()* function now executes, and the flow stops at the second breakpoint. The argument passed to *printf()* is the new value of *buf*, which should be a reversed input string. But the watch window shows us that it is not—at least not exactly.

The *buf* array now contains \054321 (followed by the previously mentioned jumble of characters and symbols). The problem is right there in the first character—a NUL character, which looks like an empty string in C. Now you know what's wrong, but you still don't know why the problem is occurring. You have, however, isolated the problem to the *ReverseString()* function.

Delete the watch expression and the breakpoints (using the Debug menu) so that you can start fresh. Move to the *ReverseString()* portion of the program source file and look for clues. With some experience, you would see the cause of the problem at once, but let's assume that it still eludes you.

A good place to look at values is the controlling expression of a loop. Let's set a breakpoint on the *while* loop that controls the string-reversal process and add watches on the values stored in the locations referenced by *p* and *q*. Simply move to the loop statement and press F9 to set the breakpoint. Then add the watches on *∗p* and *∗q*. Remember, we want the values of the characters, not the addresses.

Restart the program by pressing Shift+F5, and type the string *12345*, as before. Execution stops before the first execution of the loop and shows that *∗p* equals the digit *'1'* and *∗q* equals *'\0'*. Oops! The value of *∗q* is supposed to be the digit '5', but *q* is pointing to the wrong place. To solve this problem, add the following statement before entering the loop:

```
--q;
```

Other debugging tasks will differ in their details, of course, but they all have one thing in common. Debugging involves isolating the problem to a particular part of a program and then zeroing in on a solution. A properly partitioned program simplifies your task. And an exceptional debugger like the one built into Learn C helps you isolate bugs quickly.

The best debugging technique is to design and code your programs with care and to avoid bugs in the first place (a worthwhile goal, however rarely achieved in practice).

Questions and Exercises

1. Which of the following pointer expressions affects the value of the pointer?

```
ptr - 5          *(cp + 5) = 'A'
*cp = '?'        *cp++ != '\0'
ptr1 - ptr2      x = *ptr
ptr += 10        ptr1 = ptr2
```

2. Write a program that prompts the user for a string of text and prints it as a series of numbers (the ASCII codes that correspond to the characters in the string).

3. What is wrong with the following program fragment?

```
char str[20];
char *cp;
...
str[0] = 'R';
*cp = str[0];
```

4. Explain why the *ReverseString()* function returns a pointer to the beginning of the string it receives as an argument.

5. Write a program that reads a string from the keyboard and counts the numbers of characters in three categories: letters (a–z and A–Z), digits (0–9), and other characters. (Hint: Use character classification macros, *isdigit()* and *isalpha()*, to test the characters. These macros are defined in ctype.h.)

6. The XSORT program sorts an array of integers. Revise it to sort an array of floating-point numbers.

11: Structures, Unions, and Bitfields

Structures

Unions

Bitfields

User-defined Types

Questions and Exercises

C Programming Lessons: Structures, Unions, and Bitfields

Now that you know about pointers, you have enough knowledge about C to be really dangerous. With appropriate restraint and discipline, however, you can use the tools at your disposal to build creatively. This chapter gives you more information, ammunition you can use to build more powerful tools and programs.

In addition to arrays, C offers several user-defined data types. They enable you to create data constructs that reflect the data that confronts you in real situations:

- **Structure**—A structure is a collection of individual data items whose types can differ but which carry a common identifier.

- **Union**—A union resembles a structure in form, but its purpose is quite different. A union is a variable that can, at different times, hold data of different types.

- **Bitfield**—A bitfield is a portion of a memory word. Dividing a word into a series of bitfields allows you to pack several objects into a single memory word.

Let's give each of these C data types a fair hearing. We'll start with a look at structures because both unions and bitfields are based on the syntax of structures.

Structures

A structure is a collection of related variables that can have different data types. Optionally, a structure can be given a name, or tag, that conveniently refers to the entire collection of members and so simplifies data-handling operations.

Structure Declarations

The form of a structure—its template—is declared as follows:

```
struct [tag] {
        type1 var1;
        type2 var2;
        .
        .
        .

};
```

The *struct* keyword identifies the object as a structure. The *tag* word is optional (hence the brackets). Supplying a tag for a template provides a way to refer to the template later in your program. The structure template describes individual items, known as *members,* of the structure by listing their data types and names. This declaration does not reserve any storage unless you provide variable names in the declaration.

Using Structure Tags

Suppose you declare a structure with the tag *template*:

```
struct template {
        int number;
        char *text;
};
```

To declare a structure that uses this template, use the *struct* keyword, followed by the tag name and a variable name:

```
struct template varname;
```

This declaration reserves storage for an *int* value and a pointer to a character (or string) and attaches the name *varname* to the aggregate. Note that the variable name can represent either an aggregate, such as an array, or a single variable. Declaring a structure variable is much like declaring any other variable with a specified type—the important difference is that the amount of memory set aside by the compiler depends on the particular structure template.

Because the *template* structure was declared with a tag, you can reuse the template easily in subsequent *struct* declarations. Every time you do, the C compiler allocates sufficient memory for the aggregate.

If you don't provide a tag, subsequent declarations of the same structure must redeclare all the variables that comprise the structure. In a text editor, for example, you might declare an array variable *buffer* that uses the *template* structure you defined above. If you supplied a tag in the declaration (as shown above), you can simply declare the following:

```
struct template buffer[MAXLINES];
```

If you failed to tag the earlier declaration, you have no easy way to reuse it. Instead, you'll have to add the new variable name to the preceding declaration or declare the structure in full, as in the example that follows.

```
struct {
        int number;
        char *text;
} buffer[MAXLINES];
```

Using structure tags is much easier and less confusing than creating "one-time" structures without tags, so we'll use the tag approach in the remainder of this book.

Putting Structures to Work

Now let's look at an example of a structure declaration and the declaration of a variable of the structured type. The example is that of a card file of business contacts. Each card contains a person's name, company affiliation, telephone number, complete address, and a serial number that relates the card to an optional file in which you keep relevant documents and correspondence. Begin with the following declaration of the structured type:

```
struct card_st {
        char name[30];          /* contact name */
        char company[30];       /* affiliation */
        char phone[20];         /* includes prefixes, etc. */
        char street[25];        /* street address */
        char city[25];          /* city name */
        char state[3];          /* postal abbreviation */
        char zip[10];           /* xxxxx-yyyy */
        unsigned serial;        /* 0 means no file */
};
```

To declare a variable of this type—a form that you use for collecting data—simply type the following statement in the program source file:

```
struct card_st form;
```

Figure 11-1 shows the effect of declaring the variable *form*.

Of course, you could have declared all eight items individually, but consider how much work would be involved if you had to do this for 10 cards. Or 100. By declaring a single template, you can simply use multiple *struct card_st* variable declarations and let the compiler do the work for you, or better yet, you can use a single *struct* variable declaration of an array. For example, to create a card file with 20 cards, simply declare an array variable of this type:

```
struct card_st file[FILESIZE];
```

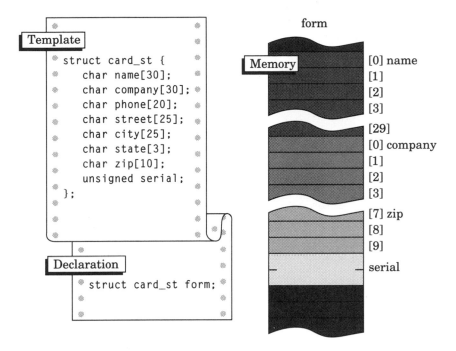

FIGURE 11-1. *Declaring structure* form *using the* card _st *template reserves storage for its members as shown above.*

Of course, you must define *FILESIZE* to be large enough for your needs and small enough to fit in your computer's memory.

Accessing Structure Members

Now that you can create data structures and declare structured variables, how do you get data into and out of them? The "dot" operator (.), lets you identify an individual member of a structure.

In the card file example, *form.name* accesses the *name* member of the variable *form*. Specify other members in the same way. For example, if you have collected data from the user and want to print the contents of the form for verification, you can show the values by typing statements such as the following:

```
printf("Company: %s\n", form.company);
```

To assign a value to a member of the *form* variable, use the same method of identifying members. For example, the following simple assignment statement assigns a serial number:

```
form.serial = 100;
```

Assigning a value to a string is more difficult. In the *struct card_st* definition, all but the last member are strings, or arrays of characters. The name of an array—*company*, for example—is a constant pointer. You cannot make an assignment to *company* because it is simply a fixed address, not a variable.

Lvalues

To better understand the impossibility of assigning a string directly to an array name, you need an introduction to "lvalues." An lvalue is an object that is acceptable as the target of an assignment. The term was derived from the fact that an assignment target is on the *left* side of an equal sign. The proposed ANSI C standard encourages the use of "locator value" as the definition for lvalue because you reference such an object to affect the value stored in its associated memory location.

In addition to their use in assignments, lvalues are required in address-of (&) expressions and in increment or decrement expressions. The & operator needs an lvalue operand because its purpose is to find the location of the operand. The increment and decrement operators require lvalue operands because the operators are, in fact, assignment statements in disguise. (Recall that *++n* is effectively *n = n + 1*).

The previously described problem with assigning a string to an array name results from the fact that an array name is not an lvalue, but a fixed address. You cannot assign a new value to it. You can use *scanf()* to read a value entered by the user directly into the array.

```
printf("Company name: ");
scanf("%s", form.company);
```

Another solution to this problem is provided by the standard library function *strcpy()*.

❑ NOTE: *Notice that the second argument in the* scanf() *statement above does not require an & operator. An array name (even when it's a member of a structure) is an address, which is what we need in* scanf().

The *strcpy()* Library Function

The *strcpy()* function copies a string from one place to another by copying individual characters sequentially. Given a receiving character array *form.company*, which serves as the destination, and an existing source string pointed to by *str*, the following program fragment shows how to use *strcpy()* to fill the array.

```
char *str = {
        "Company name not available"
};
    .
    .
    .
strcpy(form.company, str);
```

Suppose you want to copy a default string to *form.company* whenever a user fails to supply the company name on the form (by simply pressing Enter). Initially, *form.company* is undefined. Following the last statement, it contains a copy of the string pointed to by *str*. Attempting to assign the string using the following statement results in a compile-time error:

```
/* WRONG - form.company is not an lvalue */
form.company = str;
```

Initializing Structures

You can initialize a structure variable at compile time just as you can an array. Simply add one or more initializers to the declaration. Any structure members that you do not explicitly initialize are set to 0. For example, a table of silly names results from the following declaration:

```
static struct silly_st {
        char first[15];
        char last[20];
} nametable[] = {
        { "Tom", "Collins" },
        { "Wanda", "Lust" },
        { "Jerry", "Mander" }
        { "Dee", "Bugger" },
        { "Manuel", "Writer" },
};
```

Because the structure members are declared as character arrays, they reserve a fixed amount of space in memory when you declare a structure variable. The initializers fill only as many of those allocated character positions as there are characters in the string, plus a terminating NUL character. In memory, all character positions have memory associated with them, even if some are not used.

If you're concerned about memory conservation, you can store predefined strings such as those given above in a more economical fashion. You can declare members of the structure as pointers to strings, and then initialize the strings in the normal way. As depicted in Figure 11-2, each member is a pointer to a string that is elsewhere in memory. Memory that is not needed for the pointers and the strings remains available for storing more records or for other purposes.

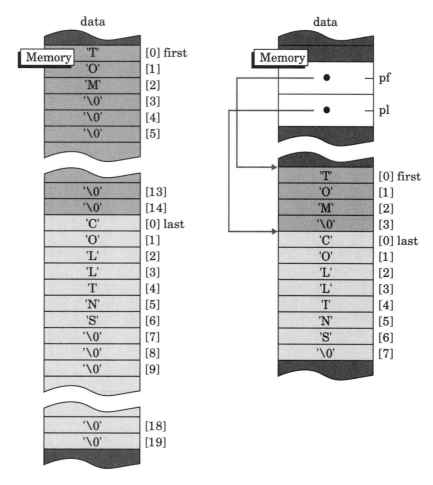

FIGURE 11-2. *Declaring pointers to arrays within a structure, as shown at right, lets you use memory more economically than declaring the (fixed-length) arrays within a structure, as shown on the left.*

The STATES Program

In a C program that manages a collection of data items, structures are often the best way to represent individual records. The STATES program illustrates this practice. The file states.h (Listing 11-1) contains the structure definition and initialization of the *States* array.

The STATES program lets you display information from the table initialized in states.h. The header contains information for only four state records. You can add others if you like by providing additional sets of initializers. Notice that the array is not dimensioned. The size is determined at compile time by the following line:

```
#define NSTATES sizeof States / sizeof (struct state_st)
```

The expression provided for *NSTATES* calculates the number of state records in the table. If you add initializers and then compile a program

```
/*
 * states.h
 *
 * Header file for the STATES program
 */

/*
 * Data structure declaration and initialization
 *
 * Initialize the state data in the array of data structures.
 * The list includes only those states the author has called "home."
 * If your state is not included, simply add the required data.
 */

struct state_st {
        char *code;             /* postal code for state name */
        char *name;             /* state name */
        char *capital;          /* capital city */
        unsigned population;    /* in thousands */
        unsigned area;          /* in square miles */
} States[] = {
        { "CO", "Colorado", "Denver", 2208, 104247 },
        { "MA", "Massachusetts", "Boston", 5689, 8257 },
        { "MD", "Maryland", "Annapolis", 3923, 10577 },
        { "RI", "Rhode Island", "Providence", 950, 1214 }
};

#define NSTATES sizeof States / sizeof (struct state_st)
```

LISTING 11-1. *Source code for states.h header file.*

that includes the states.h header file, the value of *NSTATES* reflects the new table size.

  The file states.c (Listing 11-2) contains source code that accesses the *States* array. The program prompts the user for a state code and displays the data from the row of the *States* array that contains that state code.

```c
/*
 * S T A T E S
 *
 * Use an array of structured variables to keep
 * vital information about the United States.
 */

#include <stdio.h>
#include <stdlib.h>
#include <string.h>
#include "states.h"

#define SCBUFSIZE 2              /* State code input buffer size */
int StateData(char *);

int
main(void)
{
        char statecode[SCBUFSIZE + 1];

        /*
         * Ask the user for a state code and display
         * the data, if any, or an error message.
         */
        printf("State code (CO, MA, etc.): ");
        scanf("%2s", statecode);
        if (StateData(statecode)) {
                fprintf(stderr, "%s: State not found\n", statecode);
                exit (1);
        }
        return (0);
}


/*
 * StateData()
 *
 * Display the data for a state specified by the state
 * abbreviation (postal code) supplied as an argument.
 */
```

LISTING 11-2. *Program source code for states.c.*   *(continued)*

LISTING 11-2. *continued*

```
int
StateData(char *code)
{
        int rc = 0;              /* return code */
        int index;               /* array index */

        for (index = 0; index < NSTATES; ++index) {
                if (strcmp(strupr(code), States[index].code) == 0)
                        break;
        }

        /*
         * If the index reaches the number of states in the
         * array, the code was not found.  Report an error.
         */
        if (index == NSTATES)
                return (++rc);
        /*
         * Found a state record.  Display the requested data.
         */
        printf("  State name: %s\n", States[index].name);
        printf("Capital city: %s\n", States[index].capital);
        printf("  Population: %u (thousands)\n",
                States[index].population);
        printf("   Land area: %u sq. miles\n", States[index].area);

        return (0);
}
```

The *main()* function of the STATES program prompts for the state code and reads the reply. The call to *scanf()* gathers a two-character string that is passed to the *StateData()* function as an argument.

If the user types more than two characters, the program ignores any beyond the second—note the use of *%2s* in the *scanf()* control string. In a program that loops and attempts to read the keyboard again, the residue not read by the first call to *scanf()* remains in the input buffer to be read by subsequent calls, possibly providing bad input to the program. If you need to read the keyboard repeatedly, use the *fflush()* function to empty the input buffer before attempting another input operation. The following statement uses *fflush()* to clear the standard input buffer:

```
fflush(stdin);
```

The *StateData()* function conducts a simple sequential search of the *States* table in *states.h* to find the entry that corresponds to the state code supplied by the user. *StateData()* uses the standard library function *strupr()* to force the user's entry to uppercase, in case the user entered either or both letters in lowercase. It also uses *strcmp()*, another standard library string function, to compare the input to the code member of each record in the table.

If the user types a state code that identifies a record in the *States* table, the program displays the data. If the code is not found in the *States* table, *StateData()* returns a nonzero error code to its caller. The caller can either ignore the error code or use it to control a response to the user. In the STATES program, *main()* uses the error return code to print an error message and quit (with a nonzero exit code).

Unions

A variation on the structure theme is the C *union* data type. Whereas a structure causes the compiler to reserve sufficient memory for all the declared members of the aggregate, a union reserves only the amount required by the largest member. The purpose of a union is to set aside an area of memory that can contain values of different data types at different times. In this respect a union differs from a structure. Members of a *struct* variable occupy separate memory locations. Members of a *union* variable overlap.

You probably won't use or encounter many *union* statements. Programmers use them most frequently to do system-level programming tasks. But even a beginning programmer can benefit from a knowledge of unions and their applications.

Declaring a Union

To declare a union, use a statement of the following form:

```
union tag {
        type_1 var_1;
        type_2 var_2;
        .
        .
        .
        type_n var_n;
};
```

The definition of a union resembles that of a structure; it uses the keyword *union*, however.

Declaring and Using a Union Variable

A variable declaration for a union follows the pattern of structured variable declarations:

union *tag* **varname***;*

You access union members the same way as you do structure members, but with a different purpose. As with structure members, the dot operator selects the member, as in *varname.var_1a*, or *varname.var_2*. Your program must keep track of the current "occupant" of the union variable and be aware of its size.

If you declare a *union* variable and provide an initializer, the initializer must be the same type as the first member of the union. No other member can be initialized.

The UNION_1 program (Listing 11-3) demonstrates the definition and use of a simple union:

```
/*
 * U N I O N _ 1
 *
 * Use a union to access the same area of memory
 * as either an integer or float at different times.
 */

#include <stdio.h>

/*
 * Declare the union date type.
 */
union my_union {
        float float_num;
        int int_num;
};

int
main(void)
```

LISTING 11-3. *Program source code for union_1.c.*   *(continued)*

LISTING 11-3. *continued*

```
{
        /*
         * Declare a variable union_mem to use for
         * accessing members of the union.
         */
        union my_union union_mem;

        /*
         * Save an integer in my_union and print it out.
         */
        union_mem.int_num = 29;
        printf("Current value of my_union: %d\n", union_mem.int_num);

        /*
         * Now save a float in my_union and print it out.
         */
        union_mem.float_num = 19.58;
        printf("Current value of my_union: %.2f\n",
                union_mem.float_num);

        return (0);
}
```

The union *my_union* is declared with two members, a floating-point number *float_num* and an integer *int_num*. Next, within *main()* the union variable, *union_mem*, is declared for accessing members of *my_union*. By specifying the variable *union_mem*, followed by a dot and the name of the union member, you can assign values to and subsequently access values from the union.

The UNION_2 Program

Let's define a union that gives us access to a region of memory as either a pair of unsigned characters or as an unsigned short integer. First we define a structure that has two *unsigned char* members:

```
struct bytes {
        unsigned char low;      /* low-order byte */
        unsigned char high;     /* high-order byte */
        };
```

Next, we define the union of this structure and an *unsigned short* integer as follows.

```
union word {
        unsigned short word;    /* 16-bit word */
        struct bytes byte;      /* two 8-bit bytes */
};
```

To declare the variable *data* as a union of this type, simply use the appropriate syntax:

```
union word data;
```

Figure 11-3 shows the effect of the definitions and of the variable declaration for *data* stated above. You can use the variable *data* to hold either an unsigned short integer or a pair of unsigned characters. You access the members of the union as a word, *data.word*, or as individual bytes, *data.byte.low* and *data.byte.high*.

The UNION_2 program (Listing 11-4 on the following page) shows how to use the structure and union data types to access computer memory as words and bytes. It assigns a value to the union member *word* as an integer and prints the values of *low* and *high*, the members of *byte*. In addition, it compares the value of the number represented by *word* to the value calculated from the two byte-size components.

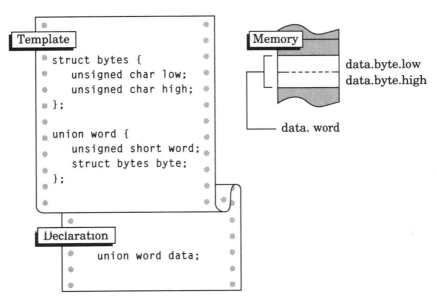

FIGURE 11-3. *The members of a union overlap in memory.*

```
/*
 * U N I O N _ 2
 *
 * Use a union to access the same areas of memory
 * as either bytes or words at different times.
 */

/*
 * Data definitions
 */
struct bytes {
        unsigned char low;
        unsigned char high;
};

union word {
        unsigned short word;
        struct bytes byte;
};

int
main(void)
{
        union word data;
        unsigned short temp;

        /*
         * Save a number in memory as a word and print it
         * in both decimal and hexadecimal formats.
         */
        data.word = 1000;
        printf("Word = %u (%04X hex)\n", data.word, data.word);

        /*
         * Print out the values of the low and high bytes
         * of the word independently.
         */
        printf("Low byte = %u (%02X hex)\n",
                data.byte.low, data.byte.low);
        printf("High byte = %u (%02X hex)\n",
                data.byte.high, data.byte.high);

        /*
         * Print out the value of the word calculated from
         * the high and low bytes of the memory word.  The
         * calculation is equivalent to (256 * high) + low.
         */
```

LISTING 11-4. *Program source code for union_2.c.*   *(continued)*

LISTING 11-4. *continued*

```
        temp = (data.byte.high << 8) | data.byte.low;
        printf("Calculated data word = %u (%04X hex)\n", temp, temp);

        return (0);
}
```

The program calculates the value of the word by adding the value of the low byte to the result of multiplying the high byte value by 256:

```
temp = (data.byte.high << 8) | data.byte.low;
```

The multiplication of the high byte value is achieved by the shifting of its bits by eight positions to the left. Shifting is faster than straight multiplication. The addition is done by performing a logical OR on the shifted high byte and the low byte. An equivalent but slower statement that does the same job is the following:

```
temp = 256 * data.byte.high + data.byte.low;
```

The *printf()* statements for the hexadecimal output use a *%0n*X format. These format specifiers cause the function to print hex values with leading zeros, which are normally suppressed.

Bitfields

One specific use of C structures is to implement bitfields. A bitfield is a collection of bits (one or more) that provide compact storage for items that have a limited range of possible values.

For example, assume that you write a large program that requires several integer variables to indicate the setting of some simple controls. (A setting of 1 means the associated control is active, and a setting of 0 means the control is inactive.) Rather than declare a separate *int* variable for each one, you can declare a single *int*-size variable, chop it into several bit-size pieces, and then address each piece individually.

Defining a Bitfield

The general form of a bitfield definition is clearly based on that of a structure, as is illustrated by the syntax that follows.

```
struct tag {
        unsigned field1 : width1;
        unsigned field2 : width2;
        .
        .
        .
};
```

Each field has a name and an associated width, which specifies the number of bits in that field.

Declaring Bitfield Variables

You declare variables and access fields just as you would for any other structure: The following fragment first defines a bitfield structure *flag_st*; then it declares a bitfield using that template and accesses a member field:

```
struct flag_st {
        unsigned mode: 1
        unsigned light: 1
        unsigned lock: 1
};
.
.
.
struct flag_st flag;

flag.light = 1;
if (flag.light == 1)
        printf("The light is on.\n");
else
        printf ("The light is off.\n");
```

The bitfield cannot span an integer boundary. Therefore, the width of a bitfield cannot exceed that of an *int* or *unsigned int*. Don't depend on any particular order of the fields because the order is implementation-specific. Also, don't use the & operator to get the address of a bitfield—it doesn't have an address of its own.

A Logic Puzzle

The FARMER program (Listing 11-5) shows how to use bitfields to keep track of a group of items. In this logic puzzle, a farmer is attempting to cross a river with a fox, a chicken, and a bushel of corn. Each of the four "players" is represented by a bitfield, the value of which indicates whether the associated player is currently on the west bank or the east bank of the river.

This program is lengthy. In addition to showing bitfields in action, it shows how to divide a problem into its component parts and package the various tasks into functions. Because *Player*, the "generic" bitfield variable (i.e. used to access all members of the bitfield), is used in so many functions, it is declared as a global data item. Figure 11-4 shows this bitfield as it is stored in memory.

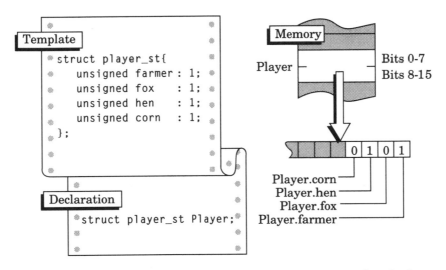

FIGURE 11-4. *Bitfield variable* Player *depicted in memory—after the first move (hint). Be aware that the order of bits is machine-specific. Don't expect a particular bitfield order.*

```
/*
 * F A R M E R
 *
 * The "farmer crossing a river" problem
 */

#include <stdio.h>
#include <stdlib.h>
#include <conio.h>

#define BEL     7
#define K_ESC   27
#define NBYTES  80
```

LISTING 11-5. *Program source code for farmer.c.*   *(continued)*

FIGURE 11-5 *continued*

```
/*
 * Player data structure (bitfield) definition
 */
struct player_st {
        unsigned farmer : 1;
        unsigned fox : 1;
        unsigned hen : 1;
        unsigned corn : 1;
};

struct player_st Player;        /* "generic" bitfield variable */

/*
 * Function prototypes
 */
void Instruct(void);
int GetMove(int);
void DoMove(int);
int CheckMap(int);
int MadeIt(void);
void YouLose(void);
void PrintMap(void);


int
main()
{
        int bank;               /* 0 means farmer is on the left bank */
        int move;               /* key code for the requested move */
        int trips;              /* number of trips across the river */
        char reply[NBYTES];     /* user response */

        /*
         * Set initial conditions.  All items are on the
         * west bank and no trips have been made.
         */
        Player.farmer = Player.fox = Player.hen = Player.corn = 0;
        bank = Player.farmer;
        trips = 0;

        printf("\n============ FARMER ============\n");
        printf("Press Esc at any time to quit.\n\n");
        printf("Do you need instructions? (Enter Y or N): ");
        gets(reply);
        if (reply[0] == 'y' || reply[0] == 'Y' || reply[0] == '\0')
                Instruct();
```

(continued)

LISTING 11-5. *continued*

```
        PrintMap();
        while (1) {
                move = GetMove(bank);
                DoMove(move);
                ++trips;
                bank = Player.farmer;
                PrintMap();
                if (CheckMap(bank))
                        YouLose();
                if (MadeIt())
                        break;
        }
        printf("Congratulations.  You made it safely!\n");
        printf("The number of trips was %d\n", trips);

        return (0);
}


/*
 * Instruct()
 *
 * Display the rules of the game.
 */

void
Instruct()
{
        puts("A farmer must cross a river in a boat.");
        puts("He has a fox, a hen, and a bushel of corn.");
        puts("The farmer can only take one thing at a");
        puts("time in the boat.  The fox can't be left");
        puts("alone with the hen because he'll eat it.");
        puts("Likewise, the hen can't be left with the corn.");
        puts("When the farmer is present, the animals are");
        puts("well behaved.  You are the farmer.  Attempt");
        puts("to get from the west bank of the river to");
        puts("the east bank with your baggage in tow while");
        puts("making the least number of trips.");
}
```

(continued)

LISTING 11-5. *continued*

```
int
GetMove(int bank)
{
        int key;

        /*
         * Prompt the user with only available commands.
         */
        printf("\nCommand: A(lone) ");
        if (Player.fox == bank)
                printf("F(ox) ");
        if (Player.hen == bank)
                printf("H(en) ");
        if (Player.corn == bank)
                printf("C(orn) ");
        printf(": ");
        while (1) {
                key = toupper(getch());
                if (key == 'A')
                        break;
                else if (key == 'F' && Player.fox == bank)
                        break;
                else if (key == 'H' && Player.hen == bank)
                        break;
                else if (key == 'C' && Player.corn == bank)
                        break;
                else if (key == K_ESC) {
                        putchar('\n');
                        exit (0);
                }
                else
                        putchar(BEL);    /* bad command */
        }
        putchar('\n');
        return (key);
}


void
DoMove(int move)
{
        switch (move) {
        case 'A':
                break;
```

(continued)

LISTING 11-5. *continued*

```
        case 'F':
                Player.fox = !Player.fox;
                break;
        case 'H':
                Player.hen = !Player.hen;
                break;
        case 'C':
                Player.corn = !Player.corn;
                break;
        }
        Player.farmer = !Player.farmer;
}


/*
 * CheckMap()
 *
 * Verify that no hostile items are left alone.
 * Return 1 if they are or 0 if not.
 */
int
CheckMap(int bank)
{
        int status = 0;

        if (Player.fox != bank && Player.hen != bank)
                status = 1;
        if (Player.hen != bank && Player.corn != bank)
                status = 1;

        return (status);
}


/*
 * PrintMap()
 *
 * Display the current map showing the positions
 * of the farmer and the other items.
 */
void
PrintMap()
{
```

(continued)

LISTING 11-5. *continued*

```
        char wc, ec;

        /* the farmer */
        wc = ec = ' ';
        if (Player.farmer)
                ec = 'F';
        else
                wc = 'F';
        printf("\n%c ^^^^^ %c\n", wc, ec);

        /* the fox */
        wc = ec = ' ';
        if (Player.fox)
                ec = 'f';
        else
                wc = 'f';
        printf("%c ^^^^^ %c\n", wc, ec);

        /* the hen */
        wc = ec = ' ';
        if (Player.hen)
                ec = 'h';
        else
                wc = 'h';
        printf("%c ^^^^^ %c\n", wc, ec);

        /* the corn */
        wc = ec = ' ';
        if (Player.corn)
                ec = 'c';
        else
                wc = 'c';
        printf("%c ^^^^^ %c\n", wc, ec);
}

/*
 * MadeIt()
 *
 * Determine whether all items have been safely
 * transported to the east bank of the river.
 */
int
MadeIt()
{
        int status;
```

(continued)

LISTING 11-5. *continued*

```
        status = 0;
        if (Player.farmer && Player.fox &&
                Player.hen && Player.corn)
                        status = 1;

        return (status);
}

void
YouLose()
{
        printf("Sorry, you lose.  ");
        if (Player.fox == Player.hen)
                printf("The fox ate the hen.\n");
        else if (Player.hen == Player.corn)
                printf("The hen ate the corn.\n");

        exit (1);
}
```

When the program starts, it asks the user if he or she wants instructions. Any reply that starts with the letter *y* or *Y* tells the program to call the *Instruct()* function, which displays a brief set of instructions. (If the user presses the Enter key without giving a specific reply, the program assumes a "yes" response.)

GetMove() receives an argument that specifies the bank on which the Farmer is standing. It prompts the user with only the currently valid moves, a better technique than prompting the user with all available moves and then having to say "You can't do that now." The *Alone* command is always active. It lets the Farmer travel in the boat without a companion. The *Quit* command (Esc key), which terminates play, is also available at any point. Other commands are available when they make sense. For example, the Farmer can't take the Hen with him if it is on the other side of the river.

Try your hand at the puzzle. (It can be solved in seven moves.) If you make a fatal move, the FARMER program tells you which player became someone else's lunch. If you get all the players across safely the program extends its congratulations, but there is no million-dollar prize. Sorry.

User-defined Types

To devise data types that model a complex situation, you need to create type definitions using structures, unions, and bitfields. C has the *typedef* keyword that lets you give symbolic names to your types. This practice enables you to reduce clutter in your source code and to provide descriptive names for the data types you define. The format of a *typedef* statement is as follows:

```
typedef type alias;
```

In such statements, the term substituted for *alias* becomes equivalent to the defined *type*.

Revising the structure that describes a text line in an editing buffer (from p. 215), you can define an alias called *LINE* as follows:

```
/* Type definition */
typedef struct {
        int number;
        char *text;
} LINE;

/* Variable declaration */
LINE buffer[MAXLINES];
```

Following the definition, you can use *LINE* as a type specifier in place of the full structure definition. To declare an alternate text buffer, for example, simply add the following statement to your source file:

```
LINE altbuf[MAXLINES];
```

Like a tag in a structure definition, the *typedef* alias lets you avoid a complete restatement at the member declarations. Notice, however, that an alias goes further than a tag to replace the data type keyword in the declaration as well. Once defined, it becomes an unofficial keyword (in the program).

This chapter covered the basic uses of structures, unions, and bitfields. For now, concentrate on the basics described in this chapter until you feel completely comfortable with them. As you progress, you can build elaborate data structures by combining these elements in various ways and by using pointers to objects of these types to create lists. You can pursue these advanced topics after you build a solid basis for programming in C.

Questions and Exercises

1. Name and describe the aggregate data types in C. What is the primary purpose of aggregate data types?

2. What is the purpose of a structure tag? Can you define a structure without one? If so, why would you use one?

3. Declare a structure that describes dates (year, month, day), declare a variable *date* of this type, and assign the date of Superbowl Sunday (January 31, 1988) to *date*. Represent the structure members, including the months, as integers.

4. Add a string member element to the data structure in the previous exercise to hold a 3-character text representation of the month (Jan, Feb, and so on). Then write a function that reads the numeric value of the month from a *date* variable and stores the text equivalent in the variable's character-string member.

5. Declare a bitfield structure that keeps track of the settings of five light switches (0 = OFF; 1 = ON). Next, initialize all the switches to the OFF condition.

6. Declare a structure that contains members for a student's last name, first name, and a numeric grade. Then write a program that prompts the instructor with each student name and collects test grades typed at the keyboard. Accept –1 as a code that the student did not take the test. After data entry is complete, print a summary table (name, grade) and the calculated average grade.

7. Write a *typedef* statement that defines a type called *SIGNAL* and declare a variable of this type. The definition should accommodate all the possible traffic signal patterns at a four-way intersection, including the possibility of a protected-turn-on-arrow from all four directions.

8. Modify the STATES program so that you can give it commands that ask for various kinds of output:

Command	Description of output
A	A columnar table of all data by state
C	A table of state capitals
P	A table of population data by state
S	Select state data by postal code
Q or Esc	Quit

(The S command is the current default of the STATES program.)

9. Write an interactive tic-tac-toe game. Use the following board layout and numbering scheme for user commands:

```
1 ¦ 2 ¦ 3
4 ¦ 5 ¦ 6
7 ¦ 8 ¦ 9
```

Use the letter X to represent a move by the user, the letter O for a move by the computer. A player specifies a move by typing the number of the square. After each move, redraw the board to show the new positions. Prevent the player from moving to squares that are already occupied and be sure to report results as soon as the player or the computer has three squares in a row in any direction.

12: File Input and Output

File input and output, usually abbreviated to file I/O, is the means for retrieving information from and storing information to files. Programs and data residing on floppy disks, hard disks, tape, and other "permanent" media are files. Even the keyboard and screen on your terminal or computer console are treated as files, as are other devices, such as printers and communication ports.

File I/O is a fundamental and necessary activity of a computer system. As your programming skills develop, you'll eventually find yourself with a need to use disk files within a program. This chapter introduces you to the topic and demonstrates how to use file I/O in your own programs.

Storage and Retrieval Concepts

In Chapter 11, we used a data structure to create a card file of business contacts. In a program that incorporated such a feature, you'd eventually find yourself with a need to store permanently the information you entered for each business contact. If you don't provide for permanent storage, you lose all the information you entered when you turn off the computer. Conversely, the business-contact information might already be stored permanently in a disk file. If you know how to retrieve that information, you can save yourself a considerable amount of typing time.

Actually, you've been working with file I/O as you've worked through this book—each time you choose the Load or Save command from Learn C's File menu, you tell Learn C to perform tasks similar to those described in this chapter. Before you can program C to accomplish those tasks, however, you need a secure grasp of some central concepts of data storage and retrieval. You'll probably find that you use many of these concepts already—with some degree of confidence.

Primary and Secondary Storage

Information stored in a computer's main memory is always at risk. Main memory, also called primary storage, is volatile, which means that anything it contains is lost if the power goes off.

Primary storage has several important attributes. It is random access read/write memory, which allows you to read and write any portion of it in any order. And it can be manipulated relatively quickly.

Secondary storage is permanent. Its chief attribute is its ability to retain data when the power to the computer is turned off. Floppy disks and hard disks are secondary storage media, as is magnetic tape. The word *permanent* does not mean eternal, however; the data can be changed easily, but if not disturbed, it remains intact for a long time.

The process of reading or writing secondary storage is usually much slower than reading or writing primary storage, but the longevity of data stored on disk and tape is, of course, of immense practical value. Figure 12-1 depicts the two types of read/write memory.

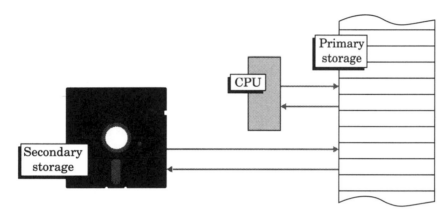

FIGURE 12-1. *Although it cannot be accessed as rapidly, secondary storage offers the advantage of permanence.*

C and File I/O

C has no built-in file I/O capabilities. This fact might surprise you, especially if you have experience with other programming languages, but keeping the details of I/O outside the language definition offers a distinct advantage. Because different computer systems use different methods of accessing disk files, and because C was designed to be a portable language, all file I/O is built into the standard library, separate from the core of C. The standard library is a collection of routines (functions and macros) that handle many common tasks.

To use standard file I/O in your program, you must use an *#include* directive to incorporate the contents of the stdio.h header file into your program source file. Once you've included stdio.h, you can use a wide variety of C routines to work with files. The header file contains needed data definitions, macros definitions, and function prototypes for the standard I/O functions.

Before we examine file I/O routines in detail, let's take a broad look at files and file I/O. We need to look at the types of file I/O routines you have available and at the two different types of files you can work with under MS-DOS.

The Two Types of File I/O

C provides two means of working with files: stream I/O and low-level I/O. Both offer a complete system of accessing files, and although they offer many similar services, they differ in several important ways.

Stream I/O, the type you'll be learning in this chapter, is the more common method of file I/O. It is much easier to use than low-level I/O because it does much of the tedious work involved in actually working with files.

Stream I/O employs a sophisticated data-buffering scheme. Data buffering provides a means of collecting, storing, and delivering data in a controlled, efficient manner.

Another aspect of stream I/O is the wealth of routines that do data conversions and formatting for you. Without these routines, your programming tasks would be far more complicated. The *scanf()* and *printf()* functions are common examples of formatting I/O functions.

Low-level I/O, often called system I/O, requires that you keep track of all the details of currently accessed files—details that are effectively hidden from you when you use stream I/O. In particular, low-level I/O does no buffering for you, so it is up to you to create and manage buffers. Low-level I/O also does no data conversion and formatting either, which shifts a considerable burden onto the programmer. It does, however, offer some advantages in terms of speed and compactness.

Two Types of Files

For purposes of learning file I/O, you need to distinguish two different types of files: text files and binary files. The difference between the two is the type of data they contain.

Text files consist entirely of alphanumeric characters, punctuation marks, and some control characters (specifically, ASCII characters in the range 0 through 127). They are the type of file with which you will usually work and thus the type emphasized in this chapter. Text files, or ASCII files, generally contain readable information; in fact, all the C source files you've encountered and any others you've created on your own are text files. Each character is represented by the lower seven bits of each byte. Within a text file, series of bytes are organized into lines.

Binary files contain 8-bit data and have no line structure imposed on them. Such files are usually incomprehensible to you and me, but they make sense to the computer. Executable files, such as the Learn C program itself, are binary files. The differences between text files and binary files are summarized in Figure 12-2.

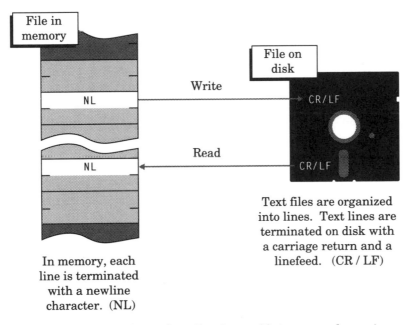

FIGURE 12-2. *Writing to and reading from a file in text mode requires a translation of line termination characters.*

A key issue in dealing with text files is line termination. The MS-DOS environment uses a two-character line-termination sequence, whereas the UNIX and XENIX environments and the standard C library I/O all use a single-character line terminator. The two-character sequence mirrors the physical realities: Terminal devices use a carriage return (CR) to get back to the beginning of the current line and a linefeed (LF) character to move down one line.

C, with its UNIX heritage, uses a single newline character (NL) to terminate a line. The thinking is that if one character can do the work of two, why use two? (Good question.) When your C program saves a file to disk in text mode, the NL characters are translated into CR/LF combinations before they are stored on the disk. Conversely, when your C program loads a file into memory using text mode, the CR/LF pairs are translated into NL characters before they are brought into memory.

Text files and binary files also differ in the way that they store numbers. In text files, numbers are stored as individual ASCII characters. In binary files, numbers are stored as they are in memory.

For example, a *short* integer value of 8134 occupies four bytes in a text file because it has four digits. In a binary file, the same number is stored as two bytes because a *short* value occupies two bytes in memory.

❑ NOTE: *Although text and binary files are distinct under MS-DOS, other operating systems, notably UNIX and XENIX, make no distinction between them. If you will be programming in different operating environments, you need to take such differences into account when you design and code your programs.*

Versions 3.0 and later of MS-DOS and versions 5.0 and later of the Microsoft C compilers use an exact size value stored in the disk directory to keep track of the number of bytes in a file. Any attempt to read past the last byte specified by the size value produces an end-of-file (EOF) condition, which means that file contains nothing else to read. Earlier versions of MS-DOS and of the Microsoft C compilers relied on an EOF character, ^Z (Ctrl-Z, hex 1A, decimal 26), to identify the EOF position.

The use of ^Z is an artifact of the original design of MS-DOS, which purposely attempted to retain compatibility with its 8-bit operating system predecessor, CP/M. The current MS-DOS and Microsoft C software versions still honor the ^Z character if they encounter it in a text file, but they do not require its use. MS-DOS stops processing a text file when it encounters a ^Z character in the input stream.

The ^Z value has no special meaning in binary files. Like all other bytes in a binary file, ^Z is simply a pattern of bits.

Essential File I/O Programming

To work with files using stream I/O, the following steps are required:

1. Declare a file pointer.
2. Open the file.
3. Access the file.
4. Close the file.

Now let's examine each step in detail and demonstrate how you accomplish them using C.

Declaring a File Pointer

A file pointer provides a means of identifying a file or stream. To declare a file pointer, use the FILE data type, which is a *struct* data type that is predeclared for you in stdio.h. The format of a file pointer declaration is as follows:

FILE *name;

where *name* is the pointer name you want to use. You need to declare a unique pointer for each file you intend to have open simultaneously. You will use the pointer name with all subsequent operations on the file, including opening the file, accessing its contents, and closing it.

The following statement declares a pointer named *fp*:

```
#include <stdio.h>
    .
    .
    .
FILE *fp;
```

The file pointer variable name is *fp*, and this statement can be read as "*fp* is a pointer (*) to an object of type FILE."

Opening a File

You must open a file before you can work with it. After declaring a file pointer, use the pointer name along with the *fopen()* function to open the file. The syntax of a statement used to open a file is as follows:

```
pointer = fopen(filename, access_type);
```

In this statement, *pointer* is the name of the previously declared file pointer, the *filename* argument is the name of the file you want to open, and the *access_type* argument is the type of file access you want your program to have. Both arguments are strings, which you can present either as literal strings or as string variables.

The following list contains the permissible file access types:

Type   **Description**

"r"   Open file for reading only. The file must exist.

"w"   Open an empty file for writing. If the file exists, it is truncated to zero length.

"a"   Open the file for writing only, appending to the end of the file. Creates the file if it doesn't exist.

"r+"   Open the file for both reading and writing. The file must exist.

"w+"   Open the file for both reading and writing. Creates the file if it doesn't exist; truncates it to zero length if it does exist.

"a+"   Open the file for both reading and appending to the end of the file. Creates the file if it doesn't already exist.

❑ CAUTION: *Use the* w *and* w+ *access types with great care. Using these access types causes any existing file with the same name to be truncated to zero length, effectively erasing its previous contents.*

The + symbol on the last three access types means open the file for *update*. When using update access, you can both read and write the file. However, you must use a file-positioning operation when switching between read and write access. See the on-line help for the *fseek()*, *rewind()*, and *fsetpos()* routines for more information about positioning.

Files are opened in either text mode or binary mode. The second argument to *fopen()*, the *access_type*, accepts a mode specifier: *t* for text or *b* for binary. If you don't provide a mode specifier, the value of the global variable *_fmode* is used. The default value is text.

The following statements declare the pointer *src_file* and open the existing file named DOGGEREL.TXT for reading only:

```
#include <stdio.h>
 .
 .
 .
FILE *src_file;
src_file = fopen("DOGGEREL.TXT", "rt");
```

Recall that the ∗ symbol in this context is the indirection operator; *src_file* is the pointer variable. The *fopen()* function returns a pointer, which you can freely assign to the *src_file* variable. Notice that the file is opened explicitly in text mode (to demonstrate the use of the mode specifier).

If the call to *fopen()* succeeds, *src_file* will contain a valid pointer to the structure that maintains data about the open file, or stream (starting position, current position, and so on). If the call fails for any reason, the value assigned to *src_file* is NULL, which, as we learned earlier, is a special pointer with a value of 0. A NULL pointer return from *fopen()* means that an error occurred. Attempting to open a nonexistent file for reading, for example, causes an error.

Your program should have code to detect possible errors and to respond appropriately. Taking our example of opening a file for reading one step further, you have three possible responses when you encounter a file-opening error:

■ Print an error message and quit.

■ Prompt the user for another filename and try again.

■ Ignore the error and bypass any file access statements.

❑ NOTE: *The last approach is appropriate, for example, if your program uses some kind of optional configuration file. If a configuration file is found, you can read it and use the values it contains. If it is not found, simply skip past the statements that would read the file.*

Accessing a File

Assuming that the *fopen()* function returns a valid file pointer, use that pointer to access the file. Statements that read and write the open file use the file pointer, not the filename, to access the file's contents. We'll look at several of the commonly used file access routines in later sections of this chapter. Don't forget that access can be only of the type requested in the file-opening statement.

Closing a File

When your program no longer needs an open file, it must close the file to prevent unwanted access and to free resources, such as buffers. Closing a file indicates to the operating system that your work with the file is finished. The action of closing a file causes the operating system to perform a series of steps: It flushes buffers used to hold information temporarily while your program runs; it breaks the connection between the file pointer and the filename, which frees the pointer variable for use with other files; and it updates the system area of the disk to reflect the current status of the file (size, location of its pieces, data and time of last modification, and so on).

To close a file, use the *fclose()* function, which takes a file pointer argument. The form of a statement used to close a file is as follows:

fclose(*pointer*);

In this statement, *pointer* references a previously opened file or stream.

The following program fragment demonstrates the statements needed to open a specific text file for reading and then to close the file when you no longer need it:

```
#include <stdio.h>
.
.
.
FILE *fp;                                    /* file pointer */
static char fname[] = { "DOGGEREL.TXT" };    /* filename */

/* Open the file for reading; quit if not found. */
fp = fopen(fname, "r");
if (fp == NULL) {
        printf("Cannot open %s\n", fname);
        exit(1);
}

/* Opened OK--the code to access the file goes here. */
.
.
.
fclose(fp);   /* Done--close the file. */
```

Notice the minimal error checking that is done in the file-opening portion of the program fragment. In this example, the program displays an error message and stops processing if it fails to open the file for any reason. The program need not close the file because it was never opened. And, of course, it cannot read anything from a file that wasn't opened, so it must not attempt any file access.

Also notice the use of a character array variable, *fname*, instead of a literal string. Using a variable gives you greater flexibility than hard-coding filenames into your programs.

Working with Files

Now that you've encountered the essential procedure for programming file I/O, you're ready to investigate some ways to manipulate the contents of a file. Let's begin by taking a closer look at reading from and writing to a file.

Buffering

Many I/O operations involve reading single characters from or writing single characters to a file or stream. When a C program reads or writes data, it is typically dealing with individual characters. Disks, on the other hand, are block-oriented devices—data is stored and retrieved in fixed-size chunks called sectors (MS-DOS) or blocks (UNIX/XENIX).

The operating system uses buffers to transfer data between a disk and the memory owned by your program. A buffer temporarily holds data being read or written. When the computer is first initialized, or "booted," the operating system sets aside a number of *system* buffers.

A buffer lets devices that function at different speeds and that manage data differently operate together. It is analogous to a water reservoir, which collects rain water and runoff as it becomes available and dispenses it later when it is needed.

Reading Characters from a File

To read from a file, your program must open the file with read access, and it must declare a variable of an appropriate data type to hold the data being read. The LIST_1 program (Listing 12-1), for example, reads the contents of the file DOGGEREL.TXT and displays the contents on the screen.

The program declares the integer variable *ch* to hold a character read from the file. This variable is an *int* value, not a *char* value, because *fgetc()* returns an *int*.

❑ NOTE: *An* int *value is required because the variable must be able to hold any ASCII character (codes 0 through 127) plus EOF. In* stdio.h, *EOF happens to be defined as having a value of −1, but other implementations of C could place it outside the range of a* char *value.*

```
/*
 * L I S T _ 1
 *
 * Display the contents of an ASCII text file
 * on the user's screen. (Bare-bones version)
 */

#include <stdio.h>

int
main(void)
{
        int ch;                 /* input character */
        FILE *fp;               /* file pointer */

        /*
         * Open the named file for reading.
         */
        fp = fopen("DOGGEREL.TXT", "r");

        /*
         * Read the contents of the file and display
         * each character as it is read.
         */
        while ((ch = fgetc(fp)) != EOF)
                putchar(ch);


        /*
         * Close the file.
         */
        fclose(fp);

        return (0);
}
```

LISTING 12-1. *Program source code for list_1.c.*

The EOF indicator is not a character, but a special code that represents a condition. If *fgetc()* attempts to read beyond the position of the last character in a file or stream, the function returns EOF. You can write your program to detect this code and use it to terminate processing or perform some other action.

The declaration of *fp* creates a pointer to a FILE data structure. The association of the file and the file pointer is made by the call to *fopen()*, which has the arguments "DOGGEREL.TXT" (the filename), and "r" (the file access type specifier).

A *while* loop controls the file-reading operation. The *fgetc()* function reads a single character at a time from the file identified by the file pointer *fp*. As each character is read from the file, the program assigns its value into the variable *ch*. Behind the scenes, a member of the structure pointed to by *fp* is updated to point to the next character to be read.

The program compares the value in *ch* to the value EOF to determine whether the end-of-file position has been reached. As long as *fgetc()* reads ASCII characters, the *putchar()* function in the body of the *while* loop prints them on the screen. After the entire file has been read, *fclose()* closes the file.

The LIST_2 program (Listing 12-2) is essentially the same program as LIST_1 except that it demonstrates how to prompt the user for a filename instead of hard-coding it in the program.

```
/*
 * L I S T _ 2
 *
 * Display the contents of an ASCII text file
 * on the user's screen.
 *
 * NOTE: This version lets the user specify a filename.
 */

#include <stdio.h>
#define MAXPATH 64

int
main(void)
{
        int ch;                   /* input character */
        FILE *fp;                 /* file pointer */
        char pathname[MAXPATH];   /* filename buffer */
```

LISTING 12-2. *Program source code for list_2.c.*   *(continued)*

LISTING 12-2. *continued*

```
/*
 * Prompt the user for a filename and read it.
 */
printf("Filename: ");
gets(pathname);
if (*pathname == '\0')   /* no name typed */
        return (0);

/*
 * Open the named file for reading.
 */
fp = fopen(pathname, "r");

/*
 * Read the contents of the file and display
 * each character as it is read.
 */
while ((ch = fgetc(fp)) != EOF)
        putchar(ch);

/*
 * Close the file.
 */
fclose(fp);
return (0);
}
```

The variable *pathname* is a character array. It is sufficiently large (*MAXPATH* bytes) to receive the user's filename input, which *scanf()* reads from the keyboard. The value of *pathname* becomes the filename argument of the *fopen()* function call. Note that FILE_2 lacks error-handling code. If the program encounters a problem (is unable to find the file, for example), it contains no statements to detect the specific cause of the error and to report the cause to the user. Run the program and enter the name of a file that doesn't exist. The program produces no useful output, but it also fails to tell you that anything is amiss. We'll deal with error handling in later programs.

Writing Characters to a File

Writing to a file involves basically the same steps as reading from a file, except of course that instead of reading data from the file into memory, data is written from memory to the file. The WRITE program (Listing 12-3) shows you how to write one line of characters to a file.

```
/*
 * W R I T E
 *
 * Write a line of text to a file.
 */

#include <stdio.h>

#define MAXPATH 64

int
main(void)
{
        int ch;                 /* input character */
        FILE *fp;               /* file pointer */
        char pathname[MAXPATH]; /* filename buffer */

        /*
         * Prompt the user for a filename and read it.
         */
        printf("Filename: ");
        gets(pathname);
        if (*pathname == '\0')  /* no name typed */
                return (0);

        /*
         * Open the named file for writing.
         */
        fp = fopen(pathname, "w");

        /*
         * Read characters from the keyboard up to a newline
         * character, then write the line to the specified file.
         */
        while ((ch = getchar()) != '\n')
                fputc(ch, fp);
        fputc('\n', fp);                /* terminate the line */

        /*
         * Close the file.
         */
        fclose(fp);

        return (0);
}
```

LISTING 12-3. *Program source code for write.c.*

The program declares three variables: the integer value *ch* to hold the character being written to disk, the file pointer *fp*, and the character array *pathname* to hold the name of the output file.

The *while* loop tests for '\n' as the current input character, which means that *fgetc()* continues to read characters until you press the Enter key. Note the use of parentheses around the left side of the control expression to force the read character to be assigned to the variable *ch* before the comparison is made. This is necessary because assignment has a lower precedence than the inequality test.

As long as the condition in the control expression of the *while* loop is met, the *fputc()* function writes the current character to the output file. (Remember, the characters are written to a buffer—they are not actually written to the file until the buffer is full or until the file is closed.) When the loop terminates, the program appends a newline to terminate the line. (The newline that you typed was read but not written.) After all characters have been written, the file is closed.

As a simple debugging exercise, try appending a semicolon to the end of the line containing the *while* keyword and run the program again. Use the LIST_2 program to view the resulting file. This exercise demonstrates a common programming error that can be frustrating to track down and correct. When you are finished, remove the semicolon to fix the bug.

Reading Strings from a File

It is often more appropriate to read input a line at a time. The program LIST_3 (Listing 12-4) duplicates the efforts of the LIST_2 program, except that LIST_3 reads and prints the contents of DOGGEREL.TXT a line at a time instead of a character at a time.

```
/*
 * L I S T _ 3
 *
 * Display the contents of an ASCII text file
 * on the user's screen.
 *
 * NOTE: This version uses string functions.
 */

#include <stdio.h>
```

LISTING 12-4. *Program source code for list_3.c.*   *(continued)*

LISTING 12-4. *continued*

```c
#define MAXPATH 64
#define MAXLINE 256

int
main(void)
{
        int ch;                 /* input character */
        FILE *fp;               /* file pointer */
        char pathname[MAXPATH]; /* filename buffer */
        char line[MAXLINE];     /* line buffer for fgets() */


        /*
         * Prompt the user for a filename and read it.
         */
        printf("Filename: ");
        gets(pathname);
        if (*pathname == '\0')
                return (0);

        /*
         * Open the named file for reading.
         */
        fp = fopen(pathname, "r");

        /*
         * Read the contents of the file and display it
         * a line at a time as it is read.
         */
        while (fgets(line, MAXLINE, fp) != NULL)
                fputs(line, stdout);

        /*
         * Close the file.
         */
        fclose(fp);

        return (0);
}
```

Notice that *fgets()* takes three arguments. The first argument is the address of the receiving array, and the second argument is the size of the array. The third argument is a file pointer, which identifies the source of the string to be read.

The size argument is necessary because we must prevent *fgets()* from reading more characters than will fit in the buffer array, *line*. The function reads characters from the source file up to and including the next newline character, or until it has read the specified number of characters. The *fgets()* function reads as many characters as are specified by the size argument minus 1, which leaves room in the array for a NUL byte to terminate the string.

After reading a line from the file, the program prints the line by calling the *fputs()* function. The function takes two arguments. The first is the string to print. The name *line*, as you learned in Chapter 9, is a constant pointer to the beginning of the array. Just what we need.

The second argument identifies the stream to which writing takes place. The *stdout* stream is the standard output stream, which usually sends output to your screen. We'll look at standard streams in greater detail shortly.

The program repeats the statements in the loop body, reading and printing lines of text until none remain. When *fgets()* returns NULL, it indicates that it has run out of input.

Finally, the program closes the file and terminates. Because DOG-GEREL.TXT is such a short file, you won't notice any difference in execution speed between LIST_3 and LIST_1. However, with large files, string-oriented operations usually provide more efficient and therefore faster processing for tasks of this kind.

Writing Strings to a File

The program WRITE_2 (Listing 12-5) shows you how to read user input and write it to a file a line at a time. To end the program, the user presses the Enter key on a blank line.

```
/*
 * W R I T E _ 2
 *
 * Write a line of text to a file. Terminate input by
 * pressing Enter on a blank line.
 */

#include <stdio.h>
```

LISTING 12-5. *Program source code for write_2.c.*   *(continued)*

LISTING 12-5. *continued*

```c
#define MAXPATH 64
#define MAXLINE 256

int
main(void)
{
        int ch;                 /* input character */
        FILE *fp;               /* file pointer */
        char pathname[MAXPATH]; /* filename buffer */
        char line[MAXLINE];     /* line buffer */

        /*
         * Prompt the user for a filename and read it.
         */
        printf("Filename: ");
        gets(pathname);
        if (*pathname == '\0')  /* no name typed */
                return (0);



        /*
         * Open the named file for writing.
         */
        fp = fopen(pathname, "w");

        /*
         * Read lines of text from the keyboard and write them to
         * the specified file. Quit when an empty line is seen.
         */
        while (1) {
                fgets(line, MAXLINE, stdin);
                if (line[0] == '\n')    /* empty line */
                        break;
                fputs(line, fp);
        }

        /*
         * Close the file.
         */
        fclose(fp);

        return (0);
}
```

The program uses *fgets()* to read input and *fputs()* to write the lines to the file. In this program, the condition in the *while* loop is the constant 1. Thus, the loop runs until terminated by a statement within the body of the loop.

The expression *line[0]* == '\n' becomes true (nonzero) when an empty line has been read. This condition indicates that the user pressed Enter on a separate line. The *break* statement causes execution of the loop to terminate. Then the file is closed, and the program terminates.

Run the program and enter a few lines to a file; then press Enter on a blank line to end input. Use the LIST_3 program to display the contents of the file.

Standard Streams

A set of standard I/O streams is opened automatically for you when a program starts running. Three are common to both MS-DOS and UNIX environments: *stdin* (standard input), *stdout* (standard output), and *stderr* (standard error). Two others are opened only in an MS-DOS environment: *stdaux* (standard auxiliary port) and *stdprn* (standard printer port). Figure 12-3 shows the five standard I/O streams that are opened under MS-DOS.

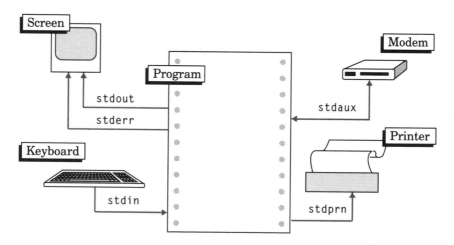

FIGURE 12-3. *Standard streams let your C program interact with its environment, including peripheral devices.*

You have been using the standard input and output streams in many programs in this book, but the fact has been hidden from you. Now the secret can be revealed.

The *printf()* function, which you have used frequently to print output on your screen, is associated with the *stdout* stream. But the *printf()* function is actually a specific case of the more general *fprintf()* function, which can write to *any* stream. The following two print statements have the same effect:

```
#include <stdio.h>
.
.
.

printf("Farewell, cruel world!\n");
fprintf(stdout, "Farewell, cruel world!\n");
```

To assure that error messages show up on the user's screen, use *stderr* as the destination stream. This stream is unbuffered to prevent messages from being held up in a buffer, and under MS-DOS it cannot be redirected, so messages don't get lost in a pipe or redirection command.

Analyzing Files

So far, we've concentrated on the basic elements of file I/O: opening and closing a file, and reading and writing characters and strings. But file I/O encompasses far more than that. Your programs can act on the incoming or outgoing stream of data to analyze its contents.

Counting Characters in a File

The CHARCNT program (Listing 12-6) demonstrates one useful task—counting the number of characters in a file.

```
/*
 * C H A R C N T
 *
 * Count the number of characters in a file.  CHARCNT
 * correctly handles only ASCII text files.
 */

#include <stdio.h>
#include <stdlib.h>     /* for exit() prototype */
```

LISTING 12-6. *Program source code for charcnt.c.*   *(continued)*

LISTING 12-6. *continued*

```
#define MAXPATH 64

int
main(void)
{
        int ch;                 /* input character */
        long charcnt;           /* character charcnt */
        FILE *fp;               /* file pointer */
        char pathname[MAXPATH]; /* filename buffer */

        /*
         * Prompt the user for a filename and read it.
         */
        printf("Filename: ");
        scanf("%s", pathname);
        putchar('\n');

        /*
         * Try to open the named file for reading in text mode.
         * Report any failure to open the file and exit with an
         * error indication.
         */
        fp = fopen(pathname, "r");
        if (fp == NULL) {
                fprintf(stderr, "Cannot open %s\n", pathname);
                exit(1);
        }


        /*
         * Read the contents of the file and increment the
         * character count as each character is read.
         */
        charcnt = 0;
        while ((ch = fgetc(fp)) != EOF)
                ++charcnt;
        if (ferror(fp) != 0) {
                fprintf(stderr, "Error reading %s\n", pathname);
                exit(2);
        }
```

(continued)

LISTING 12-6. *continued*

```
        /*
         * Report the filename and character count
         * and close the file.
         */
        printf("File %s contains %ld characters.\n",
                pathname, charcnt);
        if (fclose(fp) != 0) {
                fprintf(stderr, "Error closing %s\n",
                        pathname);
                exit(3);
        }

        return (0);
}
```

CHARCNT also demonstrates ways of adding error handling to a program. After prompting for the name of the file to open, the program tests to see whether the pointer contains a NULL value. If it does, then *fopen()* encountered a problem opening the file, and the user is informed of the problem. The program then terminates with a nonzero exit code (DOS ERRORLEVEL).

The exit code is provided by the *exit()* function. The stdlib.h header file is included to obtain the *exit()* function prototype to aid the Learn C compiler in checking function arguments and return types.

An error test is also performed after the input stream has been read. The program uses the *ferror()* macro, which returns a nonzero (true) value if an error has occurred on the stream specified by its argument. The macro returns 0 if no error occurred.

The final error test occurs near the end of the file when the program attempts to close the file. If the *fclose* statement returns a nonzero value, indicating it was unable to close the file successfully, the user is informed of the error. The program then terminates with a nonzero exit code.

The character-counting operation occurs while the input stream is being read. The variable *charcnt* is assigned a value of 0 immediately before the stream is read, and the variable is incremented with each iteration of the *while* loop. After the *while* loop terminates, and assuming that no error occurs before the end of the program, the final *printf()* statement informs the user how many characters the file contains.

❑ NOTE: *The number of characters returned by CHARCNT varies from the count returned by an MS-DOS DIR command. Recall that each line in an ASCII text file terminates with a carriage return/linefeed pair, whereas C marks the end of a line only with a single newline character. Assume, for example, that you used DOGGEREL.TXT, which consists of five lines, as the input file. The count returned by CHARCNT will be five characters less than the count returned by the MS-DOS DIR command.*

Counting Words in a File

Another useful program (especially to writers) is one that counts words. The WORDCNT program (Listing 12-7) performs this task.

```
/*
 * W O R D C N T
 *
 * Count the number of words in a file.
 * WORDCNT handles only ASCII text files.
 */

#include <stdio.h>
#include <stdlib.h>       /* for exit() prototype */

#define MAXPATH 64

typedef enum { FALSE, TRUE } BOOLEAN;

int
main(void)
{
        int ch;                   /* input character */
        BOOLEAN wordflag;         /* control flag */
        long wordcnt;             /* word counter */
        FILE *fp;                 /* file pointer */
        char pathname[MAXPATH]; /* filename buffer */

        /*
         * Prompt the user for a filename and read it.
         */
        printf("\nWORDCNT:\tType a filename and press ENTER.\n");
```

LISTING 12-7. *Program source code for wordcnt.c.* *(continued)*

LISTING 12-7. *continued*

```
        printf("Filename: ");
        gets(pathname);
        if (*pathname == '\0')
                return (0);      /* no file named -- quit */

        /*
         * Try to open the named file for reading.
         * Report any failure to open the file and
         * exit with an error indication.
         */
        fp = fopen(pathname, "r");
        if (fp == NULL) {
                fprintf(stderr, "Cannot open %s\n", pathname);
                exit(1);

        }

        /*
         * Read the contents of the file and increment the
         * counters for characters, words, and lines.
         */
        wordcnt = 0;
        wordflag = FALSE;
        while ((ch = fgetc(fp)) != EOF)  {
                if (ch == ' ' || ch == '\t' || ch == '\n')
                        wordflag = FALSE;
                else if (wordflag == FALSE) {
                        ++wordcnt;
                        wordflag = TRUE;
                }
        }
        if (ferror(fp)) {
                fprintf(stderr, "Error reading %s\n", pathname);
                exit(2);
        }

        /*
         * Report the filename and the word count,
         * then close the file.
         */
        printf("File %s: %d words\n", pathname, wordcnt);
```

(continued)

LISTING 12-7. *continued*

```
        if (fclose(fp)) {
                fprintf(stderr, "Error closing %s\n", pathname);
                exit(3);
        }

        return (0);
}
```

Like CHARCNT, WORDCNT examines the contents of a file one character at a time, but instead of counting each character, it counts words. The program has a simplistic notion of what a word is. It assumes that any contiguous sequence of printable characters is a word. Conversely, it assumes that any space, tab, or newline character or a combination of these separates words from each other.

WORDCNT looks for these special characters, called "whitespace" characters, to determine when the character-reading loop is outside of a word, and it uses non-whitespace characters to signal the start of a word. Each time a whitespace character is encountered, the *wordflag* variable is cleared (assigned a value of false). Any other character causes the program to set the *wordflag* variable (true) and to increment the *wordcnt* variable. Using a short sample phrase, work through the loop in your head or on paper to see how the *wordflag* and *wordcnt* variables change in value. Then compile and run the program using a text file, such as a program source file.

Summary

File I/O is a large and important aspect of C programming. This chapter covers enough of the topic to get you started but leaves a lot for you to explore on your own. Use the Learn C help index to explore other file I/O functions.

❏ CAUTION: *Do not use low-level I/O routines together with stream I/O routines: The two simply do not mix. Using the two types of file I/O routines together causes problems with file positioning and can result in lost data.*

Questions and Exercises

1. Describe in your own words the difference between low-level I/O and stream I/O.

2. What is the purpose of I/O buffering, and how is it obtained?

3. List and describe the primary attributes of text and binary files.

4. What are the steps required to access a file for reading? Don't leave any loose ends.

5. Alter the WRITE_2 program so that you can append characters to the file. Then, if the file already exists, its contents will not be lost. If the file does not exist, it will be created. Again, use the LIST_2 program to view the results.

6. Modify the WRITE_2 program again to allow blank lines. Require that the user type a dot (.) on a line by itself followed by Enter to terminate the program.

7. Combine the actions of the CHARCNT and WORDCNT programs and the action of counting text lines into a single program called WDC.

13: Graphics Programming

Introduction to Graphics Programming
Learn C Graphics Routines
Graphics Programming Steps
Graphics Operations
Text Operations
Clipping and Viewports

(No corresponding tutorial lesson)

One of the many application areas in which C really shines is the field of computer graphics, once the nearly exclusive domain of FORTRAN and assembly-language programmers. Increasingly, however, graphics programmers are converting to C because of its speed, flexibility, power, conciseness, and its availability in a wide range of computing environments.

Graphics programming is an important and rapidly growing field, one which is likely to continue to grow in both size and diversity for the foreseeable future. The graphics routines that accompany Learn C can help you get started in this exciting field.

Introduction to Graphics Programming

Before you attempt to construct graphics programs, you need a foundation. The material in this section describes the hardware you need and the essential software concepts and techniques upon which graphics programs are built.

As is true elsewhere in the book, the material in this chapter applies to the IBM PC and compatible hardware environments. Programs written with Learn C graphics routines are not immediately portable to other computer environments, but the concepts and techniques described in this chapter apply generally to graphics programming. Note that the material in this chapter is intended to be a brief introduction only—a thorough treatment of the subject of graphics programming is far beyond the scope of this book.

Raster Scan Images

The images on the CRT screens of our PCs are formed by one or more electron beams that are constantly scanning across and down the screen. Each pass of a beam across the surface of the screen creates a scan line. You can think of a scan line as a row of individual dots, which are known as picture elements, or "pixels."

A pixel is the smallest addressable screen object. In an appropriate display mode, your programs can address any individual pixel, turn it on or off, and even set its color (on suitable video hardware). Groups of pixels can be turned on to form objects. Even the letters of text displayed on the screen are made up of individual pixels. IBM calls display modes that permit access to individual pixels "all-points-addressable" (APA) modes.

❏ NOTE: *Until very recently, graphic images were created only on a cathode-ray tube (CRT), the type still found in most television sets. The description of raster images presented here is based on CRT technology. Gas plasma, liquid-crystal displays, and other display technologies that are used in recent vintage computers operate in entirely different ways electronically. However, the same basic terms apply to the creation of graphic images for all these display types.*

Display Modes

In general, a display mode is defined by two characteristics—its image size, or capacity, and its range of colors. To generate a graphic image that uses a given display mode, you need a suitable combination of video graphics card and monitor. Common video graphics cards, or graphics adapters, include the following:

MDA   Monochrome Display Adapter
CGA   Color Graphics Adapter
EGA   Enhanced Graphics Adapter
VGA   Video Graphics Array Adapter

The following are common types of monitors:

MD   Monochrome Display
CD   Color Display
ECD   Enhanced Color Display
VD   VGA Display

Table 13-1 on the following page lists the standard IBM display modes and shows the hardware requirements and characteristics of each mode. The capacity of the screen (in a given APA mode) is specified in pixels—the total number of pixels across the screen times the total number from top to bottom. The CGA offers its highest resolution in mode 6. The image size is 640 pixels horizontally by 200 vertically (640H × 200V), for a capacity of 128,000 pixels. Peak EGA resolution is obtained in modes 15 and 16 (640H × 350V) for a capacity of 224,000 pixels).

More pixels means more memory: The display adapter needs one bit per pixel to control monochrome images, two or more bits per pixel for color images. Thus, for a given amount of display memory, a tradeoff exists between image size and the number of displayable colors. A CGA in medium-resolution color mode (mode 4) can show each of the 64,000 pixels in one of four possible states: off, or in one of three colors. In high-resolution mode (mode 6), the same adapter displays twice as many pixels, 128,000, but displays each pixel in one of only two states, on or off.

If you run a graphics program that requests a high-resolution graphics mode that is beyond the capacity of your display system, the program will either not run or will run with diminished visual quality.

Table 13-1: Display Modes for IBM PCs and Compatibles

Mode Number	Mode Type	Adapter Type	Monitor Type	Size[1] (H × V)	Colors[2]
0	Mono text	CGA, EGA	CD, ECD	40 × 25	16 shades
1	Color text	CGA, EGA	CD, ECD	40 × 25	16
2	Mono text	CGA, EGA	CD, ECD	80 × 25	16 shades
3	Color text	CGA, EGA	CD, ECD	80 × 25	16
4	Color graphics	CGA, EGA	CD, ECD	320 × 200	4
5	Mono graphics	CGA, EGA	CD, ECD	320 × 200	4 shades
6	Mono graphics	CGA, EGA	CD, ECD	640 × 200	2 (B/W)
7	Mono text	MDA	MD	80 × 25	2 (B/W)
8	Hercules graphics	HGC	CD, ECD	720 × 348	2 (B/W)
9–10	(PCjr modes)				
11–12	(Reserved)				
13 (0Dh)	Color graphics	EGA	CD, ECD	320 × 200	16
14 (0Eh)	Color graphics	EGA	CD, ECD	640 × 200	16
15 (0Fh)	Mono graphics	EGA	ECD	640 × 350	2 (B/W)
16 (10h)	Color graphics	EGA	ECD	640 × 350	4 or 16
17 (11h)	Mono graphics	VGA	VD	640 × 480	2 (B/W)
18 (12h)	Color graphics	VGA	VD	640 × 480	16
19 (13h)	Color graphics	VGA	VD	320 × 200	256

[1] Text sizes are shown as the number of columns across by the number of screen rows. Graphics sizes are in pixels. For a given screen capacity, resolution varies with the actual screen dimensions

[2] On monochrome displays, the number of colors that can be displayed is actually the number of shades of a single color.

Graphics Concepts

In an APA video environment, the basic operations are those of reading and writing pixel values. Writing values to a designated pixel or pattern of pixels is a low-level operation known as plotting. To obtain the fastest possible display speed, the routines for plotting pixels must be extremely efficient. All other screen operations are based on those operations.

In "screen geometry," a line is simply a linear arrangement of pixels. A rectangular outline is a set of joined line segments. A filled rectangle is a set of adjacent vertical or horizontal line segments. Other graphic shapes are similarly constructed of various arrangements of pixels.

One problem associated with the pixel-composition of graphic images is the stair-step appearance of diagonal lines, an effect called "jaggies," or aliasing. The jaggies result from the fact that some calculated points along a line fall between physical pixel locations on the display. The display hardware cannot turn on a pixel that doesn't exist, so it turns on the one that is closest to the required point—an alias for the precise location.

Advanced graphics techniques called antialiasing algorithms use shading of nearby pixels to reduce the visible effects of aliasing. Also, with sufficiently high resolution, graphics display devices control enough pixels to make the aliasing effect almost unnoticeable.

The number of bits devoted to a single pixel determines the range of colors the pixel can display. A single bit allows the pixel to be either on or off. If the prevailing video attribute is green, for example, the pixel can be either black (off) or green (on).

Adding a single bit per pixel increases the color choices to four. Usually, the value formed by the two bits serves as an index into a palette, or table of colors. The Learn C medium-resolution four-color palette consists of black plus three other colors.

Color Number	Pixel Color (for a sample palette)
0	Black
1	Cyan
2	Magenta
3	White (actually light gray)

If you have an EGA or VGA display system and a suitable monitor, you can choose higher resolution or more colors (or both if your adapter provides sufficient display memory).

Learn C Graphics Routines

Learn C provides an extensive subset of the full Microsoft C graphics library. Table 13-2 summarizes all the Learn C graphics routines. The remaining sections of this chapter provide more detailed descriptions of many of the supported routines, about two thirds of the complete list.

Graphics routines that take advantage of highly compliant CGA and EGA display hardware are contained in the graphics library. The routines also provide support for selected modes of the VGA, the most recent IBM graphics hardware standard.

Table 13-2: A Summary of Learn C Graphics Routines

Routine Name	Description
Configure	
_displaycursor	Toggle cursor on and off
_getvideoconfig	Get current graphics environment
_setactivepage	Set memory area for writing images
_setvideomode	Set screen display mode
_setvisualpage	Set memory area for displaying images
Set Coordinates	
_getlogcoord	Convert physical to logical coordinates
_getphyscoord	Convert logical to physical coordinates
_setcliprgn	Set clipping region
_setlogorg	Position the logical origin
_setviewport	Limit output region; set origin

(continued)

TABLE 13-2. *continued*

Routine Name	Description
Set Palette	
_remapallpalette	Assign colors to all pixel values
_remappalette	Assign colors to selected pixel values
_selectpalette	Select a predefined palette
Set Attributes	
_getbkcolor	Obtain current background color
_getcolor	Obtain current color
_getfillmask	Obtain current fill mask
_getlinestyle	Obtain current line style
_setbkcolor	Set background color
_setcolor	Set color
_setfillmask	Set fill mask
_setlinestyle	Set line style
Output Text	
_gettextcolor	Obtain current text color
_gettextposition	Obtain current text output position
_outtext	Display text at current position
_settextposition	Set the text position
_settextcolor	Set the text color
_settextwindow	Establish a text window
_wrapon	Enable/disable line wrap
Output Images	
_arc	Draw an arc
_clearscreen	Clear screen to background color
_ellipse	Draw an ellipse
_floodfill	Fill an area with the current color
_getcurrentposition	Obtain current graphic output position

(continued)

TABLE 13-2. *continued*

Routine Name	Description
Output Images (continued)	
_getpixel	Obtain current pixel value
_lineto	Draw a line
_moveto	Move graphic output position
_pie	Draw a pie-slice shape
_rectangle	Draw a rectangle
_setpixel	Set a pixel value
Transfer Images	
_getimage	Store a screen image in memory
_imagesize	Return image size (in bytes)
_putimage	Retrieve an image and display it

❏ NOTE: *Routines that are shaded gray in the table are part of the Microsoft graphics library that are not supported by Learn C.*

In the material that follows, we examine many of the graphics routines and show how to use them in isolation. Then we combine a number of the routines in working Learn C graphics programs.

The graph.h Header File

All Learn C graphics programs must include the graph.h header file, which contains data definitions (structure templates), function prototypes, and manifest constant definitions.

If you have a serious interest in graphics programming, you should print a copy of the graph.h file, study the data structures and become familiar with the interactions among the data items and the graphics functions. For example, several routines in the graphics library set coordinate systems, current positions, and colors. Graphics routines use these data items, along with other data, to plot points, draw lines, and display text.

Manifest constants are symbolic constants that are used throughout the graphics library. As you will notice in the numerous tables that appear in this chapter, they represent an assortment of video modes, colors and other video attributes, and miscellaneous control values.

Graphics Programming Steps

Predictably, graphics programs begin by including header files (especially graph.h), declaring variables, and defining manifest constants. For the remaining executable steps, you need to write program statements to do the following four tasks:

1. Set the required video mode. You must switch to a video mode that is appropriate for your application. MS-DOS operates in text mode, so you must first switch to a graphics mode. Then, if the user's hardware does not support the required mode, provide a graceful exit.

2. Get the video configuration. If you set the mode successfully, get the video configuration parameters so that your program can know the dimensions of the screen in pixels, the number of colors that are available, and other important data.

3. Program your application. The graphics library gives you the tools to do many graphics tasks easily. This aspect of the program is your responsibility.

4. Restore the original video environment. If your program fails to restore the previous video mode before quitting, the computer might appear to lock up when the user tries to run the next program.

Let's apply this four-step procedure to a simple graphics programming project. We'll develop a set of three increasingly complex programs. Concentrate on the concepts. And use the programs as a base to build upon: They have the essential ingredients. Later, you can add whatever enhancements you please.

Setting Modes

A call to _setvideomode()_ is all that is necessary to switch to a specific video mode. The modes are represented by a set of manifest constants, which are defined in the graphics.h header file. These constants are listed in Table 13-3 on the following page.

Before you perform graphics operations, check the return value of the _setvideomode()_ function call to be sure that the mode-setting operation is successful. A return value of 0 flags an error, usually caused by a program's trying to set an unsupported video mode.

Table 13-3: Manifest Constants for Video Modes

Mode Name	Description
_TEXTBW40	40 × 25 monochrome text
_TEXTC40	40 × 24 color text
_TEXTBW80	80 × 25 monochrome text
_TEXTC80	80 × 25 color text
_MRES4COLOR	320 × 200 4-color graphics
_MRESNOCOLOR	320 × 200 monochrome graphics
_HRESBW	640 × 200 monochrome graphics
_TEXTMONO	80 × 25 monochrome text
_MRES16COLOR	320 × 200 16-color graphics
_HRES16COLOR	640 × 200 16-color graphics
_ERESNOCOLOR	640 × 350 monochrome graphics
_ERESCOLOR	640 × 350 4- or 16-color graphics
_VRES2COLOR	640 × 480 monochrome graphics
_VRES16COLOR	640 × 480 16-color graphics
_MRES256COLOR	320 × 200 256-color graphics

The following fragment illustrates a check for successful mode setting, where the 0 return value is defined as the symbolic constant *MODE_ERR*:

```
#define MODE_ERR        0
  .
  .
  .
if (_setvideomode(_MRES16COLOR) == MODE_ERR) {
      fprintf(stderr, "This program requires an EGA\n");
      exit (1);
}
```

An alternative design approach is to attempt a switch to one of the CGA modes if the EGA test fails. The program can run, though with fewer colors, on a CGA or compatible video system if an EGA is not present.

```
#define MODE_ERR        0

if (_setvideomode(_MRES16COLOR) == MODE_ERR)
        if (_setvideomode(_MRES4COLOR) == MODE_ERR) {
                fprintf(stderr, "Can't set video mode\n");
                exit (1);
        }
```

Before a program terminates, it should restore the video mode that was in effect before the program started running. Making another call to *_setvideomode()*, this time with the parameter *_DEFAULTMODE*, restores the user's previous video environment.

Video Configuration Parameters

The graphics routines require a lot of information about the hardware and the current video mode. A data structure declared in graph.h organizes the data into a convenient package. The template for structure *_videoconfig* is as follows:

```
/* structure for _getvideoconfig() as visible to user */
struct videoconfig {
        short numxpixels;       /* number of pixels on X axis */
        short numypixels;       /* number of pixels on Y axis */
        short numtextcols;      /* number of text columns available */
        short numtextrows;      /* number of text rows available */
        short numcolors;        /* number of actual colors */
        short bitsperpixel;     /* number of bits per pixel */
        short numvideopages;    /* number of available video pages */
        short mode;             /* current video mode */
        short adapter;          /* active display adapter */
        short monitor;          /* active display monitor */
        short memory;           /* adapter video memory in KB */
};
```

To capture the video configuration data in your program, declare a variable with this data type and call *_getvideoconfig()* with the address of the variable:

```
struct videoconfig vidconfig;
.
.
.
_getvideoconfig(&vidconfig);
```

Now you can find out what you need to know about the video-display-system parameters for the current mode by accessing the members of the variable *vidconfig*.

Simple Graphics Programs

The GBASICS program (Listing 13-1) shows the four essential elements of a Learn C graphics program. The program attempts to switch to a medium-resolution color graphics mode. If you run the program on a system that has a VGA, EGA, or CGA display system, the program merely displays a cheerful message and waits for a keypress before quitting. If you run the program on a system that does not support medium-resolution color graphics, it displays an error message and quits immediately.

```
/*
 * G B A S I C S
 *
 * Demonstrate the four basic steps
 * in Learn C graphics programming.
 *
 */

#include <stdio.h>
#include <stdlib.h>
#include <conio.h>
#include <graph.h>
#include <math.h>

#define MODE_ERR         0

int
main(void)
{
        struct videoconfig vidconfig;    /* configuration data */
        short x_org, y_org;              /* logical origin */
```

LISTING 13-1. *Program source code for gbasics.c.*   *(continued)*

LISTING 13-1. *continued*

```
/*----- Step 1: Set the Video Mode -----*/


/*
 * Try to set a medium-resolution color mode.
 */
if (_setvideomode(_MRES16COLOR) == MODE_ERR)
        if (_setvideomode(_MRES4COLOR) == MODE_ERR) {
                fprintf(stderr,
                        "No medium-res color support\n");
                exit (1);
        }



/*-- Step 2: Get the Video Configuration Parameters --*/


/*
 * Update video configuration members of
 * vidconfig structure.
 */
_getvideoconfig(&vidconfig);



/*----- Step 3: Your Program Application -----*/


/*
 * Display information about the current video configuration.
 */
switch (vidconfig.mode) {
case _MRES16COLOR:
        puts("Nice -- graphics and 16 colors, too!");
        break;
case _MRES4COLOR:
        puts("Tough break -- only four colors.");
        break;
default:
        /* huh? */
        break;
}


/*
 * Halt and wait for a keypress.
 */
fprintf(stderr, "\n\tPress a key...");
if (getch() == '\0')
        getch();
```

(continued)

LISTING 13-1. *continued*

```
        /*---- Step 4: Restore the Original Video Environment ----*/

        /*
         * Restore the original video mode and
         * return control to the operating system.
         */
        _setvideomode(_DEFAULTMODE);
        return (0);
}
```

A slightly more ambitious program, VMODES (Listing 13-2), embellishes the task of setting the mode and expands the application itself. The program attempts to set the best graphics mode that the hardware supports and then reports what it finds.

In VMODES, the "best" video mode is the one that gives the highest resolution with the greatest number of colors. In general, resolution is more important than the number of colors. Thus, a mode that provides 16 colors at 640×480 pixels is preferable to one that provides 256 colors at 320×200 pixels because images usually look better at the higher resolution.

```
/*
 * V M O D E S
 *
 * Show how to run a program in the best
 * mode available for the hardware configuration it
 * finds when it starts execution.
 */

#include <stdio.h>
#include <stdlib.h>
#include <conio.h>
#include <graph.h>
#include <math.h>

/*
 * Function prototype
 */
int SetBestColorGraphicsMode(void);

#define K_ESC           27
#define MODE_ERR         0
```

(continued)

LISTING 13-2. *continued*

```
/*
 * Table of video modes and names
 */
struct mode_st {
        int number;     /* internal mode number */
        char *name;     /* symbolic name */
        char *desc;     /* description */
} Mode[] = {
        0,      "_TEXTBW40",        "40x25 monochrome text",
        1,      "_TEXTC40",         "40x24 color text",
        2,      "_TEXTBW80",        "80x25 monochrome text",
        3,      "_TEXTC80",         "80x25 color text",
        4,      "_MRES4COLOR",      "320x200 4-color graphics",
        5,      "_MRESNOCOLOR",     "320x200 monochrome graphics",
        6,      "_HRESBW",          "640x200 monochrome",
        7,      "_TEXTMONO",        "80x25 monochrome text (MDA)",
        -1,     "",                 "(not supported)",
        -1,     "",                 "(not supported)",
        -1,     "",                 "(not supported)",
        -1,     "",                 "(not supported)",
        -1,     "",                 "(not supported)",
        13,     "_MRES16COLOR",     "320x200 16-color graphics",
        14,     "_HRES16COLOR",     "640x200 16-color graphics",
        15,     "_ERESNOCOLOR",     "640x350 monochrome graphics",
        16,     "_ERESCOLOR",       "640x350 color (4/16) graphics",
        17,     "_VRES2COLOR",      "640x480 monochrome graphics",
        18,     "_VRES16COLOR",     "640x480 16-color graphics",
        19,     "_MRES256COLOR",    "320x200 256-color graphics"
};

int
main(void)
{
        struct videoconfig vidconfig;   /* video config data */

        /*
         * Try to set the highest available graphics
         * resolution mode with the greatest number
         * of colors.
         */
        if (SetBestColorGraphicsMode() == MODE_ERR) {
                fprintf(stderr,
                        "No medium resolution color support\n");
                exit (1);
        }
```

(continued)

LISTING 13-2. *continued*

```
        /*
         * Update video configuration members of
         * vidconfig structure.
         */
        _getvideoconfig(&vidconfig);

        /*
         * Display information about the current video configuration.
         */
        printf("\nVideo mode name: %s\n", Mode[vidconfig.mode].name);
        printf("[%s]\n\n", Mode[vidconfig.mode].desc);
        printf("Horizontal pixels = %d\n", vidconfig.numxpixels);
        printf("Vertical pixels = %d\n", vidconfig.numypixels);
        printf("Text rows = %d\n", vidconfig.numtextrows);
        printf("Text columns = %d\n", vidconfig.numtextcols);
        printf("Number of actual colors = %d\n",
               vidconfig.numcolors);
        printf("Bits per pixel = %d\n", vidconfig.bitsperpixel);
        printf("Video pages = %d\n", vidconfig.numvideopages);
        printf("Video memory size = %d KB\n", vidconfig.memory);

        /*
         * Halt and wait for a keypress.
         */
        fprintf(stderr, "\n\tPress a key...");
        if (getch() == '\0')
                getch();

        /*
         * Restore the original video mode and
         * return control to the operating system.
         */
        _setvideomode(_DEFAULTMODE);
        return (0);
}


/*
 * SetBestColorGraphicsMode()
 *
 * Attempt to set the best available color graphics mode.
 */

int
SetBestColorGraphicsMode()
{
        int rc = MODE_ERR;        /* Assume the worst. */
```

(continued)

LISTING 13-2. *continued*

```
        /*
         * This routine assumes that
         * resolution is more important than the number
         * of actual colors.
         */
        if (_setvideomode(_VRES16COLOR))
                rc = _VRES16COLOR;
        else if (_setvideomode(_ERESCOLOR))
                rc = _ERESCOLOR;
        else if (_setvideomode(_HRES16COLOR))
                rc = _HRES16COLOR;
        else if (_setvideomode(_MRES256COLOR))
                rc = _MRES256COLOR;
        else if (_setvideomode(_MRES16COLOR))
                rc = _MRES16COLOR;
        else if (_setvideomode(_MRES4COLOR))
                rc = _MRES4COLOR;

        /*
         * Tell the calling function what was set.  A return
         * code of MODE_ERR says we struck out -- no color.
         */
        return (rc);
}
```

The *SetBestColorGraphicsMode()* function assumes the task of finding the best video mode. This function is part of our program, not a graphics library routine; however, it does use graphics library routines to do its work. As a starting point, the function sets its return code *rc* to *MODE_ERR*. Then it attempts to set each acceptable video mode, proceeding from the most desirable to the least. When it finds a mode that the hardware supports, the function returns the internal code that identifies the mode to *main()*. It returns *MODE_ERR* if it cannot set one of the requested modes.

The application part of this program prints a set of values:

■ The mode ID and a brief textual description

■ The number of pixels in the x and y directions

■ The number of text rows and columns

■ The number of colors that can be displayed

■ The number of display pages (Learn C uses only one)

■ The amount of display memory in kilobytes

An actual graphics program would not merely dump onto the screen. Instead, it would use the information to adapt its output to the hardware and so present the best possible images.

Graphics Operations

To accommodate a variety of hardware configurations, graphics programming must take place in two realms. The first is the physical realm, which is based on the specific display hardware at your disposal. The second is the logical realm, which is free of hardware constraints.

Our graphics programs rely on a logical coordinate system and on the graphics pointer, which marks the current location on the screen. Logical coordinates are, in turn, expressed relative to the screen's physical coordinate system. Refer to Figure 13-1 as we examine the coordinate systems and the graphics pointer.

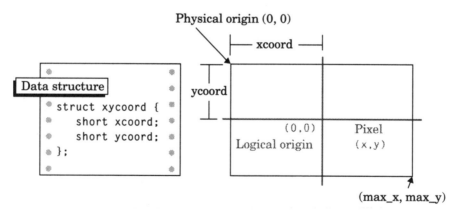

FIGURE 13-1. *The logical coordinate system is defined in terms of the physical coordinate system.*

The Physical Coordinate System

The physical coordinate system is a hardware-specific description of the graphics screen. The physical origin is located at pixel (0, 0) at the upper left corner of the screen. The values of the lower right corner of the screen depend on the graphics mode you select. For the 320×200 medium-resolution modes, for example, the maximum value of the x coordinate is 319, and the maximum value of the y coordinate is 199. Physical coordinates are always positive.

The x axis has its normal orientation—x values increase as the graphics pointer moves to the right. The y axis is inverted from its normal orientation—y values increase as the pointer moves downward.

The Logical Coordinate System

The Learn C graphics routines use the logical coordinate system. You can set the logical origin to any set of physical coordinates that is valid for the selected display mode.

Use the *_setlogorg()* function to set the logical origin. A call to *_setlogorg()* updates the members of a variable described by the *xycoord* structure. The template for the *xycoord* structure is defined in graph.h as follows:

```
struct xycoord {
        short xcoord;    /* x coordinate */
        short ycoord;    /* y coordinate */
};
```

If you don't explicitly set the logical origin, it is identical to the physical origin.

Coordinate Conversions

Two other routines provide logical-to-physical and physical-to-logical coordinate conversions. Typically, you use the routines *_getphyscoord()* and *_getlogcoord()* to convert the coordinates of a point before making an adjustment to the logical origin. These routines update the *xycoord* structure variable in your program.

To convert a pixel location from physical coordinates to logical coordinates, use the following statements:

```
short x, y;            /* physical coordinates */
struct xycoord xy;     /* coordinate variable */
.
.
.
xy = _getlogcoord(x, y);
```

To access the returned logical coordinate values after you make the conversion, use statements such as the following:

```
short lx, ly;            /* logical coordinates */
.
.
.
lx = xy.xcoord;
ly = xy.ycoord;
```

The Graphics Pointer

In graphics programming, all reading and writing operations occur relative to a specific pixel location. This location, sometimes called the graphic output position, is identified by the graphics pointer in the logical coordinate system.

After you set the logical coordinate system (or accept the default), use the _moveto() routine to set the graphics pointer position and the _getcurrentposition() routine to retrieve it.

Drawing Lines

To draw a line, use the _moveto() routine to set one endpoint of the line (x0, y0) and then draw to the other end (x1, y1) by using _lineto().

```
_moveto(x0, y0);
_lineto(x1, y1);
```

The Learn C graphics library provides complete control over line styles. A line style is a description of the way a line will be drawn: solid, dotted, dashed, and so forth. You can call the _setlinestyle() routine before calling _lineto() to set a line style mask.

The line style mask is a pattern of 16 bits in an unsigned short integer. Each bit in the mask represents a pixel in a segment of the line. Any bit that is turned on (has a value of 1) causes its corresponding pixel to be set to the current color. Pixels associated with bits that are turned off (have a value of 0) are not affected. For example, the following statements set a dashed line, which alternates every four pixels:

```
unsigned short mask;
.
.
.
mask = \x0F0F;               /* dashed line style */
_setlinestyle(mask);
```

Text Operations

Text is managed on a grid of rows and columns with row 1 and column 1 at the upper left corner of the screen. The Learn C text routines can display text in either text or graphics modes.

Setting the Text Location

Text operations take place at the current text position, which is separate from the graphics pointer. Use the *_settextposition()* function to set the current text position. The function takes two arguments: a row value and a column value.

```
short row = 20, col = 40;
.
.
.
_settextposition(row, col);
```

Following this setup, any call to the graphics text-oriented routines or to the standard I/O screen routines starts to execute at the specified text location.

Writing Text

Each text item is simply a string of characters. The routine *_outtext()* takes a string argument and writes the string beginning at the current text location.

The graphics text-oriented routines do not offer any data conversion and formatting options, so you must convert numeric values to their string representations before writing them. You can use *sprintf()* to form the needed output strings in memory before writing them to the screen with *_outtext()*.

The *printf()* function offers more flexible formatting than you can achieve with *_outtext()*, but *printf()* is not compatible with the text-windowing features of the Learn C graphics routines. We'll take a look at text windowing shortly.

Clipping and Viewports

All graphics images drawn by routines in the built-in graphics library can be clipped to specified boundaries called *clipping regions*. Clipping is a programming technique that guarantees that nothing will be written outside a specified screen region.

Assume, for example, that you draw an ellipse that falls partially outside a clipping region, as shown in Figure 13-2. The clipping feature of the Learn C graphics interface ensures that only that portion of the graphic image that falls inside the clipping region is displayed. Any points that fall outside the clipping region are not plotted. You don't have to worry about what points to plot and which to ignore. If a clipping region has been established, the graphics routines honor it.

Use the *_setcliprgn()* function to set the screen boundaries. By specifying the upper left and lower right corners of the region, you define a rectangular region of the screen. A call to *_setcliprgn()* does not affect the logical origin.

The *_setviewport()* routine is identical to the *_setcliprgn()* routine except that it also sets the logical origin to the upper left corner of the specified region. The *_setviewport()* routine, in effect, alters the user's video focus.

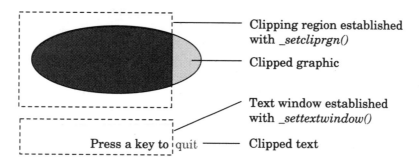

FIGURE 13-2. *Clipping regions and text windows.*

Text Windowing

Using the _settextwindow() routine is similar to graphics clipping, but _settextwindow() is used exclusively for text strings. The routine establishes a text clipping region that lies within specified row and column boundaries. You can use _outtext() to write a string to a text window. (As mentioned earlier, you cannot use a routine in the *printf()* family for this purpose.)

Now refer back to Figure 13-2. Notice that any portion of a string that falls outside the current text window is not written to the display screen. The example is accurate only if line wrap is off.

Line wrap is a feature that determines whether text that falls beyond the end of the text window is truncated (if wrap is turned off) or displayed on the next line (if wrap is turned on). When wrap is turned on, the text in the window scrolls, if necessary, to permit the display of additional text.

The wrap feature is controlled by the _wrapon() routine. The single argument is either _GWRAPON to enable wrapping (the default) or _GWRAPOFF to disable wrapping. Thus, to disable the wrap feature, use the following statement somewhere in your program before writing text to a window.

```
_wrapon(_GWRAPOFF);
```

The LCGDEMO Program

A final demonstration of graphics programming, the LCGDEMO program (Listing 13-3) shows how easily you can combine text and graphics in a screen image.

```
/*
 * L C G D E M O
 *
 * This is a Learn C graphics demonstration program.  Its purpose
 * is to show how to select a graphics mode, draw some shapes and
 * text, and then return to MS-DOS after restoring the user's
 * previous video environment.
 */

#include <stdio.h>
#include <stdlib.h>
```

LISTING 13-3. *Program source code for lcgdemo.c.*   *(continued)*

LISTING 13-3. *continued*

```
#include <conio.h>
#include <graph.h>
#include <math.h>

#define A_BRIGHTYELLOW    14
#define K_ESC             27
#define MSG_ROW           25
#define MSG_COL           2
#define MSG_WIDTH         38
#define M_NOWAIT          0
#define M_WAIT            1
#define MODE_ERR          0
#define NCOLORS           16
#define R_HORIZ           -140
#define R_VERT            0
#define R_HEIGHT          80
#define R_WIDTH           150
#define R_BORDER          0
#define R_FILL            1


/*
 * Function prototypes
 */
void Message(short, short, char *, short);
void Rectangle(short, short, short, short, short);

int
main(void)
{
        struct videoconfig config; /* video configuration data */
        short x_org, y_org;        /* coordinates of the origin */
        short x_ul, y_ul;          /* upper left corner */
        short x_lr, y_lr;          /* lower right corner */
        short x, y;                /* current coordinates */
        short x_offset, y_offset;  /* offsets */
        short color;               /* color number */
        short divisor;             /* to keep color number in range */
        short delta;               /* columnar offset */
```

(continued)

LISTING 13-3. *continued*

```
/*
 * Set up the medium-resolution graphics,
 * set the logical origin to center of screen,
 * and set up a text window.
 */
divisor = 16;
if (_setvideomode(_MRES16COLOR) == MODE_ERR) {
        divisor = 4;
        if (_setvideomode(_MRES4COLOR) == MODE_ERR) {
                fprintf(stderr, "Can't set graphics mode\n");
                exit (1);
        }
}
_getvideoconfig(&config);
x_org = config.numxpixels / 2 - 1;
y_org = config.numypixels / 2 - 1;
_setlogorg(x_org, y_org);
_settextwindow(MSG_ROW, MSG_COL, MSG_ROW,
                MSG_COL + MSG_WIDTH - 1);
_settextposition(MSG_ROW, MSG_COL);
_settextcolor(A_BRIGHTYELLOW);

/*
 * Draw a stack of rectangles in different colors.
 */
x = R_HORIZ;
y = R_VERT;
x_offset = 0;
y_offset = 0;
for (color = 0; color < NCOLORS; ++color) {
        _setcolor(color % divisor);
        Rectangle(R_FILL, y + y_offset, x + x_offset,
                    y + R_HEIGHT + y_offset, x + R_WIDTH +
                    x_offset);
        _setcolor((NCOLORS - 1 - color) % divisor);
        Rectangle(R_BORDER, y + y_offset, x + x_offset,
                    y + R_HEIGHT + y_offset,
                    x + R_WIDTH + x_offset);
        x_offset += 8;
        y_offset -= 6;

}
```

(continued)

LISTING 13-3. *continued*

```
        /*
         * Create a text window and slide the "quit" message into
         * view from right to left and then wait for a keypress.
         */
        _wrapon(_GWRAPOFF);
        for (delta = MSG_WIDTH; delta >= 0; --delta)
                Message(MSG_ROW, MSG_COL + delta,
                        "Press a key to quit.", M_NOWAIT);
        Message(MSG_ROW, MSG_COL + delta,
        "Press a key to quit.", M_WAIT);

        /*
         * Restore the original video mode and
         * return control to the operating system.
         */
        _setvideomode(_DEFAULTMODE);

        return (0);
}


/*
 * Rectangle()
 *
 * Draw a rectangle in the current color.  The type
 * parameter controls whether the rectangle is drawn
 * as a border only or as a filled (solid) object.
 */

void
Rectangle(short type, short top, short left, short bottom,
        short right)
{
        short x, y;
        switch (type) {
        case R_BORDER:
                /*
                 * Construct a box from four line segments.
                 */
                _moveto(left, top);
                _lineto(right, top);
                _lineto(right, bottom);
                _lineto(left, bottom);
                _lineto(left, top);
                break;
```

(continued)

LISTING 13-3. *continued*

```
        case R_FILL:
                /*
                 * Make a solid box from a series of
                 * adjacent horizontal lines.
                 */
                for (y = top; y <= bottom; ++y) {
                        _moveto(left, y);
                        _lineto(right, y);
                }
                break;
        default:
                break;
        }
}


/*
 * Message()
 *
 * Display the message text at the specified screen
 * location (row, col).  If wait has a nonzero value,
 * wait for the user to press a key.  When the user complies,
 * grab the character from the keyboard buffer so it won't
 * interfere with the calling program following the return.
 */

void
Message(row, col, text, wait)
short row, col; /* text position */
char *text;     /* text pointer */
short wait;     /* wait flag */
                /* (wait != 0 means wait for a keypress) */
{
        int k;          /* key code */

        /*
         * Write the prompt text at the specified location.
         */
        _settextposition(row, col);
        _outtext(text);

        /*
         * If the wait flag is set, wait for a key to be pressed;
         * then remove the code from the keyboard buffer.  Handle
         * extended codes by grabbing two bytes if the first is NUL.
         */
```

(continued)

LISTING 13-3. *continued*

```
    if (wait) {
            k = getch();                    /* read the character */
            if (k == '\0')
                    /* extended code -- get the scan code */
                    getch();
    }
}
```

The program attempts to switch to a medium-resolution graphics mode by using *_setvideomode()*. If the attempt fails, the program cannot continue, so it displays an error message and returns to Learn C.

The graphics-only portion of the program creates a set of stacked rectangles, each rectangle created by the *Rectangle()* function, one of two homegrown routines in this program. *Rectangle()* can draw either an outline box around the specified region (*type* = R_BORDER), or a completely filled rectangle (*type* = R_FILL).

A border-only rectangle is composed of four line segments drawn end to end. To compose a filled rectangle, the function simply draws a set of lines closely together.

In the text portion of LCGDEMO, the program prompts the user and waits for a keypress before restoring the original video mode and returning to Learn C. The program establishes a text window and then scrolls its message onto the screen from right to left. The simple animation effect is achieved by calls to the *_outtext()* routine (with wrap turned off) at successively decreasing column positions until the string finally originates at the left end of the text window.

The *Message()* function takes a *wait* parameter that can be set either to M_WAIT, which tells the function to wait for the user to press a key, or to M_NOWAIT, which tells the function to write the string argument without waiting for the user to press a key.

This chapter has introduced the major components of the Learn C graphics capability. The built-in graphics support considerably eases the burden of graphics programming by encapsulating commonly used graphics operations into convenient graphics routines. The routines relieve you of a tremendous amount of detailed programming work.

The routines we have covered do the bulk of the work in a graphics program, but if you have a serious interest in graphics programming, you will want to learn about image-handling functions for animation and other advanced graphics topics. To explore such routines, look through the on-line help information. In most cases, the fastest way to find what you need is to use the help index to select a topic.

Appendixes

C Programming Lesson: Tips and Techniques

Appendix A:
C Language Keywords

In the current definition of C, 32 words, called keywords, have special meaning to the compiler and are reserved. This means that you cannot use the keywords for purposes other than their defined uses. To avoid confusion, don't use a keyword with different letter case to create a new word (INT, for example).

Standard Keywords

The evolving C standard currently defines the following 32 keywords:

auto	double	int	struct
break	else	long	switch
case	enum	register	typedef
char	extern	return	union
const	float	short	unsigned
continue	for	signed	void
default	goto	sizeof	volatile[1]
do	if	static	while

Microsoft Extensions

Microsoft supports the use of the following compiler-specific keywords:

cdecl	fortran	near
far	huge	pascal

Keywords Explained

To locate a brief explanation of a keyword, you can use the index to this book or take advantage of the on-line help resources. To find an explanation using on-line help, press Shift-F1 at the Learn C edit screen and choose *C language keywords* from the list of topics. A list of keywords appears that includes both the standard keywords and the Microsoft extensions. (The keyword *huge* does not appear in that list because the Learn C compiler does not support the huge memory model.) To display the explanation associated with a particular keyword, simply choose the word from the list.

---

[1]The semantics of the *volatile* keyword have not yet been implemented.

Appendix B:
C Language Operators

The following summary of C operators, precedence, and associativity is based on the Learn C implementation. This information is fully compatible with the *Microsoft C Optimizing Compiler* versions 5.0 and later and with Microsoft QuickC products.

Complement and Unary Plus Operators

Operator	Description
–	Unary minus
~	Bitwise complement
!	Logical negation
+	Unary plus[1]

Indirection and Address-of Operators

Operator	Description
*	Indirection
&	Address-of

The *sizeof* Operator

The *sizeof* operator yields the storage requirement, in bytes, of an identifier or data type.

Multiplicative Operators

Operator	Description
*	Multiplication
/	Division
%	Modulus

Shift Operators

Operator	Description
<<	Shift left
>>	Shift right

---

[1] The semantics of the unary plus operator have not yet been implemented.

Relational Operators

Operator	Description
<	Less than
>	Greater than
<=	Less than or equal to
>=	Greater than or equal to
==	Equal to
!=	Not equal to

Bitwise Operators

Operator	Description
&	Bitwise AND
¦	Bitwise inclusive OR
^	Bitwise exclusive OR

Logical Operators

Operator	Description
&&	Logical AND
¦¦	Logical OR

Sequential-Evaluation Operator

The sequential-evaluation operator (the "comma" operator) enforces a left-to-right evaluation of its operands. [*operand1*, *operand2*]

Conditional Operator

The conditional operator (*operand1* ? *operand2* : *operand3*), C's only ternary operator, evaluates *operand1* and yields the value of *operand2* if *operand1* is logically true. Otherwise, it yields the value of *operand3*.

Unary Increment and Decrement Operators

Operator	Description
++	Unary increment
—	Unary decrement

Assignment Operators

Operator	Description
=	Simple assignment
*=	Multiplication assignment
/=	Division assignment
%=	Remainder assignment
+=	Addition assignment
-=	Subtraction assignment
<<=	Left-shift assignment
>>=	Right-shift assignment
&=	Bitwise-AND assignment
¦=	Bitwise-inclusive-OR assignment
^=	Bitwise-exclusive-OR assignment

Operator Precedence and Associativity

Operator	Associativity
() [] -> .	Left to right
- ++ -- ! ~ * & sizeof (*type*)	Right to left
* / %	Left to right
+ -	Left to right
<< >>	Left to right
< <= > >=	Left to right
== !=	Left to right
&	Left to right
^	Left to right
¦	Left to right
&&	Left to right
¦¦	Left to right
?:	Right to left
= *= /= %= += -= &= ^= ¦= <<= >>=	Right to left
,	Left to right

Appendix C:
Preprocessor Directives and Pragmas

A preprocessor directive is an instruction to the C preprocessor, which is traditionally the first pass in C compilation.

Preprocessor Directives

The C preprocessor recognizes the following directives:

#define	#if	#line
#elif	#ifdef	#undef
#else	#ifndef	
#endif	#include	

Preprocessor Operators

Two preprocessor operators are used in the processing of macro parameters, and a third is used in writing compound conditional expressions.

Operator	Description
#	Treat an actual parameter to a macro as a quoted literal string
##	Concatenate tokens ("token pasting") in actual macro parameters
defined	Used in conjunction with conditional directives to simplify the writing of compound expressions

Symbolic Constants and Macros

The *#define* and *#undef* directives are used to define and undefine meaningful identifiers. They create and destroy the associations between identifiers (macro names and symbolic or manifest constants) and their defining text.

#define	Associate an identifier with a definition text
#undef	Remove the definition of an identifier

Include Files

The #*include* directive tells the preprocessor to treat the contents of the file named by *pathname* as if they were in the including file in place of the #*include* directive line.

#include <*pathname*>   Look for *pathname* in the "standard" directories

#include "*pathname*"   Look for *pathname* in the current directory or in the specified literal path

Conditional Compilation

The conditional-compilation directives provide control over the compilation process by conditionally suppressing portions of a source file based on the values of restricted constant expressions. Such expressions cannot contain *sizeof* expressions, type casts, or enumeration constants. They can contain *defined(*identifier*)* expressions.

```
#if restricted-constant-expression
        [code-to-be-compiled]
#elif restricted-constant-expression
        [code-to-be-compiled]
  .
  .
  .
#else
        [code-to-be-compiled]
#endif
```

Line Control

The #*line* directive alters the preprocessor's internal line number (__LINE__) and optionally the internal filename (__FILE__). The #*line* directive is typically used by automatic program generators to synchronize error messages.

```
#line constant ["filename"]
```

Pragmas

The #*pragma* instruction is an implementation-defined preprocessor instruction. Its purpose is to give instructions (specified by *character-sequence*) to the compiler, such as turning a compiler feature on or off.

```
#pragma character-sequence
```

Appendix D:
Learn C Standard Library

Learn C contains a comprehensive set of built-in standard routines. The supported routines provide full support for the defacto C standard defined by Brian W. Kernighan and Dennis M. Richie in their book, *The C Programming Language,* second edition. That book was the original C reference manual and is still considered the ultimate resource for answering questions about C. The following material summarizes the supported routines by category.

To get a synopsis of any routine from the Learn C on-line help resource, simply type the name of the routine on the edit screen and press Shift-F1.

Routines Supported by Learn C

Routine Name	Description
Buffer Manipulation	
memchr	Find a character in a buffer
memcmp	Compare bytes in two buffers
memcpy	Copy bytes from one buffer to another
memmove	Same as *memcpy* but ensures that overlapping regions are copied correctly
memset	Set bytes in a buffer to a character
Character Classification and Conversion	
isalnum	Test for alphanumeric
isalpha	Test for letter
iscntrl	Test for control character
isdigit	Test for a digit
isgraph	Test for a printable character (except space)
islower	Test for lowercase letter
isprint	Test for any printable character
ispunct	Test for punctuation character
isspace	Test for whitespace character

continued

309

Routine Name	Description

Character Classification and Conversion (continued)

isupper	Test for uppercase letter
isxdigit	Test for hexadecimal character
tolower	Convert character to lowercase
toupper	Convert character to uppercase

Data Conversion

atof	Convert a string to *double*
atoi	Convert a string to integer
atol	Convert a string to *long*
itoa	Convert an integer to a string
strtod	Convert a string to *double*
strtol	Convert a string to a *long*
strtoul	Convert a string to an unsigned *long*

File Handling

remove	Delete a file
rename	Rename a file or directory
stat	Get information about a file or directory
unlink	Delete a file

Graphics

_displaycursor	Control cursor display state
_getbkcolor	Get current background color value
_getcolor	Get the current color value
_getcurrentposition	Get the logical graphics coordinate
_getimage	Save an image area in a buffer
_getlinestyle	Get current line-style mask value
_getlogcoord	Translate a physical coordinate to a logical coordinate
_getphyscoord	Translate a logical coordinate to a physical coordinate

continued

Routine Name	Description
Graphics (continued)	
_getpixel	Retrieve the pixel value at a point
_gettextcolor	Retrieve the current text color
_gettextposition	Get the current text position
_lineto	Draw a line to a logical point
_moveto	Move the current position to a logical point
_outtext	Output a string of text
_putimage	Copy a stored image to the screen
_setbkcolor	Set a new background color value
_setcliprgn	Establish a clipping region
_setcolor	Set a new foreground color value
_setlinestyle	Set a new line style mask number
_setlogorg	Move the logical origin to a physical point
_setpixel	Set a pixel to the current color
_settextcolor	Set a new text color value
_settextposition	Establish a new text position
_settextwindow	Establish a window for text output
_setvideomode	Set the video mode
_setviewport	Establish a clipping region and set the logical origin
_wrapon	Control text line-wrap status
I/O Stream	
clearerr	Reset stream's error and EOF indicators
fclose	Close an open stream
feof	Check end-of-file status of a stream
ferror	Check I/O-error status of a stream
fflush	Flush (empty or clear) a stream buffer
fgetc	Read a single character from a stream
fgetpos	Get a stream's file-position value
fgets	Read a string from a stream

continued

Routine Name	Description
I/O Stream (continued)	
fopen	Open a file
fprintf	Format and print a series of characters and values to a stream
fputc	Write a single character to a stream
fputs	Write a string to a stream
fread	Read a block of bytes from a stream
freopen	Close the current file associated with a stream and assign another file to the same stream
fscanf	Read data from a stream into buffers
fseek	Move a stream's file pointer
fsetpos	Set a stream's file-position indicator
ftell	Get the current position of a stream's file pointer
fwrite	Write a block of bytes to a stream
getc	Read a single character from a stream
getchar	Read a character from standard input
gets	Read a string from a stream
printf	Format and print a series of characters and values to standard output
putc	Write a single character to a stream
putchar	Write a character to standard output
puts	Write a string to standard output
rewind	Move a stream's file pointer to offset 0
scanf	Read data from standard input and format items into buffers
setbuf	Control buffering type for a stream
setvbuf	Control buffering type and buffer size for a stream
sprintf	Format and store a series of characters and values into a buffer
sscanf	Read data from buffer
tmpfile	Create a temporary file

continued

Routine Name   **Description**

I/O Stream (continued)

tmpnam   Generate a temporary filename

ungetc   Push back the last character read from a stream

vfprintf   Format and print a series of characters and
                    values to a stream

vprintf   Format and print a series of characters and
                    values to standard output

vsprintf   Format and print a series of characters and
                    values to a buffer

Low-Level I/O

close   Close a file

lseek   Move a file pointer

open   Open a file

read   Read a block of bytes from a file

write   Write a block of bytes to a file

Console and Port I/O

getch   Read a character from the keyboard

ungetch   Push back the last character read from the
                    keyboard

Math

acos   Arccosine

asin   Arcsine

atan   Arctangent

atan2   Arctangent (2 parameters)

ceil   Ceiling

cos   Cosine

cosh   Hyperbolic cosine

exp   Exponential

fabs   Absolute value of a floating-point value

continued

Routine Name	Description
Math (continued)	
floor	Floor value
fmod	Floating-point modulus (remainder)
frexp	Break a floating-point value into its mantissa and exponent
ldexp	Multiply a floating-point value by an integral power of 2.
log	Natural logarithm
log10	Base-10 logarithm
modf	Break a floating-point value into its integer and fractional parts
pow	Raise a value to a power
sin	Sine
sinh	Hyperbolic sine
sqrt	Square root
tan	Tangent
tanh	Hyperbolic tangent
Memory Management	
calloc	Allocate and initialize a block of memory
free	Release a block of memory
malloc	Allocate a block of memory
realloc	Change the size of a previously allocated block of memory
sbrk	Reset the memory "break" value
Process Control	
abort	Abort with an error message
atexit	Add a function to the exit list
exit	Terminate after closing files
raise	Send a signal to the running process
signal	Define system interrupt handling
system	Pass a string to the command interpreter

Routine Name	Description

Searching and Sorting

bsearch	Run a binary search on a sorted array
qsort	Sort an array using the quick-sort algorithm

String Manipulation

strcat	Concatenate strings
strchr	Search for a character in a string
strcmp	Compare strings
strcpy	Copy a string
strcspn	Find the first substring in a string composed of characters not in another string
strerror	Map an error number to a message string
strlen	Get the length of a string
strncat	Append a specified number of characters from a string onto another string
strncmp	Compare initial portions of two strings
strncpy	Copy the initial portion of a string
strpbrk	Find any character in one string that occurs in another string
strrchr	Search for last occurrence of a character in a string
strspn	Return the offset into a string of the first character found that is not in a set specified by another string
strstr	Return a pointer to the first occurrence of a string within another string
strtok	Extract tokens from a string

Time

asctime	Convert a time structure to a character string
clock	Tell how much processor time is used
ctime	Convert a *time_t* value to a character string
difftime	Compute a time difference

continued

Routine Name	Description
Time (continued)	
gmtime	Convert a *time_t* value to a GMT-based time structure
localtime	Convert a *time_t* value to a local time structure
mktime	Convert a local time structure into a calendar value (*time_t*)

Variable-Length Argument Lists

va_arg	Rewind argument list (UNIX only)
va_end	Reset argument pointer
va_list	Point to argument list
va_start	Rewind argument list (ANSI only)

Miscellaneous

abs	Find absolute value of an integer
assert	Print a diagnostic message and call the abort routine
div	Divide integers yielding a quotient and a remainder
getenv	Get the value of an environment variable
labs	Find absolute value of a *long*
ldiv	Divide *long values* yielding a quotient and a remainder
longjump	Return from a nonlocal jump
perror	Print an error message
rand	Generate random number
setjmp	Prepare for a nonlocal jump
srand	Seed random-number generator

Appendix E:
Characters and Attributes

A character code is a numeric value that is used to represent a character in computer memory and to control peripheral devices such as the console display screen, terminals, and printers. We are interested in two primary character-coding schemes: the ASCII character set, because it is the standard to which most commercial terminal and computer equipment designs adhere, and the IBM extended ASCII character set used by the IBM PC and work-alike computers.

Numeric codes are also used with terminals and PC console display devices to control the appearance of a displayed character (video attribute), to prevent specified screen regions from being updated (protect), and even to make certain areas of the screen invisible to the user (nondisplay). IBM PCs do not directly support protected fields, although our programs can simulate the effect. On a PC, a nondisplay field is one that carries a special video attribute that sets the foreground color to the same value as the background color.

This appendix is a detailed summary of the characters and attributes available to programmers of the IBM PC family of computers.

ASCII Character Codes

The ASCII (American National Standard Code for Information Interchange) character set is a table of 7-bit codes that represents a collection of control characters and printable characters. In the 8-bit environment typical of the IBM PC and similar equipment, the lower 7 bits (0 through 6) are used to represent ASCII characters. The high bit (bit 7) is used for IBM code extensions, which are discussed later in this appendix.

Figure E-1 on the following page shows the relationship between various character codes and the data bytes that hold them.

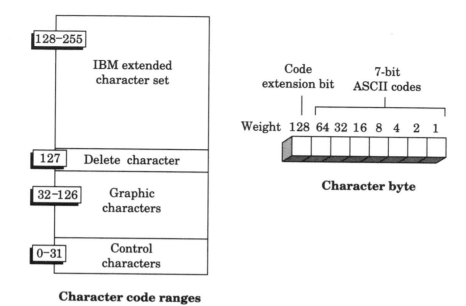

Character code ranges

FIGURE E-1. *Character codes and storage.*

ASCII Control Character Table

ASCII codes 0 through 31 and 127 (decimal) are called control codes because they are used to start, stop, or modify some action. Several control characters have meanings that vary with the context of their use, but most can be placed in one or more of the following categories:

- **Format Effector** (FE)—controls the printed or displayed layout of graphic information
- **Communications Control** (CC)—controls the operation of communication devices and networks
- **Information Separator** (IS)—controls the logical separation of information

In its design of the PC, IBM attached special meanings to most ASCII control codes so that they have displayable graphic content when placed directly into display memory. Thus, the format effector CR (code 13 decimal), in addition to its "carriage return" meaning when embedded in data streams, can also be used to place a musical note symbol on the display screen. Each control code except NUL (0) has an associated displayable symbol on the IBM PC.

Dec Code	Hex Code	Key	IBM Graphic	Name	Description (Type)
0	00	^@		NUL	Null character (CC or FE)
1	01	^A	☺	SOH	Start of heading (CC)
2	02	^B	●	STX	Start of text (CC)
3	03	^C	♥	ETX	End of text (CC)
4	04	^D	♦	EOT	End of transmission (CC)
5	05	^E	♣	ENQ	Enquiry (CC)
6	06	^F	♠	ACK	Acknowledge (CC)
7	07	^G	•	BEL	Bell
8	08	^H	◘	BS	Backspace (FE)
9	09	^I	○	HT	Horizontal tabulation (FE)
10	0A	^J	◉	LF	Linefeed (FE)
11	0B	^K	♂	VT	Vertical tabulation (FE)
12	0C	^L	♀	FF	Formfeed (FE)
13	0D	^M	♪	CR	Carriage return (FE)
14	0E	^N	♫	SO	Shift out
15	0F	^O	☼	SI	Shift in
16	10	^P	►	DLE	Data link escape (CC)
17	11	^Q	◄	DC1	Device control #1
18	12	^R	↕	DC2	Device control #2
19	13	^S	‼	DC3	Device control #3
20	14	^T	¶	DC4	Device control #4
21	15	^U	§	NAK	Negative acknowledgment (CC)
22	16	^V	▬	SYN	Synchronous idle (CC)
23	17	^W	↨	ETB	End of transmission block (CC)
24	18	^X	↑	CAN	Cancel
25	19	^Y	↓	EM	End of medium
26	1A	^Z	→	SUB	Substitute
27	1B	Esc	←	ESC	Escape
28	1C		∟	FS	Field separator (IS)
29	1D		↔	GS	Group separator (IS)
30	1E		▲	RS	Record separator (IS)
31	1F		▼	US	Unit separator (IS)
127	7F	Del	⌂	DEL	Delete (CC or FE)

Printable Character Table

The ASCII codes in the range of 32 through 126 (decimal) are called graphic characters to show that they have a visible representation on a display device. Only the meaning of code 32, space (SP), which prints or displays as blank location in a graphic sequence, is defined by the ASCII standard. The remaining graphic characters have meanings that are, in effect, enforced by consensus. We simply accept the fact that code 65 (decimal) represents the letter 'A', for example.

Dec Code	Hex Code	Key or Symbol	Dec Code	Hex Code	Key or Symbol	Dec Code	Hex Code	Key or Symbol
32	20	(SPACE)	64	40	@	96	60	`
33	21	!	65	41	A	97	61	a
34	22	"	66	42	B	98	62	b
35	23	#	67	43	C	99	63	c
36	24	$	68	44	D	100	64	d
37	25	%	69	45	E	101	65	e
38	26	&	70	46	F	102	66	f
39	27	'	71	47	G	103	67	g
40	28	(	72	48	H	104	68	h
41	29	)	73	49	I	105	69	i
42	2A	*	74	4A	J	106	6A	j
43	2B	+	75	4B	K	107	6B	k
44	2C	,	76	4C	L	108	6C	l
45	2D	–	77	4D	M	109	6D	m
46	2E	.	78	4E	N	110	6E	n
47	2F	/	79	4F	O	111	6F	o
48	30	0	80	50	P	112	70	p
49	31	1	81	51	Q	113	71	q
50	32	2	82	52	R	114	72	r
51	33	3	83	53	S	115	73	s
52	34	4	84	54	T	116	74	t
53	35	5	85	55	U	117	75	u
54	36	6	86	56	V	118	76	v
55	37	7	87	57	W	119	77	w
56	38	8	88	58	X	120	78	x
57	39	9	89	59	Y	121	79	y
58	3A	:	90	5A	Z	122	7A	z
59	3B	;	91	5B	[	123	7B	{
60	3C	<	92	5C	\	124	7C	¦
61	3D	=	93	5D	]	125	7D	}
62	3E	>	94	5E	^	126	7E	~
63	3F	?	95	5F	_			

Nothing in the standard demands that the graphic symbols be shown as Gothic or Roman or any other type style. That decision is left to the terminal/computer maker, and usually is whatever type style the producer of the video controller chip supplies. The following table shows the accepted definitions of the graphic characters.

IBM Extended ASCII Codes

Because the ASCII character set is based on a 7-bit code, the high bit of each 8-bit byte used by the IBM PC is available for other uses. When the high bit is set to 1, the character codes range from 128 through 255 (decimal). IBM uses these extra 128 codes for special characters (international symbols, line- and block-drawing characters, special symbols for mathematics, and so forth).

A complete table of the additional codes and the associated symbols and characters appears on the next page.

IBM Extended ASCII Codes

Dec Code	Hex Code	Key or Symbol	Dec Code	Hex Code	Key or Symbol	Dec Code	Hex Code	Key or Symbol
128	80	Ç	171	AB	½	214	D6	╥
129	81	ü	172	AC	¼	215	D7	╫
130	82	é	173	AD	¡	216	D8	╪
131	83	â	174	AE	«	217	D9	┘
132	84	ä	175	AF	»	218	DA	┌
133	85	à	176	B0	░	219	DB	█
134	86	å	177	B1	▒	220	DC	▄
135	87	ç	178	B2	▓	221	DD	▌
136	88	ê	179	B3	│	222	DE	▐
137	89	ë	180	B4	┤	223	DF	▀
138	8A	è	181	B5	╡	224	EO	α
139	8B	ï	182	B6	╢	225	E1	β
140	8C	î	183	B7	╖	226	E2	Γ
141	8D	ì	184	B8	╕	227	E3	π
142	8E	Ä	185	B9	╣	228	E4	Σ
143	8F	Å	186	BA	║	229	E5	σ
144	90	É	187	BB	╗	230	E6	µ
145	91	æ	188	BC	╝	231	E7	τ
146	92	Æ	189	BD	╜	232	E8	Φ
147	93	ô	190	BE	╛	233	E9	Θ
148	94	ö	191	BF	┐	234	EA	Ω
149	95	ò	192	C0	└	235	EB	δ
150	96	û	193	C1	┴	236	EC	∞
151	97	ù	194	C2	┬	237	ED	φ
152	98	ÿ	195	C3	├	238	EE	ε
153	99	Ö	196	C4	─	239	EF	∩
154	9A	Ü	197	C5	┼	240	F0	≡
155	9B	¢	198	C6	╞	241	F1	±
156	9C	£	199	C7	╟	242	F2	≥
157	9D	¥	200	C8	╚	243	F3	≤
158	9E	₧	201	C9	╔	244	F4	⌠
159	9F	ƒ	202	CA	╩	245	F5	⌡
160	A0	á	203	CB	╦	246	F6	÷
161	A1	í	204	CC	╠	247	F7	≈
162	A2	ó	205	CD	═	248	F8	°
163	A3	ú	206	CE	╬	249	F9	•
164	A4	ñ	207	CF	╧	250	FA	·
165	A5	Ñ	208	D0	╨	251	FB	√
166	A6	ª	209	D1	╤	252	FC	η
167	A7	º	210	D2	╥	253	FD	²
168	A8	¿	211	D3	╙	254	FE	■
169	A9	⌐	212	D4	╘	255	FF	
170	AA	¬	213	D5	╒			

Line-Drawing
Characters—Quick Reference

Among the IBM extended-ASCII characters are some line-drawing characters that allow us to draw boxes and other shapes that can be formed from various corners and straight line segments. The codes are somewhat scattered; to make them accessible, Figure E-2 visually groups the codes for single-line and double-line drawing characters. These design aids can be traced to Rich Schinnell in an item published in *PC World* (Nov. 1983).

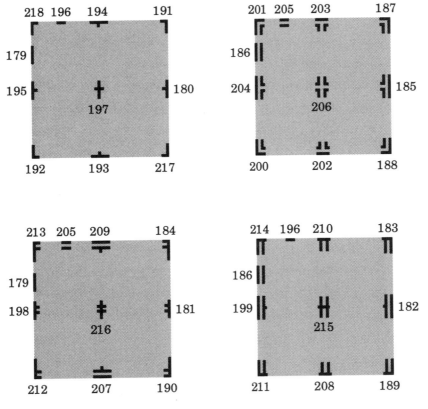

FIGURE E-2. *Line-drawing character sets.*

Block Characters—Quick Reference

The treasure trove of special characters in the IBM extended ASCII character set also contains eight block characters that you can use to good effect in screen displays. They are detailed in Figure E-3.

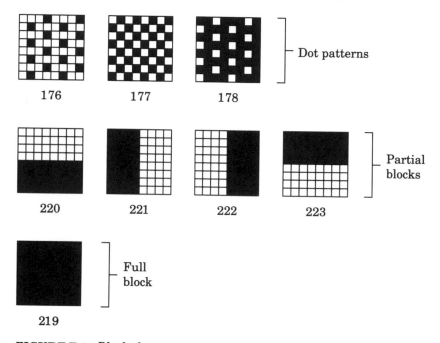

FIGURE E-3. *Block character sets.*

❏ NOTE: *These figures assume an 8 × 8 pixel character, all typical of CGA-compatible displays. Other display systems use different numbers of pixels but retain the same graphic appearances.*

Video Attributes

Both the monochrome and color display systems used with PCs give you a considerable degree of control over the appearance of characters on the screen. Each character byte in memory is accompanied by an attribute byte that specifies its visual characteristics.

Figure E-4 shows how the attribute byte is interpreted.

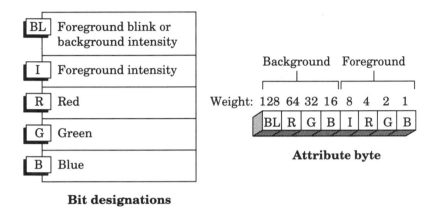

Bit designations

FIGURE E-4. *Video attribute byte interpretation.*

The following table summarizes the text mode attributes for both monochrome and color graphics systems. The codes between 0 and 7 set the foreground (low 4 bits) or background (high 4 bits) attribute. Thus, storing the code \x02 in an attribute byte produces a green foreground and a black background.

The high bit in each 4-bit (nibble) component of the attribute determines the intensity. In the foreground component, setting bit 3 causes the foreground to be high intensity; setting bit 7 of an attribute byte controls either foreground blinking or background intensity.

We can combine attribute values using bit shifting and bitwise OR operations to produce various compound attributes. For example, the combined code

```
(0x01 << 4) ¦ \x07 ¦ \x08
```

yields a bright white character on a blue background.

Primary Attributes

Dec Code	Hex Code	Binary Code	Attribute CGA	MDA Description	
				Foreground	Background
0	00	0000	Black	Black	Black
1	01	0001	Blue	White underline	White
2	02	0010	Green	White	White
3	03	0011	Cyan	White	White
4	04	0100	Red	White	White
5	05	0101	Magenta	White	White
6	06	0110	Brown	White	White
7	07	0111	White	White	White

Intensity Modifiers

Dec Code	Hex Code	Binary Code	Description
8	10	1000	High intensity
128	100	10000000	Blinking foreground (or high-intensity background).

The last entry is simply ($\backslash$x08 << 4) and is referred to as the "blink" bit or background-intensity bit depending upon whether blinking is enabled (default) or disabled.

Appendix F:
C Programming Traps and Tips

Traps to Avoid

The following traps have caught most C programmers at one time or another. Be on guard for them. The C compiler system can do little or nothing to help you with these kinds of errors because it assumes you know what you're doing!

Using Assignment Instead of an Equality Test. If you use assignment (=) in a conditional expression in which an equality test is expected, you get unwanted results. In the following example, the program always quits regardless of the value obtained from *getch()*.

```
key = getch();
if (key = 'Q') {
        Clean();
        exit (0);
}
```

Using Unnecessary Semicolons. Semicolons are not needed following macro definitions, conditional expressions in *if*, *while*, and *do* statements, or following the closing brace of a block of code. In C, the semicolon is a statement terminator (not a separator as in Pascal), and extra semicolons can have either benign effects or unwanted and surprising consequences, depending upon their locations.

Disregarding Operator Precedence. C programmers commonly use embedded assignment within a conditional expression. Note that assignment has a lower precedence than logical tests, so the parentheses around the assignment are needed.

```
if ((ch = getchar()) != EOF)
        putchar(ch);
```

If the assignment statement is not parenthesized, you have the following code:

```
if (ch = getchar() != EOF)
        putchar(ch);
```

The *ch* variable receives the logical (true/false) result of the comparison of the *getchar()* call and EOF. Thus, *ch* is assigned a value of 1 if *getchar()* is able to read a character and 0 at the end of file, and *putchar()* outputs a string of ^A codes, which print as happy faces on an IBM PC or compatible. (Not what the doctor ordered, unless you're just programming for grins.)

Forgetting to Use a *break* Statement After a *case* Body. The *switch* construct permits a fall-through from one case to the next unless a *break* statement (or *continue*, *return*, or *exit*) terminates the *case* body. Consider the following fragment:

```
switch (key = GetKey()) {
case K_UP:
        CursorUp();
case K_DOWN:
        CursorDown();
        break;
default:
        break;
}
```

In this example, the command to move the cursor up one line has the desired effect, but the effect is reversed when control falls through to the *K_DOWN* case.

Declaring Buffers That Are Too Small. To read a 20-character string, the buffer must have a size of 21 bytes to allow room for the terminating NUL byte. To avoid the problem, explicitly add 1 to array sizes in the declaration:

```
#define MAXSTR 20
.
.
.
char buffer[MAXSTR + 1];
```

Forgetting to Terminate Character Strings. A character string must have a terminating NUL byte. If it doesn't, and you hand the string to a print function, don't be surprised to see some strange output on your screen or printer. The print function marches along happily, printing everything it finds until it encounters a NUL byte, which might be at some distant location in your program data.

Confusing Size with Offset. Beginning C programmers often confuse the size of an array with the value of the array's maximum offset. Given an array called *line* with a size of 10 elements, its offsets, or array index values, range from 0 through 9. The first element is *line[0]* and the last element is *line[9]*. If you refer to *line[10]*, you are accessing data that is outside the *line* array.

Treating Pointers Like Integers. A pointer and an *int* value might have the same natural size on a particular class of machine, but they are fundamentally different data types. Don't try to use them interchangeably.

Failing to Initialize Variables Before Use. Using a variable that has been declared but not initialized can cause serious problems. Microsoft C compilers warn you about variables that are used before being initialized, but many C compilers do not. In the following example, the value of *index* upon entering the loop is indeterminate:

```
int index;

while (index < 100) {
        DoSomething();
        ++index;
}
```

The uninitialized variable *index* has whatever value happens to be in the location, not 0 as you might expect. You must explicitly initialize automatic storage.

C Programming Tips

Learn C and all other Microsoft C compilers provide a level of program checking that you specify. The primary compiler features that assist you in program checking are function prototyping and program "linting" during the compilation process.

Whereas the UNIX/XENIX environments support a separate program called *lint* that checks your code for syntax errors and questionable programming practices, the Microsoft PC-based C compilers offer such error checking as a built-in feature. In addition, Microsoft C compilers provide optional run-time stack-checking and pointer-checking mechanisms.

Function Prototyping. Until recently, C language compilers played fast and loose with regard to functions: Compilers did no checking on the number and types of parameters passed to functions, nor on the return values of functions, to see that they were used correctly.

Because compilation generated no warning or error messages for such errors, it usually finished with apparent success. A significant number of serious errors could be diagnosed only at run-time, and then only with great difficulty.

C compilers that are converging on the draft proposed ANSI C standard now offer function prototyping, which verifies that the correct number and types of parameters are passed to a function and that the return data type of a function is correct in context.

You are strongly advised to include the required header file for each standard library function that you use in your programs and to turn on the function-checking feature. Function checking is always enabled in the Learn C environment.

Warning Level. In the Learn C environment (and QuickC), the Compile dialog box offers a selection of warning levels from 0 (none) through 3 (highest). Set the warning level to at least 2. Using the maximum value (currently 3) to obtain the highest level of error checking is a good idea during the early phases of program development if you want your program to adhere as closely as possible to the proposed ANSI standard.

Pointer Checking. "Wild" pointers account for a great number of run-time errors in C programs. A wild pointer is one that accesses data outside the program's data space, an occurrence that can damage the program instructions or interfere with the operating system.

To enable pointer checking for the entire program, display the Compile dialog box and check the appropriate option. Doing so causes the program to run more slowly, so pointer checks are usually done only during the development phase of a project.

You can also enable pointer checking only during the execution of selected program instructions. To do so, surround blocks of code with pragma statements that are understood by Microsoft compilers to enable the checking only while the program is executing in blocks that are so marked.

```
#pragma check_pointer(on)
        /* code to be checked */
        .
        .
        .
#pragma check_pointer(off)
```

Stack Checking. Stack overrun can cause unrecoverable errors if it is not detected and reported. If the stack is overrun, data stored in the heap is in danger of being overwritten. As a result of a stack overrun, your program will fail to run or will run incorrectly—without alerting you to the problem.

During development, it is a good idea to enable stack checking. To do so, activate the Stack Check option in the Compile dialog box or use *check_stack* pragma statements within your source file. The usage is identical to the pointer-checking usage described above. Disable stack checking only after you are certain that your program lives within the default stack limits or after you adjust the stack size to meet your program's needs.

Glossary

The definitions in this glossary are intended primarily for use with this manual. Neither the individual definitions nor the list of terms is comprehensive.

8087, 80287, or 80387 coprocessor. Intel hardware products that provide fast and precise number processing.

active page. The area in memory to which graphics output is written.

aggregate types. A set of composite data types that includes arrays, structures, and unions.

alias. One of several alternative names for the same memory location.

alternate math library. A model-dependent floating-point library that uses a subset of the number format established by the Institute of Electrical and Electronics Engineers, Inc. (IEEE).

animation. The process of creating graphics images that move on the screen.

ANSI (American National Standards Institute). The national institute responsible for defining programming-language standards to promote portability of these languages among different computer systems.

argument. A value passed to a function.

argument type list. In a function prototype, a list of data types, separated by commas, that indicates the types of actual arguments in the function call. Used to make sure the actual arguments in the function call correspond to the formal parameters in the function definition.

arithmetic conversion. Conversion operations performed on items of integral and floating-point types used in expressions.

arithmetic types. A set of C data types that includes integral, enumerated, and floating-point types.

array. A set of elements with the same data type.

ASCII (American Standard Code for Information Interchange). A set of 256 codes that many computers use to represent letters, digits, special characters, and other symbols. Only the first 128 of these codes are standardized; the remaining 128 are special characters that are defined by the computer manufacturer.

associativity. The precedence rules that apply when multiple operators of like precedence ranking are assigned to an operand. For example, in the expression *p++, the indirection operator (*) is applied before the unary increment operator (++).

background color. The color on which all drawing and color display takes place.

base name. The portion of the filename that precedes the filename extension. For example, *sample* is the base name of the file sample.c.

batch file. A text file containing MS-DOS commands that can be invoked from the MS-DOS command line.

binary expression. An expression consisting of two operands joined by a binary operator.

binary operator. An operator that takes two operands. Binary operators in the C language are the multiplicative operators (*, /), additive operators (+, –), shift operators (<<, >>), relational operators (<, >, <=, >=, ==, !=), bitwise operators (&, |, ^), logical operators (&&, ||), and the sequential-evaluation operator (,).

block. A sequence of declarations, definitions, and statements enclosed within braces ({}).

bounding rectangle. The rectangular area used to define certain graphics operations, such as clipping.

clipping. The limiting of graphics displays to a particular region of the screen, which is known as the clipping region.

clipping region. The rectangular portion of the screen where graphics output occurs.

color value. A unique ordinal value representing a displayable color.

compact memory model. A memory model that allows for more than one data segment and only one code segment.

constant expression. Any expression that evaluates to a constant; it can involve integer constants, character constants, floating-point constants, enumeration constants, type casts to integral and floating-point types, and other constant expressions.

coordinate system. A system used to identify a screen location relative to horizontal and vertical axes. Text is positioned in a character-based row-and-column coordinate system. By contrast, graphics figures are positioned in a pixel-based row-and-column coordinate system.

core library. The library of standard C routines that is built into the Learn C programming interface.

current position. The coordinate location given by an (x, y) logical coordinate pair that defines the pixel point where the next graphics operation is to take place.

current text position. The coordinate location given by a (row, column) coordinate pair that defines the row and column junction where graphics-based text operations are to take place.

declaration. A construct that associates the name and the attributes of a variable, function, or type.

definition. A construct that initializes and allocates storage for a variable or that specifies the name, formal parameters, body, and the return type of a function.

directive. An instruction to the C preprocessor to perform a specific action on source-program text before compilation.

DOS interface functions. Run-time library routines that provide access to MS-DOS interrupts and system calls.

emulator. A floating-point math package that provides software emulation of the operations of a math coprocessor.

enumeration set. The set of valid values defined for an enumeration type.

enumeration type. A user-defined data type that specifies a particular set of valid values.

environment variable. A variable stored in the environment table that provides MS-DOS with information (the location of executable files and library files, the location in which to create temporary files, and so forth).

errorlevel code. *See* exit code.

escape sequence. A specific combination, comprising a backslash (\) followed by a letter or combination of digits, that represents white-space or nongraphic characters within strings and character constants.

exit code. A code returned by a program to MS-DOS indicating whether the program ran successfully.

expression. A combination of operands and operators that yields a single value.

external level. The part of a C program that is outside all function declarations.

file handle. A value returned by library functions that open or create files; used to refer to that file in later operations.

file pointer. A pointer that indicates the current position in an input or output stream. It is updated to reflect the new position each time a read or write operation takes place.

filling. The process of applying a fill mask to a specified area.

fill mask. An 8×8 array of bits in which each bit represents a pixel; the array defines the pattern to be used in filling figures. When a figure is filled, the fill mask is repeated over the entire area. If a bit in the array is 1, the corresponding pixel in the figure is set to the current color. If a bit is 0, the corresponding pixel is unchanged. The default fill mask is NUL, which leaves the area unchanged.

foreground color. A color used to display text and draw graphics images.

formal parameters. Variables that receive values passed to a function when the function is called.

forward declaration. A function declaration that establishes the attributes of a function so that it can be called before it is defined or so that it can be called from a different source file.

function. A collection of declarations and statements returning a value that can be called by name.

function body. A compound statement that contains the local variable declarations and statements of a function.

function call. An expression that passes control and actual arguments (if any) to a function.

function declaration. A declaration that establishes the name, return type, and storage class of a function that is defined explicitly elsewhere in the program.

function definition. A definition that specifies a function's name, its formal parameters, the declarations and statements that define what it does, and (optionally) its return type and storage class.

function prototype. A function declaration that includes a list of the names and types of formal parameters in the parentheses following the function name.

fundamental data types. A set of basic C data types that includes all integer, character, floating-point, and enumeration types.

global. *See* lifetime; visibility.

include file. A text file that is merged into another text file through use of the *#include* preprocessor directive.

internal level. The parts of a C program that are expressed within function declarations.

keyword. A word with a special, predefined meaning for the Learn C compiler.

large memory model. A memory model that allows for more than one segment of code and more than one segment of data, but that allows no individual data items to span a single segment.

level. *See* internal level; external level.

library. A file that stores related modules of compiled code. In Learn C, a major subset of the standard library routines and many special routines are built into the compiler.

lifetime. The period during program execution in which a variable or function exists. An item with a local lifetime (a local item) has storage and a defined value only within the block where the item is defined or declared. A global item, on the other hand, remains in existence until the program terminates.

line style. A 16-bit array that defines the mask to be used in drawing lines. If a bit in the array is 1, the corresponding pixel in the line is set to the current color. If a bit is 0, the corresponding pixel is unchanged. The default line style is \xFFFF (a solid line).

linked list. A data structure consisting of a list of entries, each of which includes a pointer to the next entry.

local. *See* lifetime; visibility.

logical coordinates. The coordinate system defined by the programmer. The origin for the logical coordinate system can be positioned anywhere on the screen's physical coordinate system. The default logical coordinate system is identical to the physical coordinate system, which places the coordinates of the origin (0,0) at the upper left corner of the screen.

logical origin. The origin given by the logical coordinate pair (0,0). All subsequent graphics output is relative to the logical origin.

low-level input and output routines. Run-time library routines that perform unbuffered, unformatted I/O operations.

lvalue. An expression (such as a variable name) that refers to a memory location and is required as the left-hand operand of an assignment operation or the single operand of a unary operator.

macro. An identifier defined in a *#define* preprocessor directive to represent another series of tokens.

manifest constant. An identifier defined in a *#define* preprocessor directive to represent a constant value.

medium memory model. A memory model that allows for more than one code segment and only one data segment.

member. An element of a structure or union.

memory model. One of the models that specifies how memory is set up for program code and data. *See* small memory model; medium memory model; compact memory model; large memory model. Learn C uses the medium memory model.

multidimensional array. An array of arrays.

newline character. The character used to mark the end of a line of a text file, or the escape sequence (\n) used to represent this character. In MS-DOS text mode, carriage-return/linefeed (CR-LF) combinations are translated into a single linefeed (LF) character on input, and linefeed characters are translated into carriage-return/linefeed combinations on output.

NUL character. The ASCII character encoded as the value 0, represented as the escape sequence (\0) in a source file.

NULL pointer. A pointer to nothing, which is expressed as the integer value 0.

object. A region of memory that can be examined. A *modifiable* object can also have a value stored in it (that is, it can be altered as well as examined).

operand. A constant or variable value that is manipulated in an expression.

operator. One or more symbols that specify how the operand or operands of an expression are manipulated.

palette. A mapping of the color values (the actual displayable colors) to the valid pixel values for a given video mode. The CGA modes operate with a set of predetermined palettes. The EGA and VGA color modes (among others) operate with a redefinable palette of colors.

physical coordinates. The coordinate system defined by the hardware. The physical coordinate system has the origin (0,0) at the upper left corner of the screen. The value of x increases from left to right; the value of y increases from top to bottom. The default logical coordinate system is identical to the physical coordinate system.

pixel. A single dot on the screen. A pixel is the smallest item that you can manipulate with the Learn C graphics library, and it is the basic unit of the coordinate systems.

pixel value. The 1-bit, 2-bit, or 4-bit representation of a screen pixel. It is the index into the palette of available colors.

pointer. A variable containing the address of another variable.

pragma. An instruction to the compiler to perform a particular action at compile time.

precedence. The relative position of an operator in the hierarchy that determines the order in which expressions are evaluated.

preprocessor. A text processor that manipulates the contents of a C source file during the first phase of compilation.

preprocessor directive. *See* directive.

prototype. *See* function prototype.

remapping. The process of altering the correspondence between color value and pixel value. CGA palettes cannot be remapped.

runtime. The time during which a previously compiled and linked program is executing.

run-time library. A file containing the routines needed to implement certain functions of the Microsoft C language.

scalar types. A set of C data types that includes integral, enumerated, floating-point, and pointer types.

scope. The parts of a program in which you can reference an item by name. The scope of an item might be limited to the file, function, block, or function prototype in which it appears.

side effects. Changes in the state of objects that occur as a result of expression evaluation.

sizeof **operator.** A C operator that can be used to determine the amount of storage associated with an identifier or a type.

small memory model. A memory model that allows for only one code segment and only one data segment.

source file. A text file containing C language code.

stack. A dynamically shrinking and expanding area of memory in which data items are stored consecutively and removed on a last in, first out basis.

static. A storage class that allows variables to keep their values even after the program exits the block in which the variable is declared.

stream function. One of a set of run-time library functions that treats data files and data items as streams of individual characters.

string. An array of characters terminated by a NUL character (\0).

string literal. A string of characters and escape sequences delimited by double quotation marks. Every string literal has the data type *array*, the elements of which are *char* values.

structure. A set of elements, which can be of different data types, grouped under a single name.

structure member. One of the elements of a structure.

subscript expression. An expression, usually used to reference array elements, representing an address that is offset from a specified base address by a given number of positions.

symbolic constant. *See* manifest constant.

tag. The name assigned to a structure, union, or enumerated type.

ternary expression. An expression that takes three operands. C has one ternary operator (?, :). The logical value of the first operand determines which of the other two is evaluated.

text color. The color value to be used in all graphics-based text operations.

text mode. The file-processing mode in which carriage-return/linefeed combinations are converted to newline characters on input and reconverted to carriage-return/linefeed combinations on output.

text window. A window, defined in row-and-column coordinates, in which text output to the screen is to be displayed.

tiling. The process of applying a fill mask to an area of the screen.

toggle. The action of turning an option on or off.

token. The most fundamental unit of a C source program that is meaningful to the compiler.

two's complement. A type of base-2 notation used to represent positive and negative numbers in which negative values are formed by complementing all bits and adding 1 to the results.

type. A description of a set of values that defines its range and the way its elements are displayed; for example, a variable of type *int* can have any of a set of integer values within the range specified for that data type on a particular machine.

type cast. An operation in which an operand of one type is converted to an operand of a different type.

type checking. An operation in which the compiler verifies that the operands of an operation are valid or that the actual arguments in a function call are of the same types as the corresponding formal parameters in the function definition and function prototype (if any).

type declaration. A declaration that defines the name and members of a structure or union, or one that defines the name and enumeration set of an enumeration.

***typedef* declaration.** A declaration that defines a shorter or more meaningful name for an existing C data type or for a user-defined type.

type name. A specification of a particular data type that appears in variable declarations, in the formal parameter lists of function prototypes, in type casts, and in *sizeof* operations.

unary expression. An expression consisting of a single operand preceded or followed by a unary operator.

unary operator. An operator that takes a single operand. Unary operators in the C language are the complement operators (–, ~, !), indirection operator (*), increment (++) and decrement (––) operators, address-of operator (&), and *sizeof* operator. (The unary plus operator (+) is also implemented syntactically but has no associated semantics.)

union. A set of values that have different data types and occupy the same storage space at different times.

unresolved reference. A reference to a global or external variable or a function that cannot be found. This error is often the result of a misspelled variable or function name in the source file.

usual arithmetic conversions. Type conversions performed by the Microsoft Learn C compiler on operands of integral or floating-point types in an expression to bring the operands to a common type.

video mode. The format used to display information on the screen. It defines the display characteristics.

video page. A screen image stored in memory.

viewport. A clipping region that sets the logical origin to the upper left corner of the region.

visibility. The characteristic of a variable or function that describes the parts of the program in which it can be referenced by name. An item has global visibility if it is visible in all source files comprising the program; otherwise, it has local visibility in a single source file.

visual page. The area in memory that holds the current displayed graphics output.

whitespace character. Characters that delimit items in a C source program, including space, tab, linefeed, carriage-return, formfeed, vertical-tab, and newline characters.

wildcard. An MS-DOS character (? or *) that can be expanded into one or more characters in filename references.

Answers to Selected Questions and Exercises

❑ NOTE: *In most cases, the answers show only the critical series of statements for each question that requires you to write a program.*

Chapter 3

1. Numeric equivalents:

Dec	Binary	Hex
5	101	\x5
20	10100	\x14
64	1000000	\x40
334	101001110	\x14E
1024	10000000000	\x400
31025	111100100110001	\x7931

2. Invalid C identifiers:

1_of_many	Starts with a digit
say_what?	Contains an invalid character (?)
int	Type specifier (reserved keyword)
pink.floyd	Contains an invalid character (.)

Valid but questionable:

FLOAT	Same spelling as *float* type specifier

4. Invalid constants:

0966	The leading 0 indicates that this is an octal number and 9 is not an octal digit (0–7)
0xGA	'G' is not a valid hex digit

5. Format specifiers:

3000	%d
23.67	%.2f
"Ah--What's up Doc?"	%s
'Z'	%c
−205	%d

Chapter 4

4. Declaration and assignment statements:

a. ```
int n;
n = 8000;
```

b. ```
char ch;
ch = 'Z';
```

c. ```
float ave;
ave = (3 + 11 + 21 + 66) / 4;
```

d. ```
int n1, n2, diff;
diff = n1 - n2;
```

5. Calculate the area of a right triangle (complete program):

```
/* rt_tri.c */

#include <stdio.h>

int main()
{
        float height, base;
        double area;

        height = 8.1;
        base = 4.0;
        area = 0.5 * (double) height * base;
        printf("Area = %g\n", area);

        return 0;
}
```

6. Expression evaluations:

Expression	Result
a < b	1 (True)
a != c	1 (True)
b >= c	0 (False)
a < b && c < b	0 (False)
a <= c ¦¦ b > c	1 (True)
(a += 3) < c	0 (False)

8. Invert the bits in a number (program fragment):

```
unsigned short int number;

printf("Type a number (0-65535): ");
scanf("%hu", &number);
printf("The bitwise complement of %hu is %hu\n", number,
        ~number);
```

Chapter 5

2. Echo only lowercase letters:

```
int ch;

ch = getchar();
if (ch >= 'a' && ch <= 'z')
        putchar(ch);
```

3. Show whether a digit is odd or even:

```
int digit;

printf("Type a single digit (0-9): ");
scanf("%d", &digit);
if (digit >= 0 && digit <= 9)
        if (digit % 2 == 0)
                printf("The digit %d is even.\n", digit);
        else
                printf("The digit %d is odd.\n", digit);
```

5. Odd/even test done by the conditional operator:

```
printf("The digit %d is %s\n",
        digit, (digit % 2 == 0) ? "even." : "odd.");
```

9. Reversing the digits of a number:

```
unsigned int number, digit;

printf("Type a positive whole number (0-65535): ");
scanf("%u", &number);
do {
        digit = number % 10;     /* print rightmost digit */
        printf("%u", digit);
        number /= 10;            /* get rid of right digit */
} while (number > 0);
```

11. Eliminating explicit *goto* statements.

Direct translation of the loop:

```
while (1) {
        ch = getchar();
        if (ch == 'q')
                break;
        putchar(ch);
}
```

Alternative form with embedded assignment:

```
while ((ch = getchar()) != 'q')
        putchar(ch);
```

Chapter 6

3. Descriptive names:

a. DAYS_PER_YEAR

b. BIGNUM

c. EPSILON

d. MAXROWS

e. MAX(x, y)

4. Using a DATA macro to create a table.

a. Printing a table of values:

```
int x;
printf("x\ty=DATA(x)\n");
for (x = 0; x <= 9; ++x)
        printf("%d\t%d\n", x, DATA(x));
```

b. Use parentheses around all of the variables:

```
#define DATA(x)          2 * (x) + 3
```

6. Find the minimum of three values:

```
#define MIN(a, b)        (((a) < (b)) ? (a) : (b))
#define MIN3(x, y, z)    ((MIN((x), (y))) < (z) ? \
                         (MIN((x), (y)) ) : (z))
```

Chapter 7

3. Calculate the volume of spheres:

```c
#include <stdio.h>
#include <math.h>
#include <float.h>

#define PI                      3.141592
#define MAX_RADIUS              4.0

int main(void)
{
        double radius, volume, SphereVolume(double);

        puts("SPHERE VOLUME TABLE");
        puts("Radius\tVolume");
        radius = 0.0;
        while (radius <= (double)MAX_RADIUS) {
                printf("%6.2lf\t%6.3lf\n", radius,
                        SphereVolume(radius));
                radius += 0.2;
        }
        return (0);
}
```

5. Clear the screen with repeated newline characters:

```c
void ClearScreen(int n)
{
        while (n-- > 0)
                putchar('\n');
}
```

Chapter 8

2. Corrections for the incorrect statements:

   b. Arrays in C start with element 0.

   c. Fully initialized arrays do not need a size specifier.

4. The loop control expression accesses one element beyond the end of the array.

6. Sum and average the elements of an integer array:

```
int i, n, sum;
float average;
static int array[] = { 12, 34, 56, 78 };

n = sizeof array / sizeof (int);
for (i = 0, sum = 0; i < n; ++i)
        sum += array[i];
average = (float)sum / n;
```

7. True.

9. A function that calculates the length of a string:

```
int StringLength(char string[])
{
        int length;

        length = 0;
        while (string[length] != '\0')
                ++length;
        return length;
}
```

Chapter 9

3. The *putchar()* macro prints the last value assigned to *ch* ('Z') regardless of how it was assigned (directly or through a pointer).

4. False. A pointer is not an integer.

6. Use a pointer to access the elements of an array:

```
#include <stdio.h>
int main(void)
{
        int i, elements;
        int *np;  /* pointer to number array */
        static int number[] = {
                0, 1, 2, 3, 4, 5, 6, 7, 8, 9
        };

        np = number  /* point to start of array */
        elements = sizeof number / sizeof (int);
        for (i = 0; i < elements; ++i)
                printf("number[%d] = %d\n", i, *(np+1));

        return (0);
}
```

7. The statement lacks a data type specifier (should be *char*). Also, the keyword *static* might be needed, if the statement occurs inside a function.

Chapter 10

2. To print the codes rather than the graphic representations of characters, use the %d format specifier in a *printf()* statement:

```
char *cp, line[MAXSTR];
.
.
.
/* gather input string */
.
.
.
for (cp = line; *cp != '\0'; ++cp)
        printf("%d ", *cp);
putchar('\n');
```

The space after %d in the format string puts some visual separation between codes in the output.

3. The pointer *cp* is never initialized, so it could be pointing anywhere (probably someplace dangerous!).

5. This program counts digits, letters, and other characters in an input string:

```
#include <stdio.h>
#include <ctype.h>

#define MAXSTR 80

int main(void)
{
        char line[MAXSTR], *cp;
        int digits, letters, other;

        printf(Type a string (<%d characters): ", MAXSTR);
        gets(line);
```

(continued)

(continued)

```
                    digits = letters = other = 0;
                    cp = line;
                    while (*cp != '\0') {
                            if (isdigit(*cp))
                                    ++digits;
                            else if (isalpha(*cp))
                                    ++letters;
                            else
                                    ++other;
                            ++cp;
                    }
                    return (0);
            }
```

Chapter 11

3. Date structure declaration and access:

```
        struct date_st {
                int year;               /* 4-digit year */
                int month;              /* 1-12 */
                int day;                /* 1-31 */
        };

        struct date_st date;
        date.year = 1988;
        date.month = 1;
        date.day = 31;
```

4. Extending exercise 3:

```
        struct date_st {
                int year;               /* 4-digit year */
                int month;              /* 1-12 */
                int day;                /* 1-31 */
                char monthname[4];      /* month-name abbr. + NUL */
        };

        struct date_st date;
        date.year = 1988;
        date.month = 1;
        date.day = 31;
```

(continued)

(continued)

```
        date.monthname = MonthString(date.month);
        .
        .
        .

        /* Produce a 3-character string for a given month number */
        char *MonthString(int month)
        {
                /* table of month-name abbreviations */
                static char nametab[] = {
                        "ERROR",
                        "Jan", "Feb", "Mar", "Apr", "May", "Jun",
                        "Jul", "Aug", "Sep", "Oct", "Nov", "Dec"
                };

                if (month > 0 && month <= 12)
                        return nametab[month];
                else
                        return nametab[0];   /* month out of range */
        }
```

7. Traffic signal simulation data type and variable:

```
        /* type declaration */
        typedef union {
                unsigned r1 : 1;        /* red #1 */
                unsigned y1 : 1;        /* yellow #1 */
                unsigned g1 : 1;        /* green #1 */
                unsigned a1 : 1;        /* arrow #1 */
                unsigned r2 : 1;        /* red #2 */
                unsigned y2 : 1;        /* yellow #2 */
                unsigned g2 : 1;        /* green #2 */
                unsigned a2 : 1;        /* arrow #2 */
                unsigned r3 : 1;        /* red #3 */
                unsigned y3 : 1;        /* yellow #3 */
                unsigned g3 : 1;        /* green #3 */
                unsigned a3 : 1;        /* arrow #3 */
                unsigned r4 : 1;        /* red #4 */
                unsigned y4 : 1;        /* yellow #4 */
                unsigned g4 : 1;        /* green #4 */
                unsigned a4 : 1;        /* arrow #4 */
        } SIGNAL;

        /* variable declaration */
        SIGNAL four_way;
```

❏ NOTE: *Each light is controlled by its own bit to give you the greatest flexibility in programming light patterns. You could combine the red, yellow, and green lights in a given direction into a 2-bit field if only one light will be on at a given time, but the design shown allows a green or red light and an arrow to be on simultaneously. It also accommodates a testing procedure that requires all lights to be on simultaneously.*

Chapter 12

5. Appending text to a file:

   Simply change the "w" (write) to "a" (append) to change the file access type.

6. Accepting blank lines by changing the input termination command:

   Change the test for a newline character to a test for a dot (.) as the first character of a line. A leading dot becomes the new method of terminating input.

Index

Special Characters

! (logical NOT operator) 81

!= (not equal to operator) 80

" (double quotation marks) 46, 49, 117, 162

(preprocessor directive) 116–25, *307–8*

% (percent sign)
 in format specifier 47, 51–55, 58–61
 as modulus operator 75–76

%= (remainder assignment operator) 86

& (ampersand)
 as address-of operator 63, 89, 174, 175, 218, 230
 as bitwise AND operator 83–84

&& (logical AND operator) 81–82

&= (bitwise assignment operator) 86

' (single quotation marks) 51, 52

() (parentheses) 70–71, 124, 140, 327–28

* (asterisk)
 in comments 34
 as indirection operator 89, 174–75
 as multiplication operator 72

*= (multiplication assignment operator) 86

+ (addition operator) 72

++ (increment operator) 87–89, 218

+= (addition assignment operator) 86

, (sequence operator) 89, 304

– (subtraction operator) 72, 75

–– (decrement operator) 87–89, 218

–= (subtraction assignment operator) 86

. (dot operator) 217, 225

/ (division operator) 72

/* */ (comment symbols) 34, 110

/= (division assignment operator) 86

; (semicolon) 69, 106, 139, 140, 327

< (less than operator) 80

<< (left shift operator) 85

<<= (left shift assignment operator) 86

<= (less than or equal to operator) 80

= (equal sign)
 as assignment operator 68, 72, 86, 218, 327
 in compound assignment expressions 86
 in relational expressions 80

== (equal to operator) 80

Augie Hansen

Augie Hansen started programming on IBM mainframes more than 20 years ago and since then has been involved with computers and programming at various companies, including General Dynamics, Raytheon Company, and E.G.&G., Inc. In addition, he spent seven years with AT&T Bell Laboratories, specializing in UNIX and C programming. He founded and is the president of Omniware, a company that provides academic and commercial training courses on UNIX, C, and MS/PC-DOS and offers consultation on custom programming issues. Hansen is a columnist for *UnixWorld* magazine and has contributed to several computer magazines, including the *Microsoft Systems Journal* and *PC Tech Journal*. In addition, he is the author of **PROFICIENT C**, published by Microsoft Press.

MICROSOFT® C: SECRETS, SHORTCUTS, AND SOLUTIONS
Kris Jamsa

If you're new to C, Microsoft C, or even Microsoft QuickC, you'll quickly master the basics of the language and gain the skills you need to work with variables, types, and operators; use character strings, constants, and macros; understand pointers, arrays, and structures; and master file manipulation and advanced preprocessing. And if you've already mastered the C basics, page after page of advanced information will hone your programming skills and make your Microsoft C programs fast, clean, and efficient. Jamsa shows you how to access the DOS command line, use I/O direction, enhance your program's video appearance, make full use of the MAKE and LIB tools, master dynamic memory allocation, expand wildcard characters into matching filenames, optimize your programs for increased speed, and more. Covering the fundamentals as well as the advanced topics, Jamsa provides hundreds of sample programs to support his instruction and encourage experimentation.

736 pages, softcover   7³/₈ x 9¹/₄ $24.95   ISBN 1-55615-203-5

MICROSOFT® C RUN-TIME LIBRARY: PROGRAMMER'S QUICK REFERENCE
Kris Jamsa

This handy reference provides instant access to concise information on more than 250 commonly used functions and macros in the Run-Time Library for Microsoft C and Microsoft QuickC. Each entry includes complete syntax, a brief description, details on parameters, and usually a program fragment. Also includes working examples along with notes and comments.

272 pages, softcover   4³/₄ x 8 $7.95   ISBN 1-55615-227-2

VARIATIONS IN C, 2nd ed.
Building Professional Applications with Microsoft® C
Steve Schustack

"Programmers working on large development projects definitely will want to consult VARIATIONS IN C before beginning their work." PC Tech Journal

Whether you're an experienced C programmer or new to C, with a background in structured languages, VARIATIONS IN C will show you how to develop high-quality application software. Among the hundreds of C books, this is one of the few that show, step by step, the design and implementation of a large, professional-quality application. Schustack offers an intermediate-level discussion of data types, operators, control-flow statements, data handling, and functions. Throughout, he has incorporated details of the latest versions of Microsoft C and the ANSI-approved Standard C. The heart of the book is the development of a sophisticated vendor order-entry application with over 1500 lines of code; this VARIATIONS IN C program is currently in use in many small businesses.

448 pages, softcover   7³/₈ x 9¹/₄ $22.95   ISBN 1-55615-239-6

Microsoft Press books are available wherever fine books are sold, or credit card orders can be placed by calling 1-800-888-3303.

The manuscript for this book was prepared and submitted to Microsoft Press in electronic form. Text files were processed and formatted using Microsoft Word.

Cover design by Greg Hickman
Interior text design by Darcie S. Furlan
Illustrations by Becky Geisler-Johnson
Principal typography by Lisa G. Iversen

Text composition by Microsoft Press in New Century Schoolbook with display in New Century Schoolbook Bold, using the Magna composition system and the Linotronic 300 laser imagesetter.

NOTE TO VGA OWNERS

Disk 3, the Learn C Now tutorial, does not work with all VGA cards. If your VGA card is not 100 percent IBM VGA compatible, we regret that you may be unable to use the tutorial. You can, however, make full use of the compiler and sample programs on disks 1 and 2.

If you experience problems with this book or product, please direct your questions in writing to:

Microsoft Press
16011 N.E. 36th Way
Box 97017
Redmond, WA 98073-9717
Attn: *Learn C Now* Editor